The Life I Have Lived

And Those Who Came Before Me

Hubert B. Ogle Jr.

Inspiring Voices®

Inspiring Voices books may be ordered through booksellers or by contacting:

Inspiring Voices
1663 Liberty Drive
Bloomington, IN 47403
www.inspiringvoices.com
1 (866) 697-5313

ISBN: 978-1-4624-1010-1 (sc)

Printed in the United States of America.

Inspiring Voices rev. date: 10/27/2014

INTRODUCTION

Hello, friend. I'm so glad that you have decided to come along with me on this very special journey of mine. It's always more fun to do something when you know you're not doing it alone, wouldn't you agree? Besides, without friends like you, the story of this life I have lived will never be told. Even more importantly, the lives of those who came before me will simply fade into the big black hole of time, unless friend's like you hear about them and remember. I promise to make this journey one that you will enjoy. I am not a professional writer, friend. So our conversation will be just as though we met at the grocery store, and spent some time 'catchin' up'. The people, places, and event's that I share with you will be shared from (a) my perspective, or (b) as told to me by various people who I have known, and loved, or (c) from diggin' around in old newspaper's, high school annual's and the like. Research, in other word's.

I will be the first to say that the way something is remembered is determined by the one who is doing the rememberin'. Perspective is a lot like noses. We all have'em. So don't be disapointed some day when you run across someone who remembers something differently from me. If you take all the perspectives you hear, my new friend, and consider them together in their totality, you will usually find that the truth is somewhere in the middle of all of them. I have one heartfelt desire in putting my life, and the lives of folk who came before me to paper. When I am gone, I want to leave behind me a first person account of my growin' up in the sixties and seventies. And I want folk to know about the people who shaped and molded my thinkin' as an adult. Many of them shared part's of their stories with me as I was growin' up, never dreamin' that I would one day use them in this little book of mine.

Finally friend, let me challenge you a little bit as we begin our journey together. Especially if you come from a small town as I do. The story of the small mill village town, it's way of life, it's people, with all the treasure those stories hold for the willin' ear, eye, and heart, is going to be best told by the people who lived it. There will come a time, my friend, when our grand-children will be taught the history of these little towns the way that some revisionist or apologist WANT'S them to believe it. We have a fleeting opportunity right now to tell it the way it actually happened.

I just got determined that I was going to put my ten cent's worth in while I can still remember my very small part of that history. What about you, friend? Don't you have a story to tell? The highest compliment you could pay me at a book signing some day would be to tell me that readin' my story inspired you to tell your story. I have a dream that mine will be just the beginning of the recording of mill village history as my generation saw and lived it. More people than you think will want to read it, just as you are reading this little book of mine right now. Think about it.

As we take this journey together friend it will be my prayer that God will bless your life according to your faith in Him. I pray that your life will alway's be productive, positive, and Christ centered. May you alway's have someone to celebrate your victories with, someone to cry with when the storm's of life come (and they surely will), and a voice of Christ centered reason, compassion, and wisdom when you need advice. As you climb the ladder of life, I pray that you will never forget those you pass on the way up. Remember, as they are, you once were. And as my Dad used to say, never bite the hand that feeds you. And never forget the hand that helps you up when you're down. With that friend, let us begin our journey through this life I have lived. Let us remember the special folk who came before me. By God's grace, may they never be forgotten!

I HAVE A STORY TO TELL

My name is Hubert B. Ogle Jr. But you can just call me "Brother Hugh", friend. That's what the folk at church call me, and that will do just fine for you too. I am the proud grandson of a sharecropper who was alway's at the mercy of Mother Nature, or the farmer he worked for, or both. I am the proud son of cotton mill worker's, who worked long hours in sometimes brutal conditions for crumbs from the masters table, as it were. I am a product of their sacrifice. I am also a Christian, a blood bought, born again, beloved Bible believer. I belong to the only true and living God that there ever has been, or ever will be. I am not in hell today, at least in part, because of the Godly influences that were placed in my path across the year's at Midway Baptist Church, the little church I grew up in. You will be meeting some of these precious people in this little book of mine. Without ALL of these powerful influences in my life, I shudder to think what my life would have been like before I busted hell wide open. I may never have had instilled in me the work ethic that I have used to feed my own family with. I would not have had the promise of an eternal home with my Saviour when my time on this polluted ole' earth is over. I most certainly would not have the Godly wife who has endured 26+ years with me, or the two son's who I love so much.

As I write this little book of mine, friend, I have to pause and wonder whether my son's will have such glowing report's to make about their Mother and me when it is time for them to write their own stories. It is a sobering thought indeed to realize that even as I record my story, and the story of those who came before me, I am writing in the hearts and mind's of my son's the next installment of our family's history. Will they smile when they remember their Mother and me? How about you, friend? Do these type thought's keep you up at night too? Let's you and I make a pact together as we take this journey. Let's decide to try even harder from this moment on to leave behind for our children and grandchildren the same kind of testimony that you will hear me give in this little book of mine about my parent's and other's. What do you say? Deal?

A 'SALT OF THE EARTH ' KIND OF PEOPLE

Friend, you can trace my family back as far as you want. You won't find the first Governor. You won't find the first king or nobleman. You won't find the first C.E.O. or the first high society person among us either. The late Lewis Grizzard was fond of saying that he came from a long line of used car salesmen, horse thieves, and moonshine maker's. His point was to make certain that everybody knew that he came from humble, 'salt of the earth' type people. And he was just as unapologetic about that then as I am now.

As near as I can tell, all of my people were and still are working class people. None of us make the headlines of our local paper. You won't find a story about any of us leading off the evening news on the television. But trust me when I tell you that without people like us, no company in America could have survived in the day of my parent's and grandparent's. Still can't today either. The 'big businessman' built the mill's. But the 'little man' made them run. Boss Hog pulled in the order's. But the little man got the order's out on schedule. Make no mistake, Mr. C.E.O. You can retire on your golden parachute money. But you owe a lot of that money to the little man and woman who carried you on their backs, then many time's lost their homes when you took your filthy lucre and drove off into the sunset. From the share-cropper, to the mill worker, to the metal fabricator, it is the 'salt of the earth' little man who has alway's been the glue that held together the economic fabric of this great nation of ours. Most C.E.O's started out that way too. The problem is, they forgot where they came from. Their profit became more important than their people. I'm talking about the kind of profit that causes them to put those big boats into the lake, or own multiple homes, some of which they will never live in. I'm talking about the kind of profit that allows them to walk away from dedicated, loyal people without looking back while they count the ungodly amounts of retirement money they walk away with. Before I am done with this little book of mine, friend, the 'little man' is going to get his proper due. I am going to deal with these 'son's of the golden parachute' in a very personal way. And I won't be in any mood to back down either.

It seem's to me, friend, that the sharecropper and the mill worker have become more and more nameless and faceless as the years go by. To me they are like the foundation of any home. You can't see it. But make no mistake; without a foundation, no home can stand for long, if at all. I have a firm conviction that these people built the foundation for the live's that my generation live today. I am not willing to draw my last breath without trying to make sure that these people are not forgotten. Their stories are worth telling. It is important to me that their stories be recorded for the next generation. So many of these folk are gone now. I can only hope that God will give me grace to finnish this little book of mine before ALL of them go. I am 56 now. I will be 57 or 58, maybe older when this little book of mine is in print. My generation is comming up to bat in this thing called life. I feel as though I am running a race to a finnish line that is unknown to me in distance. But I am very comfortable running this race on a life road that was paved for me by those who came before me. May I do as good a job for the next generation as the last one did for me!

DEDICATED WITH LOVE

Forgive me friend if I get a little 'mushy' right here. There are some very special people that I need to thank. Without them I could not possibly have had even the desire to write this little book of mine. Even before them, I must thank my Heavenly Father, who looked beyond the filth of my sin and accepted this undeserving sinner boy with His mercy and forgiveness on March 16, 1980. I guarantee you friend that I will be the least of the least in His kingdom when the time come's. But I know this. I WILL be there, bless His holy name. For that I am so thankfull.

Then I have to thank my wife Susan. She has tolerated me for 25+ year's now. She left a secure home and life in the great state of Delaware in 1987 and moved to this strange land called Alabama to be my life's partner. She was completely unprepared for how 'different' people can be here. But she has endured the best and the worst with equal class and perseverance. I'm not sure that I deserve the unconditional love she has shown me. I'm not sure I deserve the sacrifices she has made for me. But friend, I am more thankful for them each and every day. Through it all, she is still my 'sunshine', and she can still flash a million dollar smile at the least provocation.

Also, I must pay tribute to my precious Mother Hazel. She has enjoyed now the embrace of a loving Heavenly Father who welcomed her to Heaven as a 'good and faithful servant' on July

23, 2007. She richly deserved the mansion that awaited her when she got Home. My Mother was many thing's to me. She was my biggest cheer-leader, an encourager, a loving critic who was unafraid to let me know when she thought I was veering off onto a wrong path in life. Mother, I miss you more and more every day. But we will see each other again, perhaps sooner than later.

Finally, I pause to pay tribute to my Father. Hubert B. Ogle Sr. and I did not alway's see eye to eye in my youth and young adult years. We had our moment's, Dad and me. You'll hear all about that in the pages of this little book of mine. But you know what, friend? Long before Dad took his place in Heaven, he and I settled all account's between us. More importantly, we settled all account's with our Heavenly Father. You see friend, when we allow our Saviour to do for us what we can NOT do for ourselves, miracles happen. Any sin, no matter how dark, can be washed as white as snow. Relationships CAN be mended. Broken heart's CAN be healed. We CAN have a new beginning. So it was for my Dad and I. We forgave one another as an act of faith. But make no mistake. It was God, and God alone, who did the healing. So Dad, I wanted you to know, you made a difference in my life. You became a role model to me. You were one of my hero's in the Christian faith. You were both a mentor and a counselor. You were a calm, Christ centered voice in the middle of whatever storm of life I happened to be going through. And for that I love you. I miss you every day that I live in this polluted world of our's. By the way Dad, when you left this world, you did so not owing ANY human being ANYTHING. You forgave, and asked forgiveness, of anyone who would ALLOW you the privelege. For those who would not or could not, it's their loss. Let them go suck their unforgiving thumb's. You just enjoy the well earned rest you have had since Christmas 2008. You're just getting started!

Friend, can I tell you one more thing that I am very thankfull for? I don't say one thing about either one of my parent's in this little book of mine, that I did not say to them while they were still here with us. In that respect, I have no regret's.

THE SLOW DEATH OF INNOCENCE

My Dad would tell you that life in his day was hard, even in the fun they had or the game's they played. He would also tell you this; As hard as the share-croppers life was, as poor as they were by that day's standard, they were rich in the thing's they were taught. Those thing's ultimately enabled them to raise my generation. They were taught honesty. They were taught a good work ethic. They were taught to love and worship an amazing God,Who always loves us in spite of our flaws. Respect for authority began in the home, and was enforced without debate. Loyalty to family was expected no matter what, and was generally practiced without apology. We will explore all of these things on our journey friend, you and I.

My generation was taught many of the same thing's. But as I look back on my life, and see where our world is now, I realize something else. People my age actually witnessed the last gasp of what I call the "Age of Innocence." Innocence died a slow, painfull death right under our noses, as we grew up. Sadly, it is only now as I write this story, that I see the blow's that took it's life. Consider this one example. Even the identity of a small town now has gone from 'a community of families' to a community of 'acquaintances'. What's the difference? I'm glad you asked, friend. Let me ask YOU a question. Do you know most every family from one end of your street to the other? By name? Another question, if you please. When is the last time you had a neighbor or two over for a game night or a meal, or even to watch a ball game together? And none of that matters if you are one of the thousands who have bought a home that sit's in the middle of 5 to 20 acres of land, away from any 'next door fellowship' at all. See? We don't even want to be bothered with one another anymore.

At the age of 9 or 10 it was nothing for me to leave the little green house we lived in on the Fairfax short-cut road, and walk over to Mr. George Will Monk's grocery store, get in the wood's, walk a trail about a quarter mile, and walk all up and down the Chattahoochie River fishing. All day. I would have blackberries and spring water from Granny White Spring's for lunch. My parent's never gave it a second thought. Neither did I. In the world we live in today, carefree summer day's like that, for kids like my two boy's, are gone forever. This world is not safe or innocent anymore. To me, that is sad.

CHANGES

As a student in school, I did not have to read about integration, friend. I lived it. I was a part of the last all white 8th grade class at River View School. I don't say that with any racial pride, but for historical purposes only. I well remember my first two African American teachers, Mrs. Alford and Mr. Crook. This was a year or two before the student bodies integrated. I witnessed the sad, the glad, the good and the bad that happened as our communities left the 'separate but equal' lie and and lived the growing pains of becoming a blended community.

Friend, I watched the industry that fed 3 generation's of my family die a slow, slow death. Textiles fed our people. Textiles clothed our people. Textiles educated our people. Textiles provided our families recreation. Textiles built the towns we lived in. Friend, it is hard for me to not be bitter for the loss of our livelyhood. Textiles was not a perfect industry. It was not run by perfect people. There are thing's that could have been done differently. Still, at the end of the day, textiles did not die an internal death. It died an external death. The people who killed textiles in our Valley were 'corporate raiders' who wrapped themselves up in word's like entreprenour, who committed economic murder with a scythe called 'hostile takeover' and financed their folly with something called junk bond's. The mice who followed these pied pipers were a bunch of cattle called 'shareholders' who took the pie in the sky promises of slick self made millionaires to be prophetic. They sold out people whose loyalty and hard work they had depended on for 3 generations. Their token (at best) effort's to help 'retrain' our people were as grossly inadequate as they were surface gestures in an attempt to save face. It didn't work. Friend, they don't even HAVE a face as far as I am concerned. The best that can be said for them is that most of them have become as nameless and irrelevant as they made so many textile worker's. They are richly deserving of such a fate. These changes were very real to me as a young adult. I still feel the pain of them today.

Friend, I remember teacher's, Grand-parent's, Sunday School teacher's, my parent's, and so many others tellin' me their stories and sayin' they would not alway's be here to tell me these thing's. As a young fellow I thought (and probably said) that they were not goin' anywhere no time soon. Those word's were spoken by a very naive boy who did not have a grasp of the brevity of life that I have now. The vast majority of those folk are gone from this world. Friend, I am so thankfull to God that some of my very best friend's, even as I was growing up, were the older folk in my church and community. I know so much more than a lot of people my age know about the generation that came before me. They felt the pain of the 'changes' their generation lived through as much as we in my generation have felt the pain of our 'changes'. We will talk about many of these on our journey, you and I. But let us now begin the real 'meat' of our story with the life of the sharecropper. That was the vocation of my Fathers Dad. As you will see, it was not a life for the faint of heart. But you will have a hard time finding someone who lived that life, who is ashamed of it.

COMMING UP ON THE ROUGH SIDE

My Dad, Hubert Buion Ogle Sr., was born in Clay County, in east central Alabama. His Father's name was Albert Ogle. Albert made his living as a share-cropper. Albert was a bear of a man. He was a hard worker and a demanding head of household. He was married to the former Ora Grizzle. She was a housewife extraordinaire, even by the already hard standard of the sharecroppers life. As her husband and older children worked each day in the fields, she worked just as hard to keep the house running.

Discipline was meted out by a horse-strap if Albert did it, or by a switch if Ora was in charge. To the best of my understanding, a horse strap is the leather strap that run's from the bit in the horses mouth back to the rider. PaPa would double it up, wrap it around his massive hand a time or two, and it was revival time in the house! A switch was simply a limb off any sturdy weed that happened to be growing nearby. But don't be fooled, my new friend. It could get it's point across too. My own Mother used to call a switchin' a 'house-call by Dr. Green'. You can trust me when I tell you that Dr. Green had 'an aspirin that cures all ill's', as my Mother use to say.

Friend, I realize that all of this sound's harsh, especially to the new age 'any corporal punishment is abuse' thinker's. But allow me to tell you a little bit about the hard and sometimes harsh life of the share-cropper's family. In my Dad's youth, most families made their living primarily by some kind of agriculture. Farmers had land of anywhere from as much as 50 acres to hundred's of acres to harvest every year. Not to mention the hog's, or cow's, or chicken's, and any number of other thing's they needed or could sell. Now and again a farmer might have short term or long term difficulty getting his crop harvested in time for market. Maybe he had a small family. This would have been uncommon in my Dad's day. Dad was the oldest of seven kid's. He had an uncle who raised 12 kid's, with his wife, and sent most of them through college, on a 'farmer's living'.

Anyway, this farmer might have a small family and a big 'place'. Or maybe the farmer became incapacitated in some way. He would need some help. Many times he would have an extra house on his place. It wouldn't be anything to write home about. But it would be stable enough to host a family. The farmer would hire a man who would come with his family and live in that house. The farmer would give that man 5 acres or so to farm for his families needs. In return, that man and his family would help the farmer get his crop in on time. Thus the term 'share cropper'. So, my friend, you can see that the share-cropper had a double yoke on him at all times. He was acutely aware of his family's need's. But he had to make sure that the farmer was satisfied with his work. If that was not enough, anyone who depended on Mother Nature as the farmer and the share-cropper did, was constantly at her mercy. Not enough rain, too much rain, disease, any number of thing's could mean the difference between a bountiful harvest and a very lean year. It was the share-cropper, however, who got the low end of the business in a lean year. What, did you think the farmer was going to see to the need's of the share-cropper's family over his own in a lean year? No, my naive travel partner, that would have been wishful thinking on the part of the share-cropper. The share-cropper had to find way's to get he and his family through the winter to the next spring, with all of it's rebirth and new promise.

If that isn't enough friend, consider this. If you or I lose our job in the town we live in, we get to keep our home and our car. We can get ourselves another job, even if it means we have to commute out of town. If the share-cropper came to absolute loggerhead's with the farmer he worked for, there was the possibility that he could lose the roof over his head, and have his family without a home. I am sure that there were some times over the year's when a share-cropper would have to tolerate some less than ideal 'on the job conditions', if I can put it that way. Too, there were times when a share-cropper could be taken advantage of by a less than honorable farmer. Most share-cropper's had minimal education, if any. Albert Ogle never finnished what we call grammar school. My Dad finished high school only after his service in the Korean War, on a government program called the G.I. bill. It was only too easy at times for the share-cropper to be taken advantage of. Now friend, I don't want to have you believe that ALL farmers treated their share-croppers this way. The unscrupulous ones, as near as I can remember the stories, were in the minority. But this kind of treatment was always a possibility, as Albert would find out on at least one occaision. We will examine that incident in this little book of mine.

So as you can see friend, this life of being a share-cropper could be hard and / or harsh, in many ways. That is why a hard work ethic, and integrity, and honesty were critical to the share-cropper's very livelyhood. By today's standard's, Albert and Ora Ogle would have lost their children to the Department of Human Resources early on, on the discipline issue alone. Indeed, my Dad would later run away from home because of Albert's horse-strap. But decades later he would look back on it all, and speak of his Father in nothing but almost reverant terms. And what of his Mother? Dear friend, you would NOT have wanted to wrong my fathers Mother and have him find out about it.

I can tell you a short story from those day's that will illustrate just how strict Albert could be. There is some debate about which one of his sons was involved. But one of them was on his way back home from somewhere, and found a pretty colored button lying beside the road. It happened to be in the general front of a neighbor's home. When the son got home, at some point Albert became aware of the button. He asked where the button came from. His son told him. Albert proceeded to whip that son all the way to that home. He made his son give that button to an astonished lady of the house. Then he whipped that son all the way back home. Albert had a very simple philosophy about acquiring thing's. Folk don't adhere to this philosophy much anymore friend, not as a general rule anyway. But I guarantee you that our communities would be safer and more productive if we all went back to it. His standard was this; if it ain't yours, if you did not pay for it, if you did not earn it, keep your hands off it! He held to that thinking his entire life. He ingrained it into the hearts and mind's of all his kid's. And I remember a summer day when he taught me that philosophy in a very real, and a very personal way, friend. Let me tell you about it. It's a little story I call....

THE ROCKY FORD DISASTER

My PaPa Ogle never did but two things for a living his entire life. Even after he moved to Chambers County, he would work for whoever had a field planted with something that needed harvesting. Only when a sun stroke dictated that he cease that activity did he go to driving a taxi. And those are the only two things he ever did. When I was a child he would let his grandson's go to the field with him in the summer time and help him get in anything from butterbean's, to watermelon's, to okra, you get the picture. Looking back on all of that now, friend, I am so thankfull that I got to do that. It gave me just a small taste of what it was to depend on a crop to provide a living.

Many is the time I would spend the night at MaMa and PaPa's house the night before we went to the field. Friend, there was no need for an alarm clock at my MaMa's house. I could wake up by the sound's and smell's of MaMa's kitchen. She would make a breakfast that would include eggs, and bacon, or ham, or sausage. She made some of the biggest, best tasting 'cat head' biscuit's (that means great big 'uns for my city slicker friend's) you ever tasted. There would be home-made jelly or jam. There might be some fresh cantaloupe sliced up and oh, hush mah' mowf! My, what I would give to be able to taste just one more of those 'cat head' biscuit's! Now, tell me friend. How could a body sleep with that kind of aroma lifting you from the bed by the nose?

O.K. Hugh, back to task. On the day that I was to learn this valuable 'lesson', we finnished one of those famous MaMa breakfasts, and went off to work a little before daylight. In the memory of the child that I was, we worked on this day at a field somewhere on highway 18, just outside of West Point, Georgia, in the direction of Pine Mountain. The boy that I was remember's a stand of tree's along the road front. We entered through a gate on a dirt road. The first thing that we saw was cantaloupes. On both sides of the road. For a long way, too. Hundreds and hundreds of field fresh, ripe cantaloupes! The boy that I was asked PaPa if we could have one of those cantaloupe. After all, there were more there than the owner would ever get to market. He would be no worse off for the loss of just ONE cantaloupe. PaPa's reaction was predictable, friend. Brief, blunt, and to the point. "Nope! You didn't plant them, or work them, and you have not asked the owner's permission. Keep your hand's off them!" You know my PaPa's problem, don't you friend? He just did not have an opinion about nothing. NOT!! Well, we knew better than to sass PaPa. But on this day, our sanity would take leave of our brains. And I was soon to learn a lesson that stayed with me, well.... to this day, as a matter of fact.

Our mission that day was to pick butterbeans. Long, long row's of butterbeans. Friend, have you ever tried to pick a five gallon bucket full with butterbeans? I promise you, there was not a five gallon bucket in my childhood (and probably still isn't today) that did not have a false bottom in it. The more butterbeans you fed those things, the more they craved. They were gluttonous, really. I would sit my bucket in front of me a little ways. I would pick what I thought was a fair amount of bean's and throw them into the bucket. After a while I would peek into the bucket to check my progress. Honestly, the boy that I was spent a good bit of time wandering where a lot of these butterbeans were going. He looked around on the ground to make sure he had not missed his target. He scratched his head a bunch. But in the end there was nothing to do but to keep on picking. Needless to say, picking butterbeans never made it to the top of my 'favorite thing's to do with PaPa' list. I was reminded of a story my Dad repeated to me a few times over the year's. He would pick cotton into a great big sack till he was sure he had it completely full. He would take the sack to his Father and proudly say," Okay Daddy, I got my sack full!" His Father would ask to see the sack. He would proceed to shake that sack proper. Then most times he would say, "No Hubert, I think you can get just a little more in there." My Dad said that he would look incredulously into a sack that was now only a little over half full! The boy that I was understood Dad's story for the first time that day, picking those blasted butterbeans! As I was growing up friend, my Dad would tell me that story and get a laugh out of it. I once asked him how he could remember a story like that and smile, much less laugh. Dad said that having

30 or 40 year's of distance between you and the incident you are remembering can make all the difference in the world in whether you are laughing or crying when you remember it. Writing this now, and remembering that endless row of butterbeans, and those infernal bottomless five gallon bucket's, I can truthfully say; I understand, Dad. I understand.

Now, back to my story. PaPa would stop work for an hour in the middle of the work day for lunch and rest. He never needed a watch in the field. My PaPa could tell the time of day by where the sun was in the sky. For the boy that I was, that just separated my head from my shoulders that a person could do that. PaPa would laugh and say that we needed the rest more than he did. Now friend, we had taken the dirt road past another stand of tree's that separated those cantaloupe from the rest of the produce being grown on this place. PaPa took his break on the furthest end of the tree's. He told us we could eat anywhere we wanted. But we were to be sure we were near enough by to hear him when he called us back to work. Friend, PaPa would alway's make sure that we brought plenty of ice water or tea for lunch. He was pretty protective of his jar. It was many year's later before I found out why. You see friend, PaPa sometimes would be drinking, how shall I say this...... 'sweet tea on steroids', if I can put it like that. You know what I mean don't you friend?

Well, the boy that I was would eat his lunch quick, then spend the rest of his time 'exploring' the place. On this day he and the other kid 'explored' their way right over into that cantaloupe field. They were about to come face to face with one of satan's most effective demon's, a fellow called Temptation. It would be no contest. They were woefully unable to fight him off. And the results would be predictable. I mean, they were only going to eat ONE cantaloupe, friend. Honest injun they were. But the next thing you know, there were three, three sets of cantaloupe remains before them. I know friend, but they were so GOOD, and so SWEET. You've seen the 'tater chip commercial that say's 'nobody can eat just one' haven't you? The same principle applies to field fresh cantaloupe.

About that time we heard PaPa's voice callin' us back to work. And right back into that butterbean patch we went. In the hottest part of the day. Under a clear sky. Chunking butterbeans into that bottomless five gallon bucket. And the sun began to beat down on us. Our recently eaten dinner's began to argue with the newly arrived cantaloupe in our bellies. Our bellies soon got tired of all that fighting, and just kicked the lot of them out. Friend, that's a creative way of saying that we began to puke our gut's out. Neighbor, I've had some bad tasting stuff in my time. But back-flushing half digested food rank's right up there at the top of the list. There is never a good time for that to happen either. But on this day, the timing could not have been worse. The indignity of it all, throwing up right there in the middle of our job. In the heat. Under that summer sun.

Suddenly a shadow came across me. I started to thank God for the cloud's. But when I looked up, there were no cloud's. The shadow was my PaPa. And he was frowning.

"What's the matter with you boy's?" That was fairly obvious. I mean, the evidence was laid out right there in all it's stomach turning ugliness. It was now being soaked up by mother earth for nutrition distribution to the butterbean plant's around us. Ahh, the circle of life. From seed, to cantaloupe, to mischievous bellies, to being cast into the ground, to be soaked up by butterbean plant's, which produce the beans we pick to serve you, friend. Don't that just make you want to go heat up a bowl full right now? Anyway, PaPa took one look at this sad scene and said, "Y'all done been in the dad-gum cantaloupe, ain't 'cha?!" What were we going to say? PaPa was a tested veteran of many, many year's of working the soil for a living. He certainly knew regurgitated cantaloupe when he saw it. His action was swift, diverse, and long lastin'. He began by warming the seat of our britches proper. No sooner had we gotten our breath, than he put us right back to picking butterbeans. There was no picking around the plant's where we had lost our food, neither. PaPa said there was no use to make those butterbeans suffer just because we could not get our stomachs to hold the result of our mischief.

Later that afternoon we took the produce we had gathered to the man we were working for. When he started to give us some money, as was his custom, PaPa quickly spoke up. "You won't be paying these two today", he said.He made us tell that man what we had done. Then we were required to apologize to him. I remember that man trying to reason with PaPa. "C'mon now, Albert, they're just kid's. All kid's get into mischief, one time or another." But PaPa was having none of it. "Not when they work for me they don't," he said. "You won't be paying them today." And that was that. Nor was that the end of it. When PaPa took me home, he felt like my Dad needed to know what I did. Friend, what do you think happened then? I mean, the seat of my britches were just getting back to normal temperature from PaPa's teaching. Now then, my Daddy invited me to the bathroom, took off his belt, and flat out heated the seat of my britches up!

That day PaPa taught me the same principle that he taught his boy's, in no uncertain way; "If it ain't your's, if you didn't pay for it, regardless of where you find it, keep your hand's off it!" And you know friend, I can't help thinking that we could eliminate an awful lot of our society's problem's if folk would just once again embrace and live by that simple principle, and parent's were allowed to go back to the kind of enforcement that I went through that day. Sadly friend, some folk who will read this little book of mine will call me a wrong headed ultra conservative relic of a bygone past who need's to have his thinking enlightened. Well let me enlighten you to this. When I was a child growing up, we didn't have a Columbine. We didn't have a Virginia Tech. The real violence in our schools began, then escalated, as a direct result of serious discipline being summarily dismissed from our home's and school's as abuse.

My soul, the Bible itself teaches us that "Foolishness is bound up in the heart of a child. But the rod of correction shall drive it far from him." My Bible teaches me that I hate my boy's if I don't correct them. Oh, but I forgot, friend. The world you and I live in no longer believes the Bible, do they? The opinion I just rendered makes you and I 'closed minded', dosent it? Well, we can afford to be closed minded when we're right, ain't that right friend? And it's time for folk like you and I to tell the far left wing, elitist apologistic intelligentia academics to go suck their collective thumbs. And that's all I've got to say about that.

A LESSON IN GRACE

That day PaPa taught us a stern lesson in honesty and integrity. The following Saturday he taught us a lesson in grace. How many folk do you know friend, who would have written us off and refused to let us help again after all that? Yet the next Saturday we were right back out there with him. In fact, we were back at the same field where we were taught those lesson's. We drove by the same field of cantaloupe. We were very quiet. PaPa did not warn us again that day. He didn't have to. However, PaPa did have one more reminder for us about keeping our hand's to ourselves with the produce. He made his point too. On this day we also drove right past the butterbean rows. For this we were very thankfull. We stopped a little piece further. Getting out of the truck, PaPa said "Boy's, today we're gonna be cuttin' okra." He gave each of us a knife and assigned us a row to cut. He took a row right next to ours. I can't imagine why. Well, we started cutting that okra. Tell me, Friend, have you ever tried to cut okra bare handed? You did? How far did you get? We started noticing an itch on the first stalk. By the third stalk we were suffering. I looked over and noticed that PaPa had on a pair of gloves. He was plowing on through his row of okra like nobody's business. I called out to him, "Hey PaPa, you got any more of them gloves in the truck?" He said "Yep, I believe I do." I asked, "You think we could have a pair to use over here? Our hand's are really starting to sting." PaPa said, "Well, I thought about that. But then I thought, if I let you boy's spend the mornin' cutting okra with your bare hands, you might not have time to think about those dad-blamed cantaloupes!" His point made, we soon had a pair of gloves for our thankfull hands. And friends, it was a long time before I had another piece of cantaloupe, even at the breakfast table.

A DAY IN THE LIFE

Well, that story went on a bit longer than I expected it would. Let that be a lesson to you friend. Don't get me started on a story. Now,where was I? Ah yes, Making a living as a share-cropper. The share-cropper's day started before the sun came up. There were any number of chores that had to be done before going out to the fields. Cow's to milk. Eggs to gather. Almost certainly wood to get in. And you may be surprised to know, my dedicated reader, that breakfast was a big meal for both farmer and share-cropper families. I have heard my Dad say that you didn't eat four or five 'cat-head' bisquits with your eggs because you were famished. You ate that much because you weren't gonna be eating anything else till noon time. Between meal snacks? Don't even think about it. One, you were going to be too busy to stop and snack. And two, there wasn't enough food for that kind of extra eating.

I got a laugh at the expense of my two boy's one day. We were visiting my Dad in his home. We were talking about the share-croppers work-day. My boy's, you see, will start a work day at our house, then after an hour or so it's time for a snack, or a television break. Truthfully, from time to time their father will get in that frame of mind too. My oldest asked my Dad how long it was between breakfast and lunch. Dad said lunch was about noon. My youngest asked, "How did you know when it was noon?" His eyes got big when Dad told him that his Father could tell time by where the sun was in the sky. My oldest asked, "How long did you take for lunch?" Dad replied, "Oh, about an hour." Next question; "So when you got done eating, you could play for the rest of the hour, right?" Dad had a one word answer; "Nope". Next question; "Why?" 'Cause you had to feed and water the mules." My oldest had another one word question; "Why?" Dad answered, "Because, the last thing you wanted was to have an over-worked, underfed mule to drop dead in the middle of a plowing day.That just would not be good at all, especially if the mule belonged to the fella you was working for."

Friend, can we agree that kids today would not last but, say, a half day working the substance, the scope, or with the urgency that these people worked with every day? What about us parent's? How would we fare? My Dad vividly remembered his sisters applauding the sound of distant thunder, praying that it heralded the arrival of desperately needed rain which would give life to fast parching crops. Christmas in the home of a share-cropper was very slim indeed compared to today's standard. A good year, Dad and his siblings might get a few pieces of fruit and some candy. Many times, clothes were made by hand in the home. A pair of work boots, if you were so blessed, were to be worn till your toes grew out the end of them. New shoes, often a rare luxury, were to be worn for school and church only. And speaking of school, most share-cropper kids 'graduated' school by age 10 or 11, and studied agriculture (picked cotton), sometimes till they married.

SUPPLEMENTING THE INCOME

Many share-croppers felt the need to supplement their income, especially in a drought year. By far the most popular, and the most enterprising means was to go off in the woods and build what was known as a 'still' for making 'moonshine', also known as "corn squeezins" (the comic strip "Snuffy Smith" made this term popular), or 'boot-legging whiskey'. My PaPa had a still, I'm told. Not a very big one. Fifty gallons or so. From time to time he would 'make a run' to bring in some extra money. I don't mean to say that he did not partake of this 'fermented fury'. He did all his own 'taste testing', as far as I can tell.

I once had a sip of PaPa's home-made wine. This was years and years after his last moonshine run. And it wasn't in Clay County either. He now lived, as all his family did, in Chambers County. I was in his home one day. He brought out a large mason jar. He said, "Hugh, take a little sip of this. It will go down as smooth as a milkshake, then blow the seat slap out of your drawers." He talked me into taking one sip by telling me it was wine made from fresh black berries. Now, anything made from fresh black berries can't be all bad can it? Oh, my dear friend, don't be fooled. I never had a sip of home-brew before that day. And I have never had one since that day either. Friend, I would venture to say that had I drank a full glass of that home-brew, the seat of my britches would not have been the only thing that got 'blowed out'.

There is one story from PaPa's moonshine days that I MUST record for posterity. It has garnered many a laugh over the years. My Grand-Mother makes an appearance here. MaMa was not a big woman. But she could make her feeling's known, like most other Mom's. On the subject of alchohol, she was what was known as a 'tee-totaler'. That meant 'no alchohol in my house; no way, no how!' I don't have any evidence that any of PaPa's mixtures ever made it into their home. MaMa, as near as I can find out, put up with this 'still' business with gritted teeth.

One day, PaPa was 'making a run'. A storm suddenly blew up. PaPa was extremely wary about bad weather. There was an incident in his youth involving a bad storm that left it's mark on him for life. So when this storm blew up, PaPa headed for the house quickly. After the storm passed, PaPa told MaMa that he was going back down in the woods and finnish his 'business'. My Grand-Mother admonished him; "Now, Albert, you don't need to go back down there. The Lord's done tried to warn you." But back to the woods PaPa went. And what do you know, but the 'revenoors' (police, city folk) had done busted that still into a thousand pieces. They nearly caught PaPa too. For the rest of her life, my Grand-Mother, any time she could, would enter a discussion about alchohol by saying, "Tell'em, Albert. Tell 'em about the time I tried to tell you not to go back down in those woods that one day. But you just had to go, didn't you?" And I can still hear my PaPa say, "Aww fiddle, Ora, hush!" Towards the last years of her life though, he would say it with just the hint of a smile.

GAMES THEY PLAYED

Dad told me many times about the different thing's they did for fun. Frankly friend, It does not grieve me at all that I never experienced one particular activity I will describe to you now. They had corn cob battles. Sound's innocent, does it not? What if I tell you that they soaked the cobs first to make them harder? What's that? What did they soak them in, you ask? Well, oil was a popular soaker. If they had no oil, a good mud hole would do. If the cob battle happened during a prolonged dry spell, they would soak them in the used grass that a cow's body throws away after getting all possible nutrients out of it. And the fresher, the better. Think on it, friend. It will come to ya in a minute or two. These 'battles' were eventually banned by parent's for fear that some boy would get hurt by (a) a loaded cob, or (b) a fight started by an OVER loaded cob.

There was another favorite thing to do that could be entertaining, unless you were the person being invited to be a 'special guest' on one of these event's. They were called 'snipe hunt's.' Now friend, I did me some research on this thing called a 'snipe'. I was not real sure whether this was a REAL bird or not. Surprisingly, it is. That's the good new's. But 'snipe' could actually be one of a number of bird's. That was a little disappointing, because I had hoped to put some legitimacy to 'the hunt'. There are a species or two of this type bird that don't fly. But that is the best I can do for the 'history' of the snipe hunt. I suppose there was a time in the history of this great country of our's, when folk went on actual snipe hunt's. But from my Dad's generation through mine, for the life of me I can't find anybody. All that I have found about these hunt's were that they were all about 'fun'... or not. Let me explain.

The idea of a snipe hunt was this. You and a group of your best co-plotters, er, friends, would approach a well thought out 'victim'. Trust me, that is exactly what they were too. You would be all excited to have them go with you on a 'snipe hunt'. The soon to be changed forever soul would ask what in the world a snipe hunt was. You would say that it was a small bird. It can't fly, and it spend's it's night's holed up in ditches or ravines. All that was necessary was for one person to hold a gunny sack down to the ground while the rest of the group went to the other end of the ravine and chased the snipe down to where the sack was being held. Since the little thing's were half blind anyway, and scared to death to boot, they would run right into the sack. And boy, did they ever make gooood stew!! You would tell this unfortunate soul that you were gonna give them the easy part of just holding the sack. You and the rest would go up the ditch / ravine and do the 'hard work' of the chase. Friend, a many a fool has bought that set of lies over the generation's.

So, you would take this completely innocent person on a snipe hunt. The hunt would alway's be at night. The ravine would always be far off in the darkest part of the wood's. Your victim, who by now was salivating at being promised the first bowl of stew, would be all into the hunt, anxious to not let even one bird get away. You and your bunch of hoodlums, er, friend's, would give a last set of 'instructions' about the correct way to hold the sack, and having patience to stay with it till the snipe could be located and sent flying down the ravine. Then the lot of you would leave. And at that point you had two option's. You could just keep right on walking, all the way out of the wood's, and leave your sucker (you wanted me to say 'friend'?) to finally figure out that he / she had been had, and to get home the best way they could. The other option was a lot more fun if you had planned well. You would have stashed plenty of pot's, and pan's, and anything else that would make a racket, well before the 'hunt'. You and your motley crew would take a wide circle, come up behind the poor soul with the sack, and cause them to need a change of drawers when they got home. I don't have to tell you which option was taken most of the time in my Dad's day, now do I? With all of that now explained, I will tell you about a snipe hunt that my Dad always swore he was in on, one night after revival meeting at church. I call it....

DAD'S LAST SNIPE HUNT

You know how it is for young'uns after any church meeting don't you friend? They can't go home till Mom and Dad go home. So they find way's to occupy their time till time to go, right? Well, in my Dad's day this was a prime time for a good snipe hunt. They could walk home when the hunt was over. So on this night, after a revival meeting, the gang decided that a good snipe hunt would be an excellent way to end their evening, if only they could find someone to 'hold the bag'. Imagine how hard it was for them to contain their glee when a young lady in their midst, hearing the talk, vollunteerd to do sack duty. This was almost too good to be true for the boy's. Not just a new 'sucker', but a girl, too! With parental approval in hand, off down into the dark wood's they go. Keep in mind they are leaving church. They have their Sunday go to meeting best on. For the boy's now, that was not necessarily a bad thing. They would most likely have on over-haul's and be wearing boot's. If they were lucky, they would have on a starched white shirt. As for the young lady of that day, she may have on her only Sunday dress, painstakingly made by her Mother. So it was, Dad used to say, with this little lady.

The script went off to perfection. And which of the two normal options do you suppose the boy's chose on this night? Well, it would not be gentlemanly to just leave a young lady in the woods to find her own way home, now would it? The only honorable thing to do then, was to scare the living daylights out of her, then share a good laugh on the way home as she cussed them out. What's that? Ohhh, don't be fooled, my friend. 'Young ladies can cuss with the best of them, when the situation warrant's it. Phase one of the hunt went as planned. The boy's circled around. They were able to get closer than they ever had before to a victim. And they did have the use of long stashed noise-maker's too. When it was time to make noise, well, a high school band could not have been louder. Brother, they made the tree's shake, the deer stampede, and came darn near waking the dead. It was at that moment in time when their evening took a turn that would make it a life long memory.

The young lady bolted. I don't mean to say she ran. She bolted. I mean to say, she left that ditch so fast till the sack she was holding stayed in the air a good three seconds thinking it was still being held. Worse, when she cleared the wood's, she headed straight for the cow pasture fence that she and the boy's had gone through not that long ago. On the way to the wood's, the boy's were the very picture of chivalry, helping her to get through the strand's. Well, the boy's were not with her now, and she was not inclined to wait for them, either. She was in complete, all out 'feet don't fail me now' mode. That poor pasture fence. It never stood a chance. Hell hath no fury like a woman who is running as though it just might be the devil himself who is chasing her! Friend, I don't mean she jumped over that pasture fence. What she did was, she ran THROUGH that fence! Now her Sunday dress (you know, the one that her Mother made, BY HAND) is in shreds. She herself is scratched up from one end to the other. She looks like she just got the worst of it in a play-ground fight. We won't even talk about her hair-do. This obstruction, and the results of it, causes the addition of a couple more octaves to the aria she is already performing. She know's what her parent's reaction is going to be when they see her dress (possibly the ONLY Sunday dress she has). She still has no idea what might be behind her. She has no desire to look either. As she makes a bee-line for home, I can picture her screaming so loud that the grass / weeds before her lie down, only to be mangled in her wake.

Meanwhile, the boy's are back at the starting line, so to speak. All their jaw's are dropped, so wide as to make a fair rest stop for any bug running away from an owl. No-one moves to try and catch her. None of them think they have a prayer of catching her. To not be able to catch a girl, even in these, well, let's say 'unusual circumstances', could cause a fella a good bit of flak with the guys at school or church. None of them were willing to risk it. Never had they seen a girl run this fast! Besides, they saw her destroy that pasture fence. They have an idea that night might become a long one, once she get's home. They decide that the best thing to do at this point is to break out their running legs too, and get to the house as quickly as they can.

As they run home, the young lady get's to her own home. Her family meets her in the yard. She has already been heard. You know how it is with a train don't you friend? You hear it way before you see it, right? I rest my case. So here comes Daddy's little girl blowing into the yard, all in a mess. She's screaming. She's scratched up. Her hair looks like a milking machine has been sucking on it. They can't make out anything she's saying, EXCEPT.....The names of the boy's she was last seen with. What's a Dad supposed to think? That's his baby girl. She's crying and screaming at the same time. Her dress is torn in too many places to count. She is a walking mass of scratches. Now friend, how would that kind of math add up to you? As for this Dad, his blood pressure goes into the hyper tension zone. His face and his eyes go candy apple red. His ears start to twitch. His nostrils start to flare. His hands become two huge clinched fists. His body start's to tremble. And he bolt's for the house. You know the drill. I didn't say he ran. I said he bolted. There is a t.v. show called Smallville. It's built around the life of a young Superman, who can get from home to the scene of near tragedy in the blink of an eye. Get the picture? In a flash this Dad is out the door, shotgun in hand. He is about to see to it that these (you fill in the blank) understand that HIS daughter will NOT be handled in this way! Nor will his horses, for that matter, but especially his daughter! Then he intends to see them off into an early eternity. Explain this one to Peter at the gate, brother!!

Well, guess whose house get's the first visit? Yep, it was the home of Albert Ogle. PaPa had to do some fast talking that night to keep his own hide and save my Dad's. In the end though, they escaped with no buck shot leaks in their bodies. As for my Dad, one thing he did NOT escape was another little revival meeting led by Brother Horse-strap. You know, I've thought about this story a lot over the year's. I don't think I've ever heard my Dad talk about a snipe hunt that happened after that unforgettable night. I can't imagine why. But when I get to Heaven, I think I'll ask him. You know, just for fun!

WHEN A HANDSHAKE MEANT SOMETHING

Trust me when I tell you that I have barely touched the surface in telling you about a share-croppers life. But you should have enough information by now to know that this could be a harsh life in many ways. But there were times for fun, however devilish you might think it to be. I will say that share-cropper families, with rare exceptions, were close knit families, fiercely loyal to one another. If you were going to whip one of them, sooner or later you were going to have to whip all of them. These folk were very independent. They were not prone to accepting charity unless there was just no other way to meet a need. A share-croppers hand-shake was his contract. He did not need ink or paper. Yes, my friend, there was a time when a handshake meant something.It was like money in the bank.

I remember taking my PaPa Ogle to the doctor the day he found out he had cancer. He did not like Lanier Memorial Hospital one bit. He felt like they ignored MaMa's complaints about pain in her throat till the cancer in it had progressed too far. But sitting in Dr. Ron Shivers office that day I saw two men come to agreement where both men looked one another in the eye. PaPa signed the necessary paperwork for treatment. But before he did that he extended his hand to the good doctor. When he did that I could have cared less whether he signed anything or not. My PaPa had declared his contract with his hand. I'll tell you another thing about Albert Ogles hand-shake. He could bring a lot of present day football coaches to their knees, years after he left the fields and started driving a taxi.

DAD LEAVES HOME

Well, I told you that my Dad was the oldest of seven kids. The oldest child, and especially the oldest boy, was expected to be able to take over if illness or accident layed his Dad up for a time.

Therefore much more was expected of him in the fields and at home. PaPa being as tough as he was, his propensity for backin' up his orders with that horse-strap of his finally started wearing on my Dad. One day, when my Dad was 15 years old, PaPa strapped him with that strap. He told my Dad that he was going to town, and when he got back he was goin' to strap him again. My Dad had other ideas. He told his brother "He aint gonna hit me with that damn thing again." He had that brother to take him to the grist mill in a mule and wagon. He got off that wagon and started walking. He left a parting message thoug. "Tell Momma I'll see her soon. Tell Daddy I'll see him when flowers bloom in December." Well....

Dads life changed forever when he started to walk that day. At 15 years of age he had made the decision to live the life of a man. It is certain that he landed in a mans world when his walking ended almost three months two in Chambers County in an area called 'the Valley'. He would stop along the way and work for meals, or for a place to sleep. There was one family in particular that Dad was fond of. He stayed with them for a short while. He had long since forgotten their names the last time we talked about that part of his life. But they were very kind to him. He never forgot it either.

I'm not sure how Dad heard about Chambers County and the Valley area. It was a booming place though. Cotton mills were springing up all along the Chattahoochie River. The owners had money to spend, and they needed workers. In the beginning it wasnt easy to get people to come off the farms and these new mills. True, the jobs were indoors. True, the money would be steady and weekly. Drought or rainy season would no longer hurt a mans ability to earn a living. All well and good, but it was not always enough to convince folk to leave a way of life that had been practiced by a family for generations. Another thing that could cause the mills to be short handed was men who would work in the mills in the off season, then go back to farming in the spring.

The mill owners addressed this with what must have been a huge investment. Houses began to spring up all around these mills. These became the communities known as 'mill villages'. Friend, if you ever take the opportunity to visit the villages of 'the Valley' where I grew up you will notice that most of them still have two front doors. Thats because in the beginning two families lived in them, one on each side. The two families could tell what one anothers daily schedules were, I'm told, just by the sounds their members made. Friend, I'm gonna leave that one right there where it sits.

Now, the new houses alone were good. But other things came along that would be qualified in that day as a 'modern convenience'. For example, indoor runnin' water. No more trips to the well, or the spring, or any place else outside, often in the rain. With the advent of indoor runnin' water came along a new convenience. An indoor bathroom. And a huge tub to bathe in, to boot. Now friend, stay with me here, but I'll measure that it was right along in here, or not long after at the least, when some enterprising entreprenour came up with what became a very necessary accessory to this 'indoor bathroom' livin'. Something called an air freshener. You know what I mean, dont you friend? But really, think about this indoor bathroom thing. No more tippin' out to an out-house in the ice cold of a winter night and plantin' your warm tushie on an ice cold wooden seat. Those were the fore-runners of a toy that we call a 'whoopie cushion' today. These primitive precursors became extinct over time because of the comforts of this new modern life.

Indoor electric lights meant the home could stay 'open' longer in the late afternoons or early evenings. Tell me friend, cant you just hear that former farmer or share-cropper sayin' in wander, "My soul, Momma, you look as good in the light at night as you do in the daylight. BETTER even!" Oh, stop it Hugh. At any rate, in all seriousness any man worth his salt always wanted for his children to have more than he came up with. You feel that way dont you friend? And I imagine thats what it came down to in the end. No doubt more than a few men put a lot of careful thought and prayer into a decision to leave the farm and move to 'the village'. I dont measure that it was an easy decision.

In fact, I have wandered much over the years friend, as I have reflected on what I've heard of those times, how many proud farmers took a last walk out into the fields he had sown and reaped in, as generations of his family had. In the solitude of that moment did he allow himself a few private tears? What was it like, I have wandered, to walk out of that field for the last time. He knew he was doing the right thing for his famly, yet he was heavy hearted for a way of life that was breathing its last. Who could have known then that there would be a day when the mill worker would some day have the same feelings? But they would, and not because of any 'new way' of life either. We shal examine this much further down the road of this life I have lived, friend. And my blood pressure is rising already at the thought.

I have even mused on this line, friend. What of the fields of Clay County? If they could talk to us, would they prefer the pine thickets and subdivisions that now cover them? Or would they consider it all to be a pollution of the life they would still be living if only they got a vote on it? What stories they could tell us if only they could talk! Stories of barefoot boys bantering as they picked the cotton, about who could pick the most, or the fastest, or run the fastest, or catch the biggest fish. No doubt they would chuckle when a boy got the 'shake down' treatment from his Dad when he thought he had the sack full that he was pickin' in. Be patient with me, my fellow traveler, and I'll be done rambling here in a moment. But there were other things a share-cropper would never have to bother with, unless he just wanted to. No longer would boys have to pick black berries and sell them for ten cents a gallon to help supplement the family income. No more 'possum huntin', which could be interesting indeed. You find the possum. You hit him over the head with a stick. The 'possum curls up into a defensive ball. You pick him up and get him into a sack before he takes a taste of your flesh. Then you walk up to town and sell him for two bucks. No more would shre-cropper men and their boys have to work a whole day cuttin' a wagon load of fire wood, only to take it up town and sell it for two bucks. Whats that friend? Why, yes, the ENTIRE wagon load! The boys would make bundles of kindlin' wood to sell for ten cents each. By the way city folk, that means fire starter. Sorry 'bout that. I MUST do a better job of keepin' you all 'in the loop'.

There is a final plus to goin' to the village though, that we have not examined yet. It was potentially the most life changin' amenity of all, I would measure. It was a little thing called education. With some rare exceptions share-cropper kids rarely finnished grade school, much less high school. Albert Ogle did not finnish grade school. My Dad only finnished high school after the Korean War, on a thing called the G.I. Bill, which afforded educational opportunities to veterans. When you depend on the farmer and 'Mother Nature' to provide your sustenance, livin' often outranked education. Now, every mill village had a school. There were dormitories for the teachers. The mill owners would also pioneer the first kinder-garten programs in time. So now, the men folk could work in the mill. Some of the women would too in the early years. It was tougher for them at first. Generally the men were looked at as the bread winners for the family. Women worked in the home. So women working in the mill were often looked down on at first. They were called names like 'hussie'. That had any meaning one was tryin' to put on it. I have no desire to explore the details. So it was a hardy woman indeed who would face the 'downward look' to work in the mill.

At any rate, parents could work in the mill and know their children could get themselves an education at least through high school. Kids could do chores in the late afternoon, do their home work for school, and get a good nights rest before school the next day. And maybe, just maybe.... should a Mother or Dad dare dream? Maybe their children could go on to college! Well, now, to the village then! When I think of this time in my families history now, and look back at the complete mess I mad of any educational opportunity that was afforded me, I can almost come to tears. Much, much hard work and sweat went into what I could have done. And basically, I just spit on it all. It is a shame to me that can not be broken, even if this little book of mine sells a million copies. Think about that friend, wont you?

I want to say something to our youth who might read these words. You think it very unfair when Mom or Dad ask you to keep your room clean. When they ask you to take out the trash, or to feed whatever animals you have, you grumble. In school you do just enough to get by. You're not dedicated to being the best you can be. Lets paint this picture; you are satisfied with a burger flippin' education instead of a bank presedent education. Can I suggest a two week vacation for you next summer that might help change you outlook? What we'll do is this. We'll load a bunch of you up on a bus. We'll take you to south-west Tennessee. You will be left by twos to spend those two weeks with an Ahmish family. The Ahmish still do most things just like they did them when my Dad was growin' up. You will dress as they do. You will keep the same work day that they do.You will eat with them. You will worship with them. And you will be disciplined after their fashion.So be on your best behaviour, you hear?

No game boys, i-pads, lap tops and the like will be allowed on this little vacation. It's just as well. You're going to be too busy to use them. No cell phones either. Dont worry. It's just for two weeks. It will only SEEM like two months. Now, if you return from this vacationwith the same lack of appreciation for what your fore-bears did for you; if you return with the same lack of appreciation for what your parents, teachers, coaches,and pastors try to provide for you so that you can have a good foundation from which to spring-board yourself to a good college and career; if it dosent cause a light-bulb to sort of go off in your mind, I'll be willing to leave you to your burger flippin' future with no further comment.

The second thing I would ask you is to hear the following statement. The share-croppers, and even the early mill workers, were visionaries. Make no mistake, their first thought was for their children. But they knew their kids would be parents too some day. They knew that if they did not take advantage of the opportunities they found in the mill village, their kids and grand-children might pay the price. So they left a way of life that was a known commodity, even if it was harsh at times.They stepped into this nstrange new world of cotton mill work, which was stable enough but a complete unknown. They were the very definition of stepping out in faith. I feel as though I failed them in so many ways. Young people, you dont have to have the feelings I have unless you chose to live your educational life as I lived mine. Think about that.

DAD GOES BACK HOME

My Dad fudged on his age a bit and went to work at the Langdale Mill. But there was one time when he tossed aside his "When flowers bloom in December" message to his Dad. Someone got him word that his Mother had fallen ill. And my Dad did what any of us would have done friend. He went home to see about her. Love for ones Mother will cause many a family feud to cease, friend. When he got home Dad found that his Mother was not the only one with problems. Dad found his Father in the field. He was down. He had injured himself somehow. This was a proud man. He was use to keepin' his word. He was share-croppin' a five acre field for a man. It was not lookin' good for him. He pleaded with my dad to stay and help him get that five acres of cotton in. My Dad said it was one of the few times he ever saw his father cry.Well whats a son to do? Dad agreed to stay and help.

My Dad and his Father had an agreement between themselves. Dad would help get that cotton in. His Father, in turn, would share the profit equally with Dad when he settled up. There arose a problem though. When PaPa settled up with the man he was working for, the money was not what he had thought it would be. If he shared equally with my dad the rest of the family would be short money they needed badly. Of course Dad was having none of that. To their dying days both men believed they were badly cheated on that five acres of cotton. My Dad clearly remembered saying to his Father, "Daddy, theres something better than this out there somewhere. And I'm gonna go find it." Not long after that my Dad took his leave of Clay County for the last time. He never lived there again. In time his entire family would move to various parts of our Valley in Chambers County.

Friends, none of them had any assurance of success when they moved to a place where they were strangers. They would be working a type job they had never tried before. But they stepped out in faith. They left their old life behind. They were determined to make their new life work. For the most part they did too. Hear an old man young folk. I didnt say that my Dad and his family despised their old way of life. I have heard all of them talk wistfully of the days of hog killin', camp meetings and layin' by time. What I said is, they were not content with with that life. When opportunity called they went.They were willin' to step out of their comfort zone in exchange to make life better for their kids and grand-kids.

What would have happened to them, or to you and I for that matter friend, if they had stubbornly clung to a way of life that could still provide the basics of life, but could not afford them real future opportunities to better themselves? What if my Dad had not started that exodus of his family to a place where it was possible for a man and his wife to provide both economic AND educational opportunities for their children? There is no way that I could be writing this book right now without the chances I had to learn in our Valley where I grew up. Had I taken full advantage of those opportunities I could have done much more than write this little book of mine, which few people will probably ever see. But here I am writing it. But here I am writing it, because I dont want my boys to ever forget the hard work and sacrifice of Albert and Ora Ogle, of Hubert B. Ogle Sr and Hazel Ogle, and others who came before me. They paved the road of life I have traveled, and I am greatful for them. In leaving this portion of my book I want to include a note to my two sons, Joey and Levi. I want all young folk who might read this to consider this letter a challenge to you as well....

Dear Joey and Levi

I dont ever want you to be satisfied with being only as good as you Mom and I. The world you boys will have to be adults in will be more complexand have greater challenges for you than the world we lived in. Dont ever come to the place in life where you think you have maxed out your potential, or learned all that you can learn. Face the next challenge boldly. Reach for the stars. Dont let anyone tell you that you are not good enough to achieve your dreams.Let that kind of attitude make you even more determined. Work even harder to prove them wrong.

Dont return a hateful attitude of your own for theirs. Scripture teaches us to love our enemies, and to pray for those who despitefully use us. We're taught to not be overcome with evil, but to overcome evil with good. We're told to "Be not weary in well doing, for ye shall reap in due season if ye faint not." Remember it was Jesus Who said, "In this world ye shall have tribulation. But be of good cheer,I have overcome the world." Remember, when your Mom and I are gone,you two will still be brothers. You will have families that I pray will spend quality time with one another. Mosy importantly I pray that you will always love one another.Again, it was our Saviour Who said," By this shall all men know that ye are my disciples, if ye have love one for another.

You two have uniquely different talents that will be well suited for the trade or career you chose as adults. However, you will have more success, more satisfaction, and greater peace if you will place your talents under the hand of a mighty God Who promised through His Son, "I will never leave you,nor forsake you.In His hands you are clay to be molded into a warrior for His kingdom. Outside of His will, your life will always be just a shadow of what it could have beenif He had molded it. In the life of a child of God you will not be measurewd by how much money you make, or how big a house you live in, or how much influence you have in the community. You will be measured by (a) whether or not you ARE a child of God (remember, scripture says that not all who cry 'Lord,Lord shall enter), (b)whether you sought out His will in your life, and (c) whether you accomplished His perfect will.

It saddens me to know that I have missed out on so many golden opportunities to make a real difference in other peoples lives for Christ. My intentions were always good. But too many times I tried to accomplish my intentions in my own strength rather than following the blue-print that God has provided for His people. That blue-print is the Bible. It is not the book of the month guys. It is the Book of the ages. It is a roadmap that will get you to your Final Destination. It is a sword that will help you to fight and win the battles of life you will have along the way. You boys dont have to make the same mistakes I have made. If you will READ the word of God, MEMORIZE the word of God, LIVE the word of God, SHARE the word of God, and by doing that SPREAD the word of God, then someday when you FACE your God, you will be invited

LIVE with Him for eternity. Think about that guys. Thats a one and an infinity of zeros and commas.

On that day Joey and Levi, all of the troubles and trials you have to live through here will have been worth it. Every time you had to heal from the hurt and embarrasment of others, everyh temptation of satan that bruised you to the point of necessary repentance, and revitalization and regeneration, will have been worthwhile. You cant see it while you're going through the storm. But on Goin' Home Day you will hear your Saviour say to you, "Enter in good and faithful servant. You have been faithful in a few things. Now I will make you Lord and ruler of many things. Then guys, on that day, it will be worth it all.....

If God should call me Home early, I pray that your memories of your Dadwont be of the times that I was unkind or impatient. There were far too many of those. I pray that you will remember black-berry pickin', baseball, hiking, bowling, volleyball, and Christmas at Nannies or at Grand-ma and Grand-pas in Delaware. I hope you will remember above all else that you were raised to love Christ, to live for Him, to witness for Him, and to serve Him. Finally, know that the last breath I took on this earth was spent loving you boys and your Mother. I will expect to see all of you when God calls His church Home one glad day. On that day we can all go together and lay our crowns down at the feet of the One Who made our eternity together possible, safe from the battles we have fought here.

Lastly guys, I pray that you will remember that your imperfect father came to a placein life where he turned his heart again towards Home and tried to be both the right kind of Dad and one of your best friends besides. In the meantime guys be good stewards of of your talents. Let service to others define your life in Christ. And always stay surrendered to Hom, and for Him. I love you...

Dad

O.k., o.k., it was a short Baptist letter. Let that be a lesson to ya. Dont get me started on a story. I feel much better now that I got all of that said.

ONE-B (CONTINUED)

Seriously young folk, it's not my purpose to belabor the point. But you are reading the words of a man who failed the tenth grade three times (the last two times purposely). I literaly went to school with whole families. I crammed 12 years of school into 22 years. There will much more about this before I'm done with the story of the life I have lived. It was a total waste of three years of my life. It was a waste of my prents hard earned money and their sacrifice. It was a waste of the taslents of teachers who really wanted me to succeed. So here I am, over five decades into this thing called life, getting ever closer to that journey from which none of us can return, and just now I'm finally using what little I allowed myself to absorb in those years to contribute something positive to the world I live in.

I just dont want any of you to one day be my age and have the regrets that I have. Dont find yourself looking back with 20/20 hindsight at 30-40 years of 'what might have been' thoughts. There is still time for you. Take advantage of any opportunity to learn. Leave no stone of life not overturned in your search for an opportunity to advance your knowlege. And do me a favor wont you? Come by a book signin' some day and tell an old man that he really DID make a difference in your decision to take life just as far as you could. That would be really special.

BACK TO THE VALLEY

Now, then. Where did we leave my poor father? Ahhh yes. Lets do it like this. Lets pick his story up at the point where he leaves Clay County for the last time, friend. Are you with me? Alright then. Dad went just as straight as he could, right back to our Valley. He went back to Langdale Mill. He's sixteen now. His job is in the carding department. There were many machines, including most in the carding department of that day, that could be accidents waiting to happen for an unsafe or over-worked employee. Considering the number of hours Dad was known to work in that day, it is a wander to me that he got through 25+ years of mill work with not even one lost time accident. I have heard many rather gruesome stories over the years about deep cuts, limbs lost, and even death being the result of various accidents in the mills. My Dad was one of the fortunate ones.

Dad was a hard worker throughout his working days. He still would be today if he wasnt enjoying an eternal retirement in a Placewhere no work is necessary. He was known for his willingness to work double shifts whenever he was needed. Early on in his married life he worked 24 cosecutive hours. Only once though, mind. Mother drew a line in the sand on that one. There was another time when his second hand (supervisor for my city dwellin' readers) called him into the office. He said, "Hubert, we cant pay you all the money you have commin' this week. If we do, you'll be makin' more than the supervisors here." My Dad allowed them to defer a day of his work to the next week and took a rest day. What thinketh thou, my worthy travelin' pertner? Did my Mother get a vote in on that one too? There you go. You're gettin' the picture. By the way, what are the chances you and I would be as kind to our bosses or companies in this day? Yes, yes. My feelings exactly...

But let us think about this for a moment. Yes, the mill was extremely hot, especially in the summer. The work was never ever easy. The hours could be long, especially if you worked double shifts. But remember, the early mill work force was made up of people who were use to working a 12-14 hour work day, outside, even more exposed to the elements. For those people an eight hour shift was a walk in the park by way of comparison. As a young man especily, my Dad could stand alongside any man in terms of ability to work. Dad was a 'company man', to a fault in my opinion. He was taught by his dad, and he taught me, to never bite the hand that fed him. In my life I have strayed from that doctrine from time to time. Like everyone else who has a nose, I have an opinion on most things. And I am decidedly NOT bashful about expressin' it neither.

For example, if you are payin' me, say, $10.00 per hour, and give me a 3% raise, my pay goes to $10.30 per hour. But if you raise my health care deduction by 5%, my pay is now $9.50 per hour in money I take home. Now tell me friend, did I get a raise? Really? That is before you add in the cost of living increases in things I have to have. For the sake of our discussion, lets say that those costs went up 2%. Now, in terms of the money I actually have to spend each week, I make $9.31 per hour. Is it me, or is there a patern here? But wait, heres a better one. If I make that same $10.00 per hour, and I get a 0.005 % raise,how much am I making after that raise? I'm still making the same exact thing.Now, deduct our 2% cost to what I pay for goods, and I make$9.80 per hour in real spending money. These are two situations I have encountered in my 40+ years of working friend.There are times when it's just hard not to say something.

Now, dont get me confused with a pro union guy neighbor. I worked for one of those just once, early in my work career. I have no desire to work for one again. I just think it's time we haad an honest discussion in this country about why it is that the laborer is constantly expected to do the one who sacrifices spending power. When the price of everything we need goes up sometimes twice a year, and our real spending power is either stagnant or going backward, there should be no question why our economy cant completely turn around. Your middle class stays 'middle' only because both parents work, or both work and one works a second job. And they still try to have time with family, serve in their local chuech, and a vacation once a year, even if only for a weekend, would be nice.

Unions, in fact, dont stand a chance anymore, especially in the south. Think about this, friend. Textiles, as a mover in our economy, is extinct for the most part. In recent years various southern states especially have become adept at drawing new industries to the south. For example, the car industry.Many of these jobs are being taken by workers with textile history in their background. They use to work for $9.00 to $12.00 per hour. These days in companies that pay along that range an employee might pay as much as $100.00 per week for family insurance as well. Then they are blessed with a job at a car manufacturer that pays them as much as $18.00-$22.00 per hour. Their family insurance is half or better what it use to be. Now here comes the union rep who says "We can do better than that." And the former textile or metal worker just laughs at him. Poor union guy. He cant organize the company because the owners will just give notice and close or move the thin away. He cant organize the big companies because their employees never had it so good. Why would they want dues deducted from their checks that go in part to support political causes or candidates they done agree with?

Seems to me that we are missing some things in the work force today that were still very much in play when my Dad started working. This share-croppers son had a mind set borne of his home training. He trusted his employer to pay him in full In return he was willing to work any hours that employer needed him to work. It strikes me that if we had a mutual thing in todays workplace where management and laborers both thought the the best of one another, gave their best to one another and did their best for one another, employees would be better paid and more productive. Management would not have to worry about employees who cut corners and took advantage of of the system at every opportunity.Sadly, I'm afraid that we may never reach the level of trust we must have with one another to make all of this happen.

Now, lets leave the mill for a bit, shall we friend?When Dad got into the Valley area, the first thing he needed was a place to live. He found a room at the Hunt Boarding House in the Fairfax village. Mrs. Hunt provided meals as part of her agreement with those who stayed there. Good thing too. My Dad, bless his heart, to the day he went Home, could not boil water without stickin' some of it to the bottom of the pan.Dad remembered his time at that boarding house with great fondness.. He loved the Hunt family 'slap to death', as we say it in soth Chambers County.

The boarding house was just a short railroad track walk from his job too. Living there also put Dad near a popular hangout for folk his age in that day. That would be the Fairfax Theater right across from the mill in that village. The theater was especially popular on weekends, crowded with young folk. Trouble could be had amongst the fun from time to time however as Dad found out one Saturday night. A fella walked up to my Dad and challenged him to a fight. As I have said before, Dad did not go looking for trouble. But he was not prone to backin' down in that day either. Especially when challenged in public like that. So on this night he accepted the challenge, only to be knocked unconcious by a ball bat. When Dad came to himself and realized what had happened, he went home, got his shot-gun, and spent the better part of the balance of the evening lookin' for that fella. Had he found the guy, his insurance would have been put to good use shortly there-after, I measure.

DADS KEYS TO SUCCESS

This kind of thing could happen to Dad from time to time. He was known to be a person who never went looking for trouble. But he did not run from it either. Overall though Dad seems to have done very well for himself, living a mans life as a teenager. Though I concede that I speak with a very prejudiced tongue, I think I can speak to the why of it. As I said before, Dad was a known hard worker. Still today there is something to be said for a worker who will put his/her nose to the grind-stone, as it were. A worker who will not pout just because he cant find a job in the field of study right after college, but will do any work he can find till his 'dream job' comes open. That worker will do that job well too. When he gets the job he wanted in the first place he will appreciate it more.

Secondly, Dad was loyal to the hand that fed him, no matter who that hand belonged to. Over the years you could count on him to be one of the first in line to help whenever a friend or family member had a need. Early on in their married life Mother and Dad went to the home of a cousin of his who had passed. He had two boys who did not have suitable clothes for the funeral service. Mother and Dad took those boys to Kesslers to remedy that. While they shopped Mother noticed one of the boys admiring a belt. Dad asked him if he liked it. The boy said "My Daddy had a belt like that." He wore that belt home that day friend. Years later I was delivering Pizza part time for extra money. One night I delivered to a small home in Langdale. The young man who answered the door noticed my name tag and asked if my last name was Ogle. I said it was. He asked "Is Hubert your Dad?" I said he was indeed. And this young man proceeded to tell me the story of that shopping trip to Kesslers all those years ago. His story was exactly the story Dad use to tell me.

This type story could be repeated many times friend. I know that Dad and Mom did without more than a few times so that others could have. I once saw something written in a card sent to employees of the card/drawing department at Fairview Mill. They had made up money for him during an illness he had. I said this ; "It's always nice too be remembered. It's especially nice to be remembered when you're down". People appreciate your thoughts and prayers. But they know you mean business when you put action behind those two things. Jesus told some folk once that if you tell a hungry fella that you sure hope he gets a belly full of food, but you do nothin' to make that happen, why, you realy aint done nothin.' I learned to help take care of my fellow man by watchin' my parents do it. And I am very thankful for that.

Thirdly, my Dad was honest. In every job he ever had, he was trusted because of his honesty. When Doss Leak left the River View Recreation Department to take leadership of Community Service west Point Pepperel owned it's own vending service in that day) he added Dad to his work force at his earliest opportunity. He said of my Dad "Hubert is as honest as the day is long." You know friend, there are times in life where a less talented but more trustworthy person is to be preferred over a more talented person with less integrity. It strikes me that if corporate America had adhered to this kind of policy instead of the 'get ahead at any cost' policy that still prevails today, sadly enough, we might have avoided some of the corporate scandals that have so damaged our credibility and economy over the years.

I would also say that my Dad was a person who did not meet strangers. He could strike up a conversation with with anyone. It did not matter whether it was a pauper or a millionair. He was just as comfortable talking with the CEO as he was the bathroom cleaner. This is just another one of the lessons Dad learned as the son of a share-cropper. A man, by any other defination, is still just a man at the end of the day. The millionair can buy all the luxuries of life that a pauper can only dream of. But they both will be held to the same standard when they stand before Christ some day. And they both will leave this world with the exact same thing they entered it with... nothing.

So Dad looked every man in the eye. He measured no man by any secular or economic or proffessional standard. He wanted to know whether that person was a hard worker. He wanted to know whether that person was honest. He wanted to know whether that person was honest, and whether that person could be loyal. And finally, could that person look him in the eye when they spoke. And he was appreciated for it.

GOSPEL MUSIC

One of dads favorite things, from his youth on up, was gospel music. He grew up on camp meetins' and convention style sigins' in Clay County. Dad took us back to his ole stompin' grounds about a year before he went Home. I was surprised when I saw his old home church. It was a tiny Holiness Church. We were raised in a Southern Baptist Church. This little church still looked much as it had when Dad was growin' up. It had cement block walls. It was painted white. Like most churches nowadays it had added the almost obligatory ' fellowship hall.' But it was pretty much the same building Dad led his first singing in. It sit's up on a little hill. Standin' in front of that little church and lookin' out across the road, there is a beautiful view of the woodlands. In Dads youth, I imagine that land would have been planted in cotton or corn or some such thing. I got a little tickled to myself thinkin' about that fateful 'snipe hunt' that almost certainly ended Dads 'snipe hunt' career all those years ago. I wandered which direction from this little church they went in when they left this little church yard that night. I couldnt bring myself to ask him though.

Dad was involved in gospel music in one fashion or another for over 50 years. He sang solo, duets, trios, quartets. He directed choirs for every age from beginner to youth to adult. He directed a church music program at Midway Baptist where I was raised for over 20 years. Revivals, weddings, funerals, home-comings, Bible schools, there just isnt much dad did not do in music. I have a picture of Dad from early on in his singing career. He's in a radio station with another man and two ladies. They are singing for a one hour gospel music show. Dads love for gospel music would lead him to be able to be involved in some pretty amazing things in the years to come. But it all started at this little holiness church in Clay County. Watching him that day, as we visited all too briefly where Dads faith in an all seeing, all knowing God began, I couldnt help but notice the look in his eye. He was back to his roots. He was home. And he was glad. You know what I mean, dont you friend?

GOSPEL MUSIC - NEVER A DULL MOMENT

Well friend, before we get too far down the path of life my Dad is now traveling in his youth, I thought you might enjoy a tale or two I remember, or that Dad told me across the years, about the life of the traveling part time gospel music singer. Some folk tend to think that all gospel music singers are well to do folk who do singing as a hobby. Au contraire my long sufferin' travel partner. They were, for the most part, workin' class folk just like you and I. Gospel music was not ever 'just a hobby' for them. It was a way of life, a ministry if you will. Their very heart was for the message in a song to make an eternal difference in some life at one of their singings. Never doubt that.When you are working a full time job and juggling a calendar full of singin' dates friend, things can get gut bustin' funny from time to time. Of course, the real 'funny' part comes when you look back on it all years later. So I include here a small set of stories about some... ahem...'adventures' some of these singers...including my Dad, had over the years. I hope you enjoy them. Let's start with a group on the way to a singin' out in the country on a Saturday night...in the winter...AFTER a time of snow, snow melt, and a dirt road. I'm smilin' already.

This group traveled as most did in the early days of the popularity of Saturday night singings. They used their personal vehicles. They went to their singin' already dressed in their suits. On this particular late afternoon they will be going to a church far out 'in the cuntry' as we use to say. It's winter. It's cold. A snow has fallen and half melted on the dirt road they are trying to navigate. The road is 'fresh peeled onion' slick. And one of the cars slips off into a shallow ditch. Normally this is not a challenge. But on this day, with everyone already dressed to sing, and the road 'fresh mud slick', it's another matter.There are three cars in the singin' groups little convoy. Several of the wives are along. Of course, all the cars stop and the men start to look over the situation. They decide that if they have someone to steer the car they can probably push the car out of the ditch and be on their way. One of the wives vollunteers to steer so that all the men can put their collective brawn into pushing the car. A second wife vollunteers to sit on the passenger side and 'be the ears' of the driver on that side of the car. Y'all with me now?

The steering vollunteer get's instructions from her husband. "When we get the car out of the ditch, I'll say 'hit it!', and you hit the gas just a little. The car should come right on up out of this ditch, and we can still be on time." The men get behind the car and start pushin'. Just as they are startin' to move the car a bit, the man on the right side of the car slips, his elbow strikin' the bumper rather hard. Before he can contain himself he starts to testify...rather loudly. Well, it's HIS wife 'bein' the ears' for the steerin' vollunteer. She hears all this testifyin'. Shae aint NEVER heard her husband testify like this before. She leans out of the window. Her husband is shaking his arm wildly. She asks "What in the world you done went and done to your arm to make you testify like THAT?!! He hollers back "I HIT IT!!!" The pore lady doin' the steerin' now, she thinks she missed the signal and is being told again, emphatically, to give some gas to the car. Unfortunately she over reacts, giving the car more gas than she was told to. By the way, the men are still behind the car. All of a sudden, they are not dressed to sing after all.....Mother said there would be days like that...

KEEP IT REAL SIS

The following story I tell in honor of and in memory of my oldest Sister Veritha. She fought a three year battle with breast cancer like a true warrior. Frankly, friend, if a persons last name is Ogle, you can be sure that we love life. We live life to the fullest that we possibly can. And at the end of it all, we will fight for the last breath we take. So it was with Veritha. My sister, when we were growin' up, was quite the live wire. She was the life of the party wherever the party was. Sometimes she started BEFORE the party, friend. She once showed up for a 'surprise' 16th birthday party almost 40 minutes early with a big ole grin sayin' "Wheres everybody at?" Mother and Dad got around to teachin' her to drive, not knowin' that she had been drivin' since the age of 14 or so. I smile now as I wonder how she managed to pretend that she was the one doin' the learnin' durin' that time. How Mother and Dad never caught on is a mystery to me.

There was an occaisional time however, when Verithas mischief didn't end with a laugh. This is the story of a singin' she went to with Dad one night that I assure you she never forgot. Nor did Rhonda, her friend who went with us that night. Nor did I. I want you to understand, my attentive reader, that I am not makin' fun of a denomination in this story. I tell it all in good fun. I think Veritha would get a real hoot out of it. After we were grown she never failed to laugh out loud when this story was retold again.

Please understand friend, that we were raised in a conservative southern Baptist church. We tend to be a bit more reserved I'm afraid, in terms of the type services we have. There IS a bulletin, and we WILL go by it. Everything decent and in order. There is not one thing wrong with that either. Y'all don't have to worship the way a Baptist does. Nor does the Baptist 'reform' his or her worship to mimic yours. After all, when you get right down to it salvation is all that really matters, is it not? Soooo... Dads group, on this Saturday night, was to be singing at a Holiness church. WAIT, DON'T START LAUGHING YET! NO FAIR! Awww, it's okay. I'm smilin' a bit myself. Dad showed up at the church early, as was his custom. He would get the equipment all set up, then do a sound check which lasted till he thought the system jibed with the building they would be singin' in. When the group was all there, a song or two would be practiced. Then it was off for prayer time before the service started. The guy who let us in the church that night seemed just like many others we had met at singings on other Saturday nights. Nothing out of the ordinary at all. We were completely ignorant of the type service we were about to be indoctrinated to.

The church was a small cement block type building on the outside. It had just a simple sign out front announcing the denomination of the church. I was impressed at the crowd. The boy I use to be and I agree that the little church was full that night. I could tell that this service was going to at least be different from what we were use to from the beginning. Even during the congregational music there was all kinds of clappin' hands and shoutin' and I don't know what all. And friend, these folk could flat out sing! Presently it was time for the featured singers to begin their sets. And then commenced a service that even now, over 45 years later, I can call back from my memory as though it was last weekend.

It took all of three songs for this service to go wide open. The first thing I saw was a woman...a woman, now, flat foot jump from the pew she was in to the pew in front of her, just'a shoutin' to beat the band all the while. Soon I heard a commotion to the front and the right of the church. Three or four fellas had another guy pinned up against the wall. One of them had his hand on the guys forehead. The others had their hands on his shoulders or his back. And friend, they were holler shoutin', at the top of their lungs. And the pinned up fella, he was havin' a seizure. He was just'a shakin' and mumblin' nothin' I could understand. But he looked like he was in a lot of pain. At this point neighbor I was looking for an exit strategy. It was then I saw a window, and remembered that this little church was a one story affair. If I jumped out the window I would land in grass not three feet off the ground. Good. But before I could act on that idea I heard womens voices in the rear of the church. They were so loud, and so quick, till I yanked my head around to see what was goin' on. And I'll be a big bowl of 'nanner puddin' left uneaten, if they were not doin' the same thing to some young lass as the men were doin' to the poor guy up front. Only this young lady was feeling the effects of 'hands on' far more than the guy up front. She passed slam out, neighbor! I mean, she hit the floor like a rock and layed there shakin' like she was out in winter weather without a coat. And them other ladies, they aint even slowed down their hollerin'. If anything, they were now even louder!

Well friend, my toast is completely done now. I'm goin' out that window, and fast. Before I could make my move though, I heard the voice of the pastor, just'a bellerin', "Anybody who is ready to get somethin' from Gaaawd jes line up right here in front of me." Well, just feed me a half a watermelon on a hot summer day and call me satisfied, if that line didnt start forming almost before the pastor could get the words out. With all that was goin' on around me I thought by now folk would be makin' for the door. But my astonished friend, these folk, why, they almost seemed to be jockeying for position to see who could get up there first. This preacher now, he had one hand up in the air. He had in the other hand a small bottle of a yellow liquid. When someone got to him, the preacher would holler, "Are you ready to get something from the Laaawd tonight?" And person after person friend, ever single one'a them people would say "OH YEAAAAH!" That preacher would put some of that yellow liquid on his fingers, and he would tap the person in front of him on the forehead. Friend, that was a powerful tap. I was right glad he did not flat out hit them. Every time he tapped somebody, he or she would just fall out in the floor. They would just twitch and turn and contort their bodies this'away and that'away, and say things that I declare, to this day I can't tell you what they were.

Thats it, I thought. I am solid gone now. Then I thought of my sister Veritha and her friend Rhonda. Where were they? How were they takin' this 'church service'? Well it did not take me long to find them. And when I did friend, I got cold chills all over my body. They were up about four rows from me and to my left. And friend, they were just'a jumpin' up and down, and yellin', and I don't know what all, just like most of the folk in the place were by now. That was REALLY it neighbor. I thought, OHHH NO, THEY DONE WENT AND GOT VERITHA AND RHONDA!!! FEET DON'T FAIL ME NOW!! I went out that window so fast friend, till I can not remember if I even scraped the side of it on the way out. I made a bee line for the van that my Dads group carried their equipment in. I dived into the back of that van. I covered up with a quilt and stayed out of site. The only reason I came out was when I heard my Dads voice some time later. Boy, was I glad to see him! As for Veritha, she did not have such a good end to her night. When Dad saw that she and Rhonda were apparently 'in the spirit' he was so proud of her. That is, till he heard, as Paul Harvey use to say it so well, "the REST of the story". When the pastor started that line in the front of the church, Rhonda asked Veritha what that line was for. Veritha said, "Thats the line for anybody NOT participating in the other stuff goin' on around us. I 'spek we better get busy!" And the two of them started just'a jumpin', and shoutin' and all of that.

That night it was not MY name that was called to a bathroom revival friend. And if I told you I am sorry about that, I would be tellin' you a big ole lie. I really would. I will always miss my sister. She and I had our moments when we were teenies and in our young adult years. But at her passing we had restored ourselves to an open and honest, and sometimes frank, relationship. She was a fighter to the end in the matter of living life. I admired her strength. These days I find myself a tad jealous actually, of the reunion she has had with Mother and Dad. I look forward to my reunion day. Don't you, friend?

IT'S THE SNAKES FAULT!

This last story comes from my own short time in quartet music. My Dad gave my name to a fella lookin' for a singer. And I always had wanted to give it a go, just once. It involves a singin' we did on a Saturday night way out in the country somewhere. Neighbor, I have wished many a time that I could remember where that little country church is. I would love to go back there and visit. At any rate, I must set this story up properly. First of all, we traveled in and old use to be school bus. We had the back two seats on each side taken out for equipment storage.

In those days we had our equipment, of course, set up at the front of the church. But our sound was run from the back of the church. There was a long cord that ran from the sound board up to the mikes, speakers and so forth. Our manager called this cord a 'snake.' He had just bought a brand new one. And he was right proud of it too. Are you ready, friend? Here we go!

I remember that the side of the church we parked on was inclined just a tad. We pulled up that tiny slope and began to unload equipment. As we went about our buisness, I looked and saw a small car coming into the driveway. About that time someone came out of the front door of the church calling out, "Hey, we can't find the snake!!" Our manager called back, "Well, we have GOT to find that snake! We can't have service tonight without that snake!" Came back the answer, "Well, we done looked all over the place, and in every box too. And we can NOT find it!"

While all of this is going on the riders are getting out of the car. Turns out it was four senior ladies, come early to get a good parking place and a good seat. Friend, they heard every word of this back and forth between our manager and group members. Then they heard someone call out "Okay, we found it! It was under one of the pews! Someone took it out of the box too early!" Wait, friend, are you laughing and crying at the same time? Me too, me too. But we are not through yet. Our manager is now relieved and back to talking about the singing soon to commence. He never sees the little old lady who has apparently been selected to speak for her friends, slowly toddling up behind him. She tapped him on the shoulder. He turns around, and seeing her and smiles, saying"Hi there young lady! How are you this evening?" This lady has a simple question; "Excuse me, but thats not really a snake you y'all have in there, is it?" Our manager, not realizing what he is saying, and VERY proud of this newest piece of equipment, says "Ye ma'am, and it's 75 feet long too!"

Poor lady. She meekly said "Thank you", and toddled back down to their car. These ladies huddled for about one minute. Then they all got right back into that car. They backed out of the parking lot. Then they started back down that dirt road. Friend, by now I was laughing so hard till I mite-near rolled down that little hill we were parked on. I said to our manager, "You know you just broke up tonights singing, right?" He asked "Well how did I do that?" I asked "You really don't realize what you said to that lady do you?" I repeated their conversation, told him about their huddle before leaving. I said, "Every one of those ladies are going to get on their phones and call all their friends. They are going to tell them about this crazy singing group that brought a snake with them to the Saturday night singing. Don't expect a huge love offering tonight." And friend, I'll never forget what he said as the little car went from view in the dust behind that car. "Bless her heart. I didn't mean to scare her, not at all..."

I could write a book friend. I could write a book, indeed. But let us get back to my Dad, shall we?

THE GREAT WATERMELON CAPER

Believe it or not, even after that disastrous snipe hunt from his youth, Dad still had the disposition to the occaisional prank at the expense of some unsuspecting soul. I guess he felt more freedom now that he was away from home, far from his Dads horse-strap. However, one incident reminded Dad, in a very forceful way, that whether at home or on your own, there is always someone to answer to. There can be consequences anywhere and anytime you step across the line of what is reasonable. Or legal. Friend, I can hear the 'talky-talk' person asking me," Hey, was your Dad not saved at this point?" As a matter of fact he was. And would you like to tell me that you have never gotten into one moments mischief after your salvation decision? Did you suffer consequences? Careful now. God is listening.

One of the things that young fellas like my dad just could not seem to resist from time to time was to satisfy their craving for a field fresh watermelon at the expense of some farmer in the community. Remember, for a long time there were still farmers around the perimeter of the villages. A few of these farms were still pretty good sized. There was just such a farmer in the Valley area nearby to the villages. He had a field that he planted watermelons in each year. And each year a fair nimber of them would just take legs and walk right outta that field! You just would not believe it. Well, this farmer let it be known that this particular year he meant to put a stop to this 'walkin' melon' syndrome if he had to do it with his shotgun. O.k. friend. Are ya with me here? Do yhou need a hint about what is fixin' to happen?

There was a house on one side of this field. It was a two story house. It was empty as my head. Dad and his friends decided to play a practical joke on a fella. The idea was, they would take him out to this field, ostensibly to go on a 'melon raid'. They sent one of their number ahead to go into that empty house and plant himself by an upstairs window. He had a shotgun with him. The rest of the group, with their sucker...errr, victim in tow, would enter the field a little after dark. They would tip out to the middle of the field, within hearin' distance of the house. There was a set signal for the fun to start. Someone would call out, "Lookie heah, ahh got me a great big'un!" And at that pre-set signal, heres what happened friend. First, the fella in the second story window of that old house yelled out the window, "Ahhh said ahhh meant to keep my melons from tippin' outta mah field even if'n ahh had to do it wif a shtogun. And ding-dang it I mean to do just that!" And he fired that shotgun...BLAM!!

Then came the real 'coup' of the prank. A fella in the 'raidin' party' friend, had a light colored shirt on. That shirt, just by happenstance now mind, had a pocket on the left side. When the shotgun blasted, he sreamed, "ARRGGHHH!! The dang fool done went and shot me!!" He hit that shirt pocket, which just happened to be loaded with a very ripe small tomato. It looked for

33

all intents and purpose as though a murder had been committed. The 'victim' of that murder did the best death fall, followed by a very realistic death stare, that you ever did see, friend. Now then, the 'raiders' planned a fake pandemonium scene whereby they all would run as fast as they could to the other side of the field. There they would all stop and say "GOTCHA!!" to their friend, then laugh as he cussed them out on the way home.

Thats not quite the way it happened though friend. All went as scripted till they got to the other side'a the field. When they stopped to say "GOTCHA!" the poor guy never slowed up. He was plowin' up ground for spring plantin' just like the young lady in our snipe story. Dad and the guys called after him for a moment, but the young fella was solid gone,friend. So Dad and his little 'band of brothers' decided to just go on home. They could get their cussin' out on the morrow. On the whole, it had been a good night. And not one melon had walked outta that field. But look out. Mornin' is comin'. The 'victims' will be different then.You see, their 'victim' was absolutely convinced that he had witnesed a bonee-fidee killin' friend. He ran just as hard as he could run. He ran a good two miles. All the way to the police station.

Imagine the surprise on the faces of the nights 'raiders' when they are called rather briskly back to the melon field the next mornin'. Imagine their shock to find that field just crawlin' with police, who are looking for a 'body'. And standin' right in the middle of all that madness stands their 'victim' of the previous night. By now he has figured out exactly what happened the night before. But he aint about to say NUTTIN'! Who are the victims now? Poor Dad and his 'raiders'. All they wanted to do is to have a little good clean fun with a 'buddy'. Now the joke is on them. Only the police are not laughing. You know, I've thought about that incident more than once over the years. I don't think I've ever heard my dad speak of a melon raid that took place after that night. I cant imagine why. But when I get to Heaven friend...when I get to Heaven, you KNOW what I'm gonna have to do right? Yeppers, I'm jes gona HAVE to ask him. Whats that friend? Well of COURSE just for fun. Why else?

THE WAR DAYS

The sands of time shift again. Dad is near to twenty by now. He's lived in a mans world now as a teen for several years. He is about to finnish his growin' up. The hard way. I can almost see my Dad as he gets his mail on this particular day. He's just mindin' his own business, not bothering anybody. Then he opens up a letter. It's from an uncle oh his. Dont laugh. He's your uncle too. His name is Sam. When you are dealin' with your Uncle Sam, the picture he paints for you of your 'responsibility' often dosent match the reality of what you have to do to keep your responsibility.

Sam wanted to send Dad on an all expense paid four year vacation. Thats the good news. The bad news is that he wanted to send dad to something called a 'camp for boots'. Which made no sense coz at this 'camp' he would be taught how to shoot a fella before the fella could shoot him.

Friend, tell me if you can why that kind of 'paid vacation' would appeal to ANY of us? He would have to have a 'kill to keep to bein' killed' mentality each and every day he was there. I mean, hows a fella to get a decent tan, much less a good date? Dad would love to have just turned the whole thing down flat. But you know how persuasive uncles can be. And Sam, now, he can get downright onery AND persuasive when a body tries to turn him down. You know what I mean dont you friend? So, Dad accepted Uncle Sams offer. Off he went for six weeks of basic training. He went from our Valley to Montgomery, then on to Fort Jackson, South Carolina. After basic training he spent some time in the Phillipines. Then it was off to Korea to fight in the war.

Oh, but I forgot. Korea wasnt a war, was it friend? It was...how do they say it... a 'police action' right? There was no formal declaration of war, right? And who got to decide that this was not a war? I guarantee you this; it most certainly was not the young men like my Dad who ducked bullets and artillery, or tried to negotiate mine fields. It was not the soldier who came back from there minus a limb or two. It was not the soldier like an uncle of mine who left here young and strong only to come back scarred emotionally or mentally or phsycologically, never to be the same. It was politicians and governments friend. They got to call this a 'police action' without cracking a smile. Civilized nations (which would leave out North Korea and China) have some built in law or so called ethic which limits the circumstances under which a president or prime minister and so forth can ask for a declaration of war. In a situation like Korea, nobody wanted to take that kind of responsibility. So the words 'police action' were born.It is still used today. But friend, to families like yours and mine it is all the same. They send our young men and women to do their dirty work. Any action that calls for exchangng live fire, and results in the killing and maiming of our young people, is indeed war, regardless of the politically expedient explanations of any politician.

We lost multiple thousands of our nations best in Korea. Many more thousands came back wounded. And for what? What was gained? There was no final victory. The enemy never surrendered. What there was, was a truce, which only means everybody agreed to stop shooting. And thats the way it remains, even today over 50 years after the last shot was fired.Technically North and South Korea are still at war. Was it worth the massive loss of life and injury suffered by our military families? Not only that, but we did not learn any lesson at all in this 'police action', did we friend? If we had, we may have spared ourselves the next of our 'police action' calamities. You remember that one dont you friend? It was called Viet Nam.

My Dad, like most men who have gone off to war over the years, never spoke much about his time in the hell that was Korea. Generally, I know that he was slightly wounded once. He had a scar just above the hairline on the right side. On the rare occaision that you might get him to speak of it, it was clear that he thought there were other things our nation could have been doing. However, once his 'uncle' called, there was no question he was going to serve. As I have said before in this little book of mine, we dont raise draft dodgers, flag burners, and assorted other traitors in our family. Dont even bother with your apologistics right here neighbor. I aint budgin'! Just go ahead and start suckin' your thumb...

At any rate, my Dad made it through his time in Korea in reasonably good shape. When it was time to come home, home was our Valley, in Chambers County. Home was the same boarding house in Fairfax, with Mrs. Hunts good cookin' and all. And it was back to Langdale Mill, where Dad would work till he went to the River View Recreation Department. He pretty much settled into the regular routine of a normal life. When I consider what war, or 'police actions', do still today to many well serving military service members, it is remarkable to me that Dad was relatively unscathed by it all. He was blessed with good health over the years for the most part. He always did what was necessary to keep a roof over our heads, food on the table, clothes on our back, just little things like that. And he got little thanks for it too many times.

Dad had the same kind of social life most of his friends had. There was no shortage of dates. He still had a love for gospel music. He worked hard every day he was needed in the mill. He's in his early twenties now. He's beginning to think about a day when he will settle down. That day would be on him sooner than he would think. You see friend, when love strikes, it almost always does so in ambush style. I'm not talkin' about the surface stuff so popular in todays world. I'm talking about love that you are just sure will last a lifetime. It happens to all of us sooner or later. And so it was to be for my Dad.

MOTHER - LIFE IN THE VILLAGE

My Mother was born on August 8, 1934 in Langdale, in Chamber's County, Alabama. She was born in the family home. This was not uncommon in that day. George H. Lanier Hospital was still year's away. Doctor's still made house call's. The only hospital at that time was a long white building that sat across the road from the Langdale United Methodist Church. It has been gone for some year's now. My Mother's Mother, Ludie Yarbrough, was highly distrustfull of that hospital. A relative of her's had surgery at that hospital. In that day they used something called ether to put folk to sleep. In this case they administered too much of it, and her relative died. Miss Ludie never got over it. Actually, the old hospital looked more like a motel or an inn to me when I was a small boy. I remember well when it was torn down. Many folk never gave it a second thought. But I knew that a little bit of Valley history was gone. It lives on now only in stories like mine. God forbid that we ever forget it. That little hospital was the seed out of which George H. Lanier Memorial Hospital would later grow. For that reason alone it deserves to be remembered.

The home Mother was born into was a simple white frame house, roughly fashioned after the mill village homes. There is a little bridge that crosses Moores Creek where the road lead's up to Red Dirt Hill there in Langdale. Just before you cross that bridge, on the left, there use to be three of those white frame houses. Sadly, they are all gone now. If memory serves me right, Mother said it was the middle of these houses where her family lived at the time of her birth. Dr. Marshal was the doctor who delivered her. Dr. Marshal was one of the last 'community doctors' of the mill village era. This man was loved all over the Langdale Mill village. I've never heard a cross word said about him. Mother's parent's named her Hazel Raye. She was named after a nurse that her Mother knew and thought well of. I am sorry to say that I know nothing of this nurse other than Mother's brief mention of her in a keep-sake book she filled out for me called "A Mother's Memories To Her Child." I do know this. If Ludie Yarbrough thought enough of a nurse to name a child of her's after her, she was a special lady indeed. I'm sorry I never found out more about her.

My Mother's Dad was Albert Corbett Yarbrough. His friend's either called him A.C. or Corb. In the pronunciation of south Chambers County Alabama, it sounded more like 'Cawb.' He was a remarkable man in many way's. For example, he never learned to drive. Yet he could take apart the motor of any car on our street and put it together again. The same with lawn mower motor's. I wander sometimes how he would have done with today's 'computerized car's'. My guess is that he would have figured them out and done quite well. My PaPa had one downfall in his life, even on into my growing up year's. He enjoyed his beer. Occasionally he would have a go at the more high octane stuff too. As you can imagine, his entire personality changed when he had the brew in him. He could be verbally abusive. He could use some word's that would confuse a dictionary. When he was at his normal self though, he could be very giving of his time, his money, and anything else he thought would help another human being. Even at his worst, he had a big heart. He loved his family.

Both of my Mother's parent's were cotton mill worker's. But they both came from farming families. Miss Ludie's parent's were Emory and Julia Ann Colley. They moved to the Valley area from the Clay County area, just as my Dad's people did. Together they raised twelve kid's. Grandpa Colley was in Heaven before my time on earth began. I picture him as a bit of a ham. I have a good picture of him in his Sunday best. He has his hat off and doffed up in the air. And I swear I think I see a twinkle in his eye. I think he would have been fun to know. I do have some memory of Granny Colley from early in my childhood. She lived in a house in the village of Fairfax, behind Mr. Cheese Goggan's store. My Aunt Lorene lived with her. When Granny got tickled, her belly would just shake and shake. Funny what a child remember's, is it not? Another thing I remember is frollicking in a number ten washtub and thinking we were in a small pool. Go ahead and laugh friend. But it was fun to us, so a hearty suck of the ole thumb to ya! Grandpa and Grandma Colley lie at rest in a cemetary at Plant City, which is now a part of Lanett, Alabama.

Mr. Corb's family came from the Tallapoosa County area, not too far from where I live now. I do know that my great-great Grand-father fought in the Civil War with a unit from Alabama. He sustained a wound during that conflict that caused him to walk with a pronounced limp for the rest of his life. His last name was Monroe. PaPa use to tell us that his Grand-pa could not work in the fields to the same degree that the kid's could. But what he could do was hop into the house and tattle on who-ever was not holding up their end of the day's work. Which brought a result that would cause our 'new age' thinkers to have a seizure, friend. So we won't do it to them.... yet....but wait, we already hit them once with PaPa Ogles horse-strap, right? Poor undisciplined souls. Prob'ly still suckin' their thumbs. Which is o.k. by me.

My Grand-pa's Dad was named Bunk Yarbrough. His wife's name was Sudie Mae. They were farmers. My PaPa use to tell me that when my Mother was born he thought once or twice they might have to give her to his parent's. They doted on Mother, apparently. They did not live an easy life. But as in my Dad's case, I never once heard my PaPa vocalize any regret's about his raising. They were a proud, close knit bunch. Grandpa Bunk left this world in a painfull way. A big knot came up on his neck. The doctor thought it was a 'rising.' These could become 'boils' if left untreated. Think of a 'rising' as a huge ant bite. Think of a 'boil' as wet slimy puss that comes out of the top of that bite if it is left untreated. Get the picture? The common treatment for this was to 'lance it'. That is to say, cut it and let it drain. Only this was not a 'rising'. It was a tumor. Cancer. PaPa remembered well his Father saying to him, "You know, this thing came on me to kill me." And so it did. He, and a lot of PaPa's family, are buried at Eagle Creek, near Dadeville Alabama.

Something I always want to remember about PaPa's family is how they tried to stay in touch. I sat in Aunt Canvas (PaPas sister) and Uncle Lussie's apartment many time's when I was a boy. The Yarbrough's had family reunions every year till I was a young adult. They didnt go to a church or a park either. They went to one another's homes. My sibling's and I havent been in the same room together, all at one time, but twice in the last 15 plus year's. Once at my Mother's death. And once at my Father's death. We had a brief reunion this year. It was not an especially joyous one. We were at my oldest sister Verithas side when she fought her last minutes against cancer. I was not there for her last breath. Looking back now, I am glad for that. But at her last breath I lost my 'reunion' spirit friend. I will go to one, and be glad, too. But I just can't get myself to try and organize one again. That spirit left me when Veritha went to a well deserved rest in her new Home. I have tried more than once to initiate change in that regard. But to no avail. My son's have never been able to grow up regularly interacting with their cousins. Yessir friend, the world it has changed in my generation. But The sand's of time continue to shift. And I must move on.

MOTHERS FAMILY

My Mother was the youngest of four children. She had two sister's. The oldest died as an infant. Her name was Ruby Jim. Mother's brother was the next oldest. His name was Lee Preston. He came to be affectionately known as 'Pep' to all who loved him, and there were many. The sister Mother grew up with came along next. Her name was Flossie. They were life long best friend's as well as sister's. We shall see a good bit of their relationship as we travel through this little book of mine, friend.

Ruby Jim is buried in the old portion of the Langdale cemetary, at the top of the hill next to the road. It's just a small headstone. There wasnt even enough room to put her whole name on it. It says simply, 'YARBRA BABY.' Mother would make an occaisional point of our walking up there. Looking back on it now, I think Mother saw it as important that Ruby not be forgotten. And friend, she won't be. Mother never could remember the story of why Aunt Ruby went Home so soon. But as I look around the old part of that cemetary now friend, it is amazing to me how many head-stones there are just like Aunt Rubies. Many a bitter tear must have been shed on that hill over a life given too little time to develop. Some years ago, after Mother's Home-going, I looked at the possibility of having Aunt Ruby moved down to be with the rest of the family. It just wasn't meant to be. One, many year's ago the building that housed the record's of burial's there burned. So there is no way to prove that Aunt Ruby is who Mother said she was. Two, in my research a man told me that the casket as well as the body might well be dust by now. After all, in that day, 'embalming' was a primitive art by today's standard's. And caskets were almost always nothing more than wood. He offered to test the grave site. But in the end I decided against it.

You see friend, the rest of the family had dubious feeling's on the subject. They were not sure they wanted to move a body on my Mother's word only. Especially since she was no longer here to 'confirm' Aunt Rubies story. Friend, you take anything out of that you want. As for me, I know this. Mother's family are all awaiting our arrival Where they are now. And the older I get, the more I look forward to the day when "the dead in Christ will rise first. Then after that we who are left will be caught up to meet Him in the air." Then we will be with our Saviour forever. This is the most important thing, friend. I have had to come to realize that not everybody see's things just exactly like I do. Some thing's are worth the battle. Some thing's are better left to eternity. But Aunt Ruby, you are remembered. And you will be remembered by many, every time someone read's this little book of mine.

TO FIGHT FOR LIFE OR NOT?

Friend, I mentioned marveling at the number of small head-stones there are in the old part of Langdale Cemetary. But think about this. In my Mother's childhood, vaccination's against thing's like smallpox, measels, mumps, and the like did not exist. Add in accident's of all kind's, and it can cause you pause to imagine all those broken hearted Mother's and Dad's who stood on that hill and wept sore for the little lives, in those tiny caskets, that would never mature and bear fruit.You know friend, I think of people like these who fought for all they were worth to save little live's that were considered precious. Then I think about the climate of the world we live in today. It is perfectly acceptable, even legal, to take a life before it even see's the light of day, in killing centers called abortion clinics. And I shudder to think how our generation is going to be judged in eternity. Consider this friend. If someone shoots a dog with a pellet gun, or hits it with a rock, or even neglects to take proper care of them, they can be prosecuted to some degree. Yet we have come to the place in society where a baby can be judged unfit to live. All in the name of 'choice.' Tell you what. Steal the egg of an eagle. Bust it, and get caught. Congratulations, you just donated your 401k, in effect, and garnered yourself some time in the cross-bar hotel. Why? Well, there was an EAGLE in that egg, thats all. Friend, do you see there the hypocracy of the anti-life movement?

Yet folk like me who have the unmitigated gall to defend the right of these little creations of God to actually HAVE life are called 'right wing extremists', or 'anti choice.' You want a discussion about 'choice', friend? Did that baby have a voice, or a choice? Oh, but long ago liberal society dehumanized the baby by giving it a 'scientific' name, fetus. In my lifetime I have heard of judges who will hold a person in contempt of court if they dare to use the word 'baby' instead of the word 'fetus' in their court-room. A person of some influence once exclaimed to the Apostle Paul that too much learning had made him crazy. In my opinion that argument could more accurately be made of the secular humanist's of our world. God is no longer in charge of when life begins. We are willing to let Him provide life, of course. But we reserve the right to snuff it out if it does not fit the 'special circumstances' of life. Is that not right friend? In the end, the abortion debate is about one thing, and one thing only. Will we allow that BABY to have an opportunity to see life, to grow and develop into whatever God want's it to be, or will we allow 'normalcy' to include the legality of tossing that precious body, in whole or in part's, into a trash bin with the rest of lifes rubbish? Well friend, I just lost a sizable portion of my readers right there. They can go suck their thumbs, the lot of them. This won't be sorted out with any finality till God does His judging at the Great White Throne. On this issue, I have no fear in facing Him. Do you, friend? Think it over.

My, my Hugh, you really must get back on task. A.D.H.D. strikes again. Now, where was I? Ah yes, I was talking about my Mother's family. Ruby Jim, we must leave you for now. But your nephew is on the job. We shall meet again.

FROM 'GINNY BRANCH TO THE MEADOW

My Mother's family had moved to the Langdale Mill Village long before my Dad left Clay County. We know they were there when Mother was born. From Mother's earliest memory both of her parents worked at the mill. The home I spoke to you of near Red Dirt Hill was the earliest home Mother remembered. Miss Ludie always had rabbits or chickens or both in the yard.

Mother remembered that whenever the rains were long and hard enough to put (Mr.) Moores Creek in a foul mood, she would have to go up under the house and gather chicks from time to time so that they would not drown. Mother always enjoyed playing with the chicks. But she felt sorry for them, coz she knew what their final end would be. In time though the family would move a short distance away to a place affectionately known to this day as the 'Ginny Branch.

The 'Ginny Branch was nothing more than a small feeder stream that emptied into Moore's Creek. It was forced into service by Mother Nature from time to time as a kind of holding place for water from the creek during heavy rain or flood conditions. Let me explain it like this. Moore's Creek begins very near the Chattahoochie River, just north of West Point Georgia. It empties into that same river just south of Langdale Mill. So, if the rain has been long and hard, the river would fill up, sometimes to flood stage. Ole Man River would then force water into streams like Moore's Creek. Those streams in turn would force water into tiny feeders like the 'Ginny Branch. In my lifetime I have seen water running freely in the street's of West Point. I have seen Moores Creek running up under Langdale Mill. I have seen the waters of Mr. Moore run out into Highway 29. 'Mr. Moore' was not to be trifled with, thats for sure. So, my travel partner, it should not surprise you to find that most every home on the branch side of that street had it's back yard under water more than a few times over the years.

The 'Ginny Branch hardly has any life at all now. Moore's Creek is a shadow of it's former self. Oh, he can still kick up a fuss every now and again. But he's not the same now. One only has to see a picture of the creek as it was in my Mother's childhood, then view it as it is today. It's sad really. But not as sad as the end suffered by the meadow. In my Mother's childhood the meadow was also a pasture for the cows many mill village families still had. Later, on the north side of the meadow there was a ball field. That field was once home to a baseball team sponsored by Langdale Mill. All of the villages had mill sponsored ball team's in the early day's. I remember playing softball on this field. For many years the annual Boy Scout jamboree was held in the meadow. Three days of camping and team competitions that all scout's looked forward to each year. The fishing on the creek was pretty good at one time too. I guess you could say that the meadow and Moores Creek acted together to provide a whole lot of happy recreational moments for both young and old.

Time passed though. I once heard it said that the only inevitable thing in life is the inevitability of change. And so it has been for the meadow. Someone had the idea at some point to build a road right through the middle of the meadow to relieve traffic on Highway 29. So what came to be called Fob James Drive years later was born. Year's later the people of the villages voted to join themselves together by creating one city, which was named Valley. When they built their city hall complex they built it right on top of the Langdale ball field. If you call yourself a progressive all of this is positive change. If you are a traditionalist you might call these things a mutilation of good things for the sake of progress. With the hindsight that the passage of year's bring's, and hopefully a wisdom that comes with age, I long ago accepted these changes as necessary. I suppose that most thing's, and most places, and even most people, are bound to change at some point. All of the change hasn't been bad. Over the year's a branch of Southern Union State Junior College has located here. The City of Valley built a really nice sportplex along this road. It is the envy of many towns of the same size. A bustling business area can be found there. Chambers County Board of Education built a brand new Ram Stadium there, along with soccer facilities and several ball fields that cater to both softball and baseball for youth. Apartments can be seen along this road near the sport plex. There will be much additional usage of these lands in the future. Of course this is good for the community. More recently a Christian college called Point University has relocated to nearby West Point Georgia. They play their home football games at Ram Stadium. They made arrangements to use a portion of the nearby apartments for their students. This has been a blessing to the entire community.

But you know what, friend? There is a part of me that mourns the loss of a simple way of life, when a person could swim, or fish, or boat literally yard's from their back door, when tent's sprang up once a year and the meadow came alive with the sounds of care-free boy's who met to camp and compete, but most importantly to have fun. Cows grazed here in my Mothers childhood. Kids picked blackberries here. Now there is concrete and asphalt. There is just enough grass for the life sized Manger scene to be shown each year at Christmas. And tired old Moores Creek, a ghost of it's former self, has become an afterthought. That is, unless the rains have a turn at rousing him once or twice a year. Go ahead neighbor. Sue me. I have become a sentimental old cuss. In some way's I have become similar to the main character in 'How Green Was My Valley'. In his case he was leaving his home town forever due in part to his home place being slowly swallowed up in a mining pollution called slag. That pollution was enabled by anger, spite, and vengefulness. In my case it's not all that. But I miss the simplicity of mill village life. I miss the structure of it. I miss the people who stood together, took care of one another. The changes that continue to take place here are a necessity born of increased population and a forced diversification of industry brought on by the death of king cotton. But those mill villages, and the people who inhabited them, paved the road of life I talked about in the beginning of this little book of mine. And you can be sure, my faithful friend, that I will never forget them. I will pass them, and their stories, along in this book. In that way my word's can last far beyond my time on this earth, and the generation of my son's will have reason to remember.

ADVENTURES ON 'THE BRANCH'

Friend, you're just going to have to get use to me 'chasin' rabbit's' like that. The Langdale Meadow, 'Ginny Branch, and Moore's Creek were all a good sized part of life on the 'Ginny Branch street where Mother and her family lived for a time. Another thing even more important to them was the presence of other family. Mother had family on both end's of the street. The Colleys, and to a lesser extent the Yarbroughs, once they got to the Valley area, tended to put down root's and stay. Mother did have one aunt, Luline, who lived in the Montgomery area. But most of this family called the Valley area home in that generation. Many of them are buried there now.

I told you friend, that mill village kid's were expected to do chores and study as well. Miss Ludie was on the second shift, which would have been the 4:00- 12:00 P.M. shift. Mother use to tell me that she well remembered her Mother getting her and her sister out of bed at night when she got home and giving them a 'switching' for some infraction or another. Some times it would be something they just KNEW wasn't known to anyone other than themselves. Miss Ludie would say "Little birds tell me these thing's." Many year's later I would have my own experiences with these "little bird's." But we'll wait till then to talk about that. What? I got to keep you reading, don't I friend? :)

Thinking back now, I remember a story or two that Mother shared with me from this part of her life. Even in the village danger could lurk at the most inopportune times and places. There is a malady that still occurs in our day. If it is treated immediately, it can be beaten. And there IS effective treatment available too. In my Mothers childhood however, not so much. This particular affliction could carry a death sentence very easily. The mention of it evoked fear. This affliction was called hydrophobia. The most common way to be infected with this dreaded affliction was and still is to be bitten by an animal that was already afflicted with it. Rabies was the common name for it. The animal that most commonly passed rabies on to a human was a dog. But in my years I have heard of rabid squirrels, or raccoons. Really, no animal is immune. As near as I can understand it, hydrophobia attacks the nervous system and the brain.Near the end, the animal will be frothing at the mouth and will become extremely vicous and violent. Your pet will not know you then. You will be only a target to it. Your pet will become akin to a horror movie animal. And if it bites you, you are in mortal danger. In my Mother's childhood, and especially in her Dad's, the outcome was often death. And a horrible one at that.

That said, one day Mother and some other kid's were in the street playing. Someone came running down the street yelling, "Mad dog,mad dog!!" Friend, that meant "Get off the street!!" Mother said all of the kids got off the street as fast as they could. Still, it seemed that they were no sooner on the porch than the dog came loping by. It ran beyond the end of the street and into the wood's. Some of the men tracked it down and shot it. A tragedy was narrowly averted. In my PaPa's generation, when a person bitten by a rabid animal had even less chance of surviving, PaPa told me that he once knew of a man who was bitten by a rabid dog. His fate effectively sealed, he begged to be tied to a tree so that he would not be a threat to anyone when the rabies did it's evil work. Just before he fell into the madness that is rabies, his wish was honored. And there he died a death that I imagine is the closest thing to hell on this earth.

You know friend, it strikes me that none of us are guaranteed tomorrow. And when our time comes to take the journey from which none of us can return, we will arrive at one of two destinations. There is no middle ground. No holding place. Scripture tells us that to be absent from the body is to be present with the Lord. That is, if we BELONG to Him when we take that journey. If we don't, our journey will end in the one place where we will be tortured more than the man in the story I just told you went through. What think ye, my traveling partner? If that man had known for sure that his leaving this world was imminent, and he found himself to be outside the loving embrace of a Righteous God, do you think he would have made preparations to meet Him? Now, what about you, friend? Are YOU prepared to meet Him? Do you KNOW that you will see tomorrow? Give it some thought, would ya?

THE LAST APPLE RAID

I just have to tell this little story about my ONLY experience at the 'Ginny Branch street. I was just a small boy. I was either second grade age or a tad younger. I've told you, my faithful travel partner, about the ball field that sat on a hill on the far side of the meadow. Remember now, at this time the meadow had not been mutilated by 'progress'. So there was nothing but meadow between the ball field and the houses on the 'Ginny Branch street. My dad coached softball at the time. He spent a fair amount of time at the Langdale ball field either coaching or scouting some team he might have to play. I was allowed to pretty much have the run of the ball field / meadow area as long as I could hear my Dad when he called me. I put that to the test one night. Some older boys were talkin' about an 'apple raid'. It seemed a couple of folk had apple trees in their back yards just across the branch. The guys enjoyed an occaisional romp across the meadow during a night ball game. They would place some of their number outside the fence of the back yards. Others would jump the fences and take apples off the ground. A brave one or two would even shimmy up the trees and toss apples to the fellas outside the fence. The whole operation could be done and over with in twenty minutes max.

On this night I got brave enough to ask if I could tag along. Of course friend, on an apple raid the more raiders you have, the quicker you can be done with the thing. So I was allowed to become a 'raider' for the night. Is it not crazy, frend, the way that fate places us sometimes in places where we know we have no business being? And this case is no different. Yes, we were stealing. That is reason enough for me to not be in on this 'raid'. But on the way down the hill, one of my fellow raiders pointed out the two houses that were to be visited. I began to have a feeling of dread, because one of these houses belonged to an uncle of mine. Thats TWO reasons for me not to have been there. There was a third reason though, one I did not know about at the time. My uncle, Benny Colley, and his neighbor had seen apples leave their yards more than one summer. They were not very fond of the loss of fried apple pie making fruit. So they had created a defence for their yards and their apple trees. Both of them aquired B.B. guns before apple season. They intended to send a message if the opportunity presented itself. And this particular night, it did.

Anytime there was a ball game going on at the field, these two diligent neighbors would darken the lights in their houses. They took a position at a window at the back of their homes. Can you see them, friend? Can you see their trigger fingers tighten up as they watch this motley crew of 'raiders' coming down the hill from the ball field and wade across the branch? They followed the usual plan. A few outside the gate, a few inside working the trees. One or two up in the trees. These two men waited till the raiders were in the middle of their fun. Then they simultaneously cut down on them with those B.B. guns. The raiders were caught in a cross-fire. There were b.b.'s flying everywhere. Can you see the chaos that ensued as the raiders fell all over themselves trying to retreat from those yards?

One of these raiders took a b.b. in the side of the head, just enough to stick there. Just enough to scare the daylights out of him and his co-horts, including the boy that I was. You dont have to ask me about this one in Heaven, friend. I'll go ahead and tell you that this was my LAST apple raid. My first too. I will say however that it was not the last time I engaged in mischief. There would be other opportunities as I grew older. But you will see them soon enough, if you keep reading this little book of mine.

BROTHER JERRY HAD IT RIGHT

Friend, I know that I have strayed far away from Randolph Hill at the moment. But while we are talking about education,(AGAIN, you are probably saying,my new friend) I want to share one of the best rebuttals I ever heard to apologists and enablers who constantly try to 'dumb down' students who are deemed to be economically or socially disadvantaged. It was spoken, interestingly enough, by one of the funniest Christian comedians I ever heard. His name was Jerry Clower.Many of you remember several years ago when there was this national debate on the subject 'Why Johnny can't read',don't you? It seemed that all of academia, government policy wonks, and social special interest groups had opinions about 'Why Johnny can't read'. Brother Jerry got in on that debate on one of his projects. He was just a country boy who "growed up pore" as he liked to say. And he had a refreshing way of cutting through the static special interest gobbledy-gook and getting to the point in a way that left a lot of these 'learned people' frustrated and gasping for breath. I want to let part of what he said stand for the way I have tried to raise my two boys:

"A lot of people are arguing these days about why Johnny can't read. I have come to the conclusion that too many times the REAL reason Johnny can't read is, Johnny don't give a care whether he can read or not...... Look, I growed up dirt pore. We lived in a shotgun house. I come from a broken home. If some of todays learned 'experts' had been around in MY day, they would have told me how pore I was and how underpriveleged I was, and maybe I wouldn't have never went to Mississippi State University and graduated with a degree in agriculture...... look,this is the United States of America! And if you want it bad enough, and if you have some of that bull-dog, hang in there foreverishness in you, In THIS country, you can be a WINNER!!!"

Amen, Brother Jerry. Amen. I had the chance to shake hands with this warrior of faith a couple times. You could go to a concert of his and just laugh till you cried. And not one time did you even hear the hint of a profane word, or an off color joke. But he always tried to use whatever fame or notoriety he had to reach out to his fellow man and to encourage all of us to be the best we could be, to fight the fight regardless of the obsticals we might find in our way. By the time this little book of mine is published, I will have almost 6 years invested in the writing of it. More than once I have been tempted to abandon the attempt. But here we are, friend. You are reading this, so that means that I made it! Ask ANYONE I went to school with if they thought I would EVER be able to write a book. Watch them laugh at you. But here I am.

Both of my boys are A.D.H.D.,something we knew nothing of when I was a boy. My oldest son has Aspergers too. I do not let them use what this world calls a 'disability' as a crutch. They both have their own strengths. The youngest is a potential builder. The oldest is excellent with numbers and categorizing things. Both have been athletically inclined to a degree. I have always taught my boys to reach for the stars. I have taught them to follow their dreams wherever they lead. If someone tells them that their dream can't be accomplished, I say tell them to go suck their thumb, then go get it anyway. Then turn around and stick your tongue out at them.

Last statement on this, I promise. For now,anyway. All of you kids and young folk who feel like you have messed up too much to catch up, listen up. Everything right I have done in life, I have done later than is considered 'normal'. I didn't get my drivers licence till I was 18. Didn't have my first date till I was 18. Never went to a high school prom. Didn't marry till I was 30. Didn`t become a father till I was 35. My wife and I adopted our second son when I was 50. I`ll have kids in college till I'm well into my 60's. And here I am, I`ll be 58 when this little book of mine is published. What are you trying to say, Brother Hugh? Just this; (a) nothing in life really worth having is going to come easy, and you are not going to get there on a 'fast track' fable. It will take perseverance, dedication, and determination; (b) You can succeed in spite of past failures. You have read already of how I spent 3 years in the 10th grade. I've done my share of stupid things. But if you are reading this, I have become an author, full-filling a long, long dream of mine!!! Now,what is YOUR excuse? It is time to stop sucking your thumb and get on with it! Friend, believe me, YOU CAN DO IT!!! And when you get there, give Brother Hugh a call, or drop me a note, or send me an e-mail and tell me your story. There may just be another book to write some day!!

BACK TO RANDOLPH HILL (FINALLY!!!!)

There is much to talk about concerning Mothers years on Randolph hill. There is a line in a movie or a poem, I can't remember which, that says "It was the best of times, it was the worst of times". I think that could be fairly said of the Randolph Hill years. Before I have anything to say about the hill, I have decided to allow my readers to enjoy a special treat, and a very personal one to me. I am going to allow you to hear right from my Mothers own pen about what it was to finnish growing up on Randolph Hill. She wrote me two separate letters several years before she went to be with her Savior. You will not only hear about this ole' hill. You will hear some golden nuggets about Langdale Mill, the theater, and so much more. And you will see how very close she was to her Mother, what a special bond they shared. It's a bond I know well. And like my Mother before me, I never knew just how close that bond was until I could no longer tap her wisdom anytime I wanted. Even sharing these two letters with you friend is an emotional thing for me. But I think my Mother would have gotten a hoot out of it. Hazel Ogle, you will now be remembered for generations to come, every time someone reads this little book of mine. Enjoy, all! This first letter was written on September 12, 2001.

Dear son

First of all let me say, I love you very much and am very proud of you and what you stand for. Don't ever let anyone or anything turn you away from the Lord. Now, I'd like to tell you a little something about your Grand-Mother, Ludie Yarbrough. She was born on May 11, 1898 to Emory David and Julia Ann Colley. She was one of 14 children. They had a hard life as children, but were loved and cared for as best Grandpa and Granny could.

Mama wasn't a 'fat' person. She was (just) big boned. Like Granny and some of her sisters, she had a "pot-belly". She use to pat her tummy and say, "if I'm pregnant, it's one of Gods children." It took a lot for Mama to use the word 'pregnant' because such things as that were just not to be discussed.

Mama was a hard worker at home and in the mill. She worked in the Spinning Room at Langdale Mill. Sister and I used to have to take her a quart of sweet tea down to the mill every afternoon at 5:00. She'd be at the gate, and we'd better not be late. She'd give us a nickle a piece when she had it. We'd go to the 'coffee shop' (a little place at the top of the hill just by the mill) and buy us some candy. Boy, that was a treat! Then we'd walk back home on Randolph Hill and get our chores done. If we didn't (Mama) would get us out of bed at 11 P.M. when she got home from work and whip our behinds.

Many's the time we'd be gotten up and given a whipping because we had done something we had been told not to, maybe go into a neighbors yard to play or some other thing. But when Mama told you to do or not to do something, that's the way it was. We always wondered how she would know when she was down in that mill. All she'd ever say was "a little bird told me". If she told you she was going to whip you, you may as well go ahead and start crying, 'cause it was comming. When Sister and I were smaller, before we moved up on the hill, when we knew we were in for a whipping, we'd stoop down and pull our dresses up over our leg's. (We'd) start hollering, and she wouldn't even be touched us yet! She'd whip us and we'd cry, then she'd whip us till we stopped

49

crying. She sent me and Sister out to get her a switch to whip us with one time. We brought back a small weed-like thing that we thought wouldn't hurt so bad. Big mistake! She got her own and didn't send us to get another one. On the other hand, she`d send Uncle Pep to get her a switch to whip him with, and he'd bring back a great big one. Mama would whip him and he'd just stand there and not move or cry. When she got through whipping him, she'd go off in the bathroom and cry. She always told us that it hurt her more than it did us. I never understood that until I had children of my own.

Mama was an honest person. Everyone knew knew they could trust her and depend on her. If she told you something for you, you could take it to the bank. She was a woman of her word. She worked hard, she liked to have fun, and she took care of her family. She loved babies. Everyone around the hill who had babies soon learned that if their baby suddenly disappeared, go to Ludies house and they would find their baby. She would take them home and play with them. If they were big enough to eat cookies or ice cream, she'd get them in a good mess and them take them home. (She'd) tell their Mom's that they needed a bath.

I remember one time she took one of mine or sisters doll's that looked just like a real baby. (She) wrapped it in a baby blanket and laid it on the bed. Shortly after, the insurance man came to collect. He knocked loudly on the door. Mama went to the door and told him to be quiet (or) he'd wake the baby. Naturally, he wanted to see the baby. So she took him over to the bed. He leaned over and pulled the blanket back. He said something like "good God, Ludie, that's just a doll!" He was embarrased and Mama had a good laugh.

(Mama) and 'Miss Willie', Snookies Mom (Editor's note; 'Snookie' is Janelle, a life-long friend of Mothers who would become Mrs. J.D. Stodghill as a young adult.), both worked on the second shift. 'Miss Willie' and Mr. Rob were one of the first on the hill to get a T.V. set, black and white of course. Well, one night they came home from work at 11:00 P.M. Miss Willie asked Mama to come in and they would watch the T.V. Well, they turned it on and there was nothing but 'snow' on it (you know, like when your cable goes off). Well, they didn`t know you had to adjust it. They watched a while. (Then) Mama told Miss Willie she was going home, and if that was all a T.V. would do, she didn't want one. Of course, later when they learned that it just needed adjusting, they had a good laugh.

Mama would lay down in the floor, put both legs in the air,wrap one arm around each leg, and roll all over the room. This was called the'punkin roll'. When we'd kill a hog, Mama and Aunt Margaret would clean the chitlings, plait(??) them, boil them a short while, then fry them. Boy did those things smell bad! Mama would laugh and say, "Oh boy, I`m gonna have the house to myself today". We'd know she was going to cook those stinking things. We'd go down to Snookies. 'Course you could still smell them. I think everybody on the hill could smell them.

Mama and one of our neighbors would get out in the road in front of our house and take turns riding down the hill in a red wagon. It wasn't big enough to hold both of them at the same time. 'Miss Francis' Mc Cain was the neighbors name. She and Mama did 'fun thing's, but it was good clean fun. (Mama) enjoyed playing practical jokes on people, (but) never anything to do any harm. A cousin of Uncle Harlons (Harlon Peek, who would become 'Sisters' husband) used to come up from Tallassee with him when he'd come to see Sister. He would date Snookie. Well, Mama found out that he was scared of bugs. Yep, she tortured that boy. She could run him all over the hill with just a 'rolly-polly' (remember those?). He stuttered real bad. When he was scared it was worse. Sometimes she wouldn't even have a bug. She'd just cup her hand like she did (have one), and he'd take off running. Uncle Harlon would laugh like crazy!

Mama also liked sweet potatoes. (She) kept some baked all the time. She'd eat them before going to work, then go off to work giggling, saying "I'm gonna have fun today"! She would. She'd get in an alley and 'pass gas'. Hers would peel the paint off the wall. The fixer would come around on her job and say something like, "good God, Ludie, there's a dead rat around here somewhere!" She'd help him hunt the 'dead rat' and never crack a smile. I've often wandered if they ever caught on that it was her. She'd come home and tell us about it and have a good laugh. Mama had the misfortune to be working when a man got killed in her department. A belt on one of the spinning frames broke. It caught him and slammed him against the ceiling. Mama said that even when they painted it, his impression was still there.

My Mother was never one to complain about how she felt. She had high blood pressure and a heart problem. But to see her going about her job, whether it was working, taking care of her family, or helping someone in the community in time of sickness, Mama did it with a smile. She always put others first. During those times, everyone had to have a 'rest day' (at the mill). Mama hated to be sent back home. Sister got so she'd tell Mama when she started off to the mill, "They're going to send you back today." Mama would say, "Hush Sister, you know I need to work." But it seemed like every time Sister said it, no matter what day it was, in a little while we'd see Mama comming up the hill. Her boss came to the house before the funeral. As he looked at Mama, he said he wished he'd made her rest more.

Often times I'd wake up in the middle of the night. I'd be 'floating' through the air. Mama would have me, taking me and putting me in bed with her. It would have come up a bad storm, and she wanted me and Sister and her to be together. She loved animals. She grew chickens and rabbits. She'd raise the chickens to 'frying size'. Then she'd kill them, dress them, and we'd eat them. We enjoyed playing with the rabbits and the baby chicks. But we felt sorry for the baby chicks, 'cause we knew what their fate was. She loved her flowers too. She could grow anything.

She had flowers all over the yard. She knew what each one was and where they were. If anyone stepped on one of them, (and if) Mama knew it, that person got justly reprimanded.

I just wish (though I know I shouldn't because it was God's will) that I could have had her more than 17 years. Her one dream was to see her 'girls' graduate from high school. I honestly don't know if she got to go to Sisters graduation or not. I think she did. However, in my senior year, on March 17, two months before my graduation, she went Home to be with the Lord. So my graduation was not a happy occaision for me. In fact, 1952 was not a good year for me at all. I have wished so many times that I had my Mother to talk to. I still wish I could talk to her and tell her I love her one more time. So this coming March 17, 2002, Mama will be gone 50 years. May 11, 2002 would have been her 104th birthday. Son, I know I have rambled on and maybe none of it makes any sense. But I just thought you'd like to hear a little bit about your Grand-Mother. You kids really missed a blessing by not getting the chance to know her. I think the two of you would have enjoyed each other very much. So I always encourage anyone who has a living Mother to go see her. If they can't, call or write. It really grates on my nerves to hear anyone talk badly about their Mother. That`s the best friend you'll have here on this earth. I just wish I had been a better Mother to you kids. I know I failed all of you in so many ways. But I can't go back and undo the things that were done. One thing you can be sure of though is my love for you. May God bless you and keep you in his care.

Love and God bless

"Mom"

Dear friend, every time I read that letter I go from laughter to tears and back. I have been over our life with this precious Mother with a mental fine toothed comb. For the life of me I can not find any failure of ANY kind what-so-ever in our raising, or in our relationship with her as adults, not on her part anyway. This was one of the most self sacrificing people I ever knew. Like her Mother before her, it was always about others first. Truly this apple did not fall far from the tree. But Mother wasn't through with me yet. The very next day she penned a second letter. It is almost as powerful as the first. For a lady who professed to not being good with words, she really knew how to get at this son's heart-strings. Read on:

September13, 2001

I'm back! I thought of something else I meant to tell you. I don't remember how old I was, but we had moved up on Randolph Hill. One day a lady came to see Mama. I can't remember if it was a neighbor or a sales lady. Anyway, as she was about to leave, she and Mama were out on the front porch. I wandered out there too. Something was said about 'business'. This lady looked at me and said, "You don't know what business is, do you? "Me with my big mouth piped up and said, "Yep, It's something you're supposed to keep your nose out of if it's somebody elses". You can bet I never opened my mouth again when I wasn't supposed to. Mama 'tended' to me. I knew better but I guess I was just feeling spunky that day. There are so many stories I could tell about my Mama. I might write some of them down as I think of them some time. If it hadn't been for my Mama I don't know what us kids would have done. We didn't have the best clothes to wear or the best food to eat at times, but Mama was a good cook. (She) could make most anything taste good. She always saw that we had food and was warm. (She) saw that we had what we needed.

Uncle Pep went in the navy at an early age. Mama and Daddy had to sign for him to go in. Mama worried about him. She was so afraid that her boy would get hurt or killed. Sometimes it would be months before we would hear from him when they were at sea. When he'd come home on leave, he'd take every dish out of the cabinet. He'd take every spoon, fork, knife, every pot and pan and pile them on the table. Sister and I would have to wash and dry them to his satisfaction. Goodness knows, if they had passed Ludie Yarbroughs inspection, they should have been clean enough for anybody. We had to heat water on the stove and use two aluminum pans; one to wash them in, and one to rinse them in. If the water got the least bit greasy, we had to pour it out and get more. Sometimes Sister and I weren't too happy to see our brother. We loved him though and really were glad when he got to come home.

Yes, Hugh, your Grand-Mother was a wonderful lady, someone you could be very proud of. The last memories I have of her other than seeing her in her casket was the morning she died. She came home after Daddy went to work. She had been staying down at Grannies for a while. She'd take the little "dinky" bus that ran from one end of the Valley to the other after Daddy went to work and stay with me till time for her to go to work. This particular morning, March 17, she came home. I was in the kitchen making bisquit's. She came in to see what I was doing. (She) told me she was going to lay down and rest. She never waked up. That morning Daddy had not gone to work. I still don't know where he was. He came in after Mama laid down. (He) went to the bed and shook her by the shoulder to wake her up. I told him to leave her alone and let her rest. But he shook her several more times with no response. That's when we knew she was dead. That was a horrible time.

So son, you can know that your Grand-Mother was a wonderful person. She was of the 'old school', as I said before. She was strict, loving, dependable, hard working, and much more. So again, I'll sign off, hoping I have helped you to know your Grandma a little bit.

Love and God bless

Mom

MY TURN

You know friend, I do get a chuckle or two when I read Mothers rememberances of the Randolph Hill years. I stand at the top of this hill and marvel yet again when I picture Miss Ludie going down that hill in a red wagon. First of all, how in the world do you control that little red wagon going down a hill that steep? Much less make the turn at the bottom of the hill to keep from taking a dip in Moores Creek. And this kind of fun from a Mom who my Mother told me never let her learn to ride a bike for fear that she would wreck and get hurt. Say what??

I have a sobering thought too when I read about Miss Ludies love for children. Consider this; in those days if a small child came up missing, the Mom would chuckle and go or send to Miss Ludies house to fetch their young 'un home. About the worst thing that would result would be some aggravation that the child would be full of ice cream or candy. In our world, if a child comes up missing, we put out an Amber alert. Scores,sometimes hundreds of people will come to participate in a desperate search, hoping for the best but fearing the worst. Tell me now friend, if you can. Tell me how we are better off in todays world than Mother was in the world she was raised in? How is our society so improved on hers? Many people will try to sell you that bill of goods. Me, I'm havin' a good bit of difficulty cipherin' that one out.

Then, I can get just a bit indignant when I read these remembrances. Indignant of todays new age thinking that calls discipline 'abuse' and spanking 'hitting'. It is amazing to me that even people of faith have joined this misguided club. I suppose they went and cut out the verse in Proverbs that says "Foolishness is bound up in the heart of a child, but the rod of correction shall drive it far from him". Let me hasten to say that I am fully in agreement with doing things to a person who commits child abuse that can't be printed in this little book of mine. I have no use at all for anyone who causes the hospitalization of, or the death of, or the mental or emotional breaking down of ANY child. But you have read my own Mothers words about the discipline meted out to her by her Mother. You will read in this little book of mine examples of the discipline meted out to me by my own parents. But you also see in my Mothers letters her absolute devotion to and love for her Mother. You hear no regrets about the discipline she received. Like-wise, you will hear no negativity from me about discipline I received. If you really want to start a verbal fight with me, just start in on either of my parents. I am a better man today because my parents loved me enough to punish me when it was necessary. So you "new agers" who will want to send me all kinds of negative messages about my "backwards view" of this thing called DISCIPLINE, don't waste your time. I ain`t budging! You all can go and suck your thumb!

I just had a memory of something that my church family got involved in many years ago in this ugly area of child abuse. A family moved into our community. They lived just up at the top of the road we lived on, in Mr. Tommy Hamers old home. There were 2 girls and a boy. Their parent's wouldn't come to church. But they were only too happy to have the kids to come. It was obvious that these folk were poor. For example, it was winter time when they moved into our community. The kids were coming to church in short sleeves and maybe a light sweater, sometimes no sweater. When we found out they did not own winter coats, a bunch of us pooled our money and bought them new coats.This kind of thing alone would be enough to warrant concern. But one Sunday morning the kids got to church, and someone noticed 3 small patches of hair missing from the little boys head, as though somebody had started 3 times to give him a G.I. haircut, then thought better of it. When he was asked how that happened, he said that his daddy did it to him. Friend, you have probably noticed that in this little book of mine that about every time I use the word 'Mother' or 'Daddy' I use capital letters, right? Did you notice that I did NOT do that in this story? That was on purpose, friend. And the words I would have used prior to my salvation experience would not be fit for this little book of mine anyway.

Of course we alerted D.H.R. right off. We had 2 problems, as I look back on it now. One, the 'wheels of justice' did not move as fast as they are capable of moving now when the right people are in charge. Secondly, once the parents knew that D.H.R. was on their trail, they moved. Their first move was to Langdale, somewhere behind the Rica Motel. It was not long before they were found out. But before anything could be done, they moved. Again. No, they vanished. Nobody ever saw them in our Valley again. I have wandered many times across the years how life turned out for those 3 precious kids. They certainly deserved a better fate than what they got during their stay in our Valley. As for their so called 'parents', I really hope and pray that they came to know Christ as their Saviour and became REAL parents to those children. Otherwise they deserve the same chance in eternity that a snow-ball would have in the hottest corner of hell.

Anyway friend, I have SEEN abuse in my lifetime. I hate it with everything that is in me. But "the rod of correction" still has it's place. In my humble and obviously biased opinion, a lot of the breakdown of social order that continues to harass us in America today can be traced back to a root called 'lack of discipline', beginning in the home. I know that thought just sent you modernistic, secularistic, apologistic, new age "thinkers" into another frenzy. But let's be friends, o.k.? I am allowed to disagree with your opinion just as much as you are allowed to force "wuss parenting" down the throats of folk like me who think like I do. The first amendment says so. So get used to it, because I done got too old, fat, and onery to give a care about the red faces you have right now or the screaming you are doing. Say, since you are already red faced and screaming anyway, there is one more thing you all can do that will complete your "somebody stole mah' suckuh" countenance. You know what that is, don't you friend? That's right. Open mouth, insert thumb, suck real hard. There now. Feels better already, don't it? I'm not really as mean as I may seem right now, friend. I'm really not. I really love ALL of my readers, really I do. I`m jes' sayin'.......

THEM STANKIN' THANGS

I know some of y'all will accuse me of not being 'real' country because of what I`m fixin' to say. But I have to be honest. My Mother had it right concerning these thing's called 'chitlins'. I had the opportunity to smell 'them stankin thangs' just once in my life. Thank God! I am convinced that you could cure any 24 hour bug known to man just by tying a person to the stake in a yard, then boilin' a big ole pot of chitlins nearby. I can't think of a bug that I don't think wouldn't RUN out of a body being forced to inhale that kind of aroma! And before you even get TO the smell of them stankin' thangs, do you chitlin eaters REALLY know just where them thangs have been? Don't even bother tellin' me how well you cleaned the thangs before you cooked 'em. The smell alone tells me you didn't clean'em quite well enough. Besides, I don't care if you DRY-CLEANED them ole' nasty thangs, neighbor. It would not be enough to get me to put any of that mess into my mouth! Surely the first person who thought to eat chitlins had to eat them or starve, right? O.K. friend, calm down just a bit. This little diatribe was all in good fun. All in good fun. But still, I'm jes' sayin'............

TRAGEDY ON THE HILL

Friend, I'm going to fill in some blanks for you concerning the tragedy on Randolph Hill. At the time of her goin' Home, Miss Ludie and PaPa were separated. My PaPa was not an expressive man as a general rule. At least not verbally. He expressed his friendship, his loyalty, thing's like that, through acts, not word's. Once you were called his friend, you were his friend for life unless you did something to show yourself unworthy of the title. These character trait's defined my PaPa every day of hi life, UNLESS...........he was drinking. As you know friend, a person who is under the influence of alchohol is prone to all manner of deed's that he / she would not do when not under that influence. In PaPa's case, the personality change could be volatile. He could be verbally abusive. He could be threatening, though I have no information or reason to believe that he committed any physical act of violence. There was one time where that possibility was averted when Uncle Pep went and got him off the street. He was walking up and down that street with a shotgun, waving it around and daring anyone to come out of their house.

But in my Mothers senior year of high school, things must have gotten worse in some way, because Miss Ludie felt compelled to leave Randolph Hill, with Mother. She moved in with her Mother (Granny Colley) one village south, in Fairfax. But one day, PaPa showed up down there, "under the influence", and threatened to burn the place down if some-body didn't come back to Randolph Hill to live. My Mother finally vollunteerd to go back home. She had the least to fear from PaPa. So she went back home. She stayed in school. She kept up her studies. And she had to run the house to boot. Many, many people both then and now give up hope and quit trying over less adversity than that. But My Mother was having none of it. This was her senior year. She didn't come these 12 years to lose the prize at the end. Her Mother was counting on her. She would be the last of her siblings to graduate high school. She and her Mother were SO looking forward to that day. In the spring of that year, just a few weeks before she was to graduate, Mother came down with a bad case of the mumps. She told me once or twice over the years that both sides of her face had the same look as that of a squirrel as he gathers acorns for the winter. Since mumps is contagious, Mother could not go to school. The mumps, then, were the reason that Miss Ludie came up Randolph Hill for the last time that fatefull day to see her baby girl. Mother told me once that a neighbor said she knew something was amiss with Miss Ludie, because she called out to her as she passed by on her way up the hill. Miss Ludie, always full of her fun, this day said nothing.

Flossie ('Sister' to Mother) had already left to 'come home' for a visit when the family called to tell her the news. A different neighbor called to her as she made her way up Randolph Hill. She said "I'm so sorry about your Mama". Flossie, knowing that her Mother had been sick, but not knowing the terrible truth that awaited her at the top of the hill, said "Well, these things happen". Many years later, I would come to know all too well the feelings that Flossie must have gone through that day. Dear friend, I wouldn't wish that on my worst enemy. Uncle Pep was at sea at the time that his precious Mother vacated her earthly clay shell. In those days it took much longer to get news of a family emergency to a service person who was overseas than it does now. Frantic efforts were made to get word to him and get him home. Still, they were just about to close the casket for the last time when he got home. I won`t even try to put into words how that must have made him feel.

As for my PaPa, I would imagine that he found himself dealing with more than a few regrets during this dark time. My Aunt Flossie once told me of seeing him sitting at the kitchen table. Like all of the family, he was in shock. Aunt Flossie told me that she vividly remembered him saying softly to no-one in particular, "I didn`t want it to be this way." Please hear the words of a man who has been both wise and a fool in this area over the years. Friend, if there is someone who you love, who you have been on the outs with, who you know you need to reconcile with, and if you have put it off over and over again, please don't just ASSUME that you will have tomorrow. The past is a memory. The future is not guaranteed. There is the 'today' of your life that you can use to heal and to bring healing to that person you used to call family or friend. With God's help, it can happen if you will only set aside your silly stupid human pride. I know more than one person, friend, who wasted what turned out to be their last opportunity to put aside past hurts and start a relationship over fresh. These are tortured people who have more regrets than they will ever admit to. I am so glad that I am no longer in that number.

In that day, it was a common custom to bring the body of a loved one back home one last time before the final goodbyes. In fact, many people in my Mothers day preferred that. So it was with Miss Ludie. It must have been hard, and extra hard for my poor Mother. Remember, she had the mumps. So I am pretty sure that she got a fraction of the hugs she really needed. She had been unashamedly a 'Mama's girl', and Mama's baby to boot. Miss Ludie was her Mother, her mentor, her best friend. For the last 7 year's I have known the kind of consuming pain that my Mother must have been feeling. I must say, Mother handled it a lot better than I did. Friend, there is more to tell about this sad event and it's aftermath. But I find myself needing a little break right about here. As you can imagine, this is a very emotional part of my family's story. So I'm going to take a break and try to get you and I to smile a bit, if that's o.k. Or even if it's not. There are a few more stories that Mother told me across the years about life on the hill. Let`s give it a whirl, shall we? I'll call this little set.........

ADVENTURES ON RANDOLPH HILL

THE BULL ADVENTURE

The area across the road from the house on Randolf Hill was pasture in my Mother's childhood. Today, I'm sorry to say, it is almost totally developed. Houses everywhere. But in my Mother's childhood, the pasture could be a real adventure. On occasion, it could also turn dangerous. The old Ginny Branch I spoke of earlier ran up through there somewhere. There was a swimming hole thereabouts too that Mother and friends would visit on occasion. Keep in mind that in this was pasture there were several cows, and a bull who didn't take real good to human visitors. The trick was to visit the swimming hole at a time when there was no beef around. Mother told me this story about a near miss experience with the old bull. Mother and a friend, with her friends little brother in tow, had gone to the swimmin' hole for a dip. All went well until they heard an ominous sound. It was the sound of that bull, pawin' the earth. He was not happy. There was a hill jes' beyond the swimmin' hole. The pawing sound was coming from just beyond that hill. Now friends, if you can hear a bull pawin' the ground, but you can't see him, that's a good thing. That means you all get a head start. And if you're smart, you will take advantage. Nobody had to explain that to my Mother and her co-horts. The two girls lit out pronto, each with a hand on the little guy whose feet, Mother used to tell me, probably only touched the ground two of three times from the swimming hole to the fence. By the way, they never saw the bull. And for the life of me I can't remember her telling me of another trip to that particular swimming hole after that day. You know what I`m going to have to do when I get to Heaven don't you, friend? Yep, I'll have to ask, just for the fun of it.

Friend, I'm havin' a 'silly fun' moment. Some of you might even call it 'stupid fun'. But I can't help myself. Have you ever wandered how animals react to us silly humans when we're reacting to their indignant warnings to leave their space? Can't you jes' see that ole' bull eye-ballin' Mother and her friends that day? Suppose he duck's behind that hill before they can see him. And he say's to himself, "I'm gonna break these human's from suckin' egg's once and for all". So he begins to paw the earth as hard as he can. Maybe he throws in a few grunts just for good measure. Hearing splashin', then the sound of runnin', he look's over the hill to see the panicked retreat of the tresspassers. "Heh-heh-heh, that'll teach'em", he thinks to himself. About that time he notices one of his favorite cow's has walked up beside him in time to witness the fun. "Good one, Henry. Look at'em go!", she say's. "Thanks Bess. Yeah, I don't think I've ever seen humans run that fast before". Bess says,"Not only that, but apparently some of them can fly too. Look at that little one in the middle. I ain't seen his feet touch the ground yet!" Henry say's "Jes' like them human's. Always full of surprises!"..........Oh, stop it, Hugh! Let`s move on now, shall we?

THE OLD MOVIE THEATERS

From time to time Miss Ludie would give the girls money to go see a movie at the Langdale Theater. I think Mother told me it cost a quarter to get in. For a dollar you could see a movie, have popcorn and a drink, and still get back a little change. Every mill village had a movie theater, compliments of "The Company." The old Langdale Theater is still there today. It has been salvaged and remodeled in the style of those early years, and is now used for concerts, dramas, and the like. It has been added to a list of historic buildings in the state of Alabama. Good thing too, because all the others are gone now.

I remember having school assemblies in this old building when I attended the elementary school next door. We also attended gospel singings here. There was a well known gospel group called Wendy Bagwell and The Sunlighters who once recorded a live concert at the Langdale Theater. My parents were in attendance that night. Friend, try to find a copy of that album today. It's a rare treasure indeed. There were three people who could make you laugh till you cried when I was growing up. They were Jerry Clower, Wendy Bagwell, and Grady Nutt, who was known as "The Prime Minister of Humor" on the old Hee-Haw T.V. show. Brother Wendy was well known for his 'Rattle Snake Story'. He and the ladies could flat out sing too. The Langdale Theater was all the richer because Brother Wendy and his group recorded there. I remember something Brother Wendy said during that concert. He was relating to the audience that a recording friend had asked him the previous week when he was going to record again. He told him, "As a matter of fact, we're going to record next week, live in Langdale, Alabama". This friend said "Langdale; I don't believe I ever heard of Langdale". Brother Wendy said "Well, don't you let that worry you none, 'cause I already checked down there. And they ain't never heard of you, neither!" Amen, Brother Wendy. Amen! Brother Wendy sings in Heaven these days. In fact, Brother Wendy is in good company in that Place of Eternal Rest. Grady Nutt got there a little ahead of him. Brother Jerry got there some time after. Friend, with these three guy's around, Heaven HAS to be quite the lively place, don't you think?

I did attend a movie or two at the Fairfax Theater before it closed. In fact, into my teen years that particular theater was still quite the hangout. When it was no longer used for movies, it was rented out for gospel singings and various other social functions. I well remember going to something that c.b. radio clubs used to call 'coffee breaks'. These were social gatherings usually sponsored by one of these clubs or the Rescue Squad. A good one could be a "Hee-Haw" variety show with singing talents, skits, and so forth. There would be refreshments, sometimes free, sometimes for a donation. Then there was a truly bizzare spectacle called a "woman-less beauty contest". Men, friends and neighbors, this was men dressed in evening gowns, and swimmin' suits, and doing a 'talent' (don't get me started), with a grand winner at the end. Sometimes even with a crown. You could not watch one of these things without shedding some tears. From laughing so hard. I saw more than one of these shows at the Fairfax Theater. Come to think of it, I went to an annual Hee- Haw show put on by the Valley Rescue Squad at the Langdale Theater several times. Those were some good days, my friend. They tore down the theater in Fairfax several years ago. It was a loss that I feel still today. Thank God for the people who saved the Langdale Theater! It is the last link to a day when you could get a movie ticket, a sack of popcorn, and a piece of candy with a fifty cent piece and get a bit of change back. If you're ever in my Valley, friend, you might just go by and have a look-see. It is, now, truly, one of a kind.

I would say that I have some small memory of going to a school assembly or two at the River View theater building the first year or two that I attended school there. So I count it a special privelege to have been inside three of the mill village theaters in my growing up years. Sad it is that my generation is the last one that will ever be able to say that. But what an honor.

'MISS LUDIE ' TAKES A BOAT RIDE

PaPa enjoyed the river. I don't think there is one square inch of it that he didn't fish from Langdale to River View. At this point in his life he was known to put in a rowboat at the old boat landing down below the mill and row over to an island about sixty yards away. That boat ramp doesn't exist anymore. It's been replaced by a newer one, and a handicaped fishing area has been added. Good. I do remember one story PaPa used to tell me about. It was the one (and only) time he talked Miss Ludie into getting into the boat with him for a row over to the island. If I were her, I expect it would have been my only time, too. PaPa had this little mutt of a dog, see. I have long since forgotten it's name. But PaPa and this dog were inseperable. Where you saw him, except for work, you were most likely to see this mutt. On the day that PaPa convinced Miss Ludie to go for a row with him, they somehow got away from the house without the dog. In a little while, the dog figured out that nobody (specifically PaPa) was at home but him. Not to worry. This little guy knew all of PaPa`s hang-out`s. Since PaPa walked everywhere he went, he wasn't hard to track.

By the time the little mutt caught up with PaPa, he and Miss Ludie had already put out into the river. Now, y'all have to picture this. Miss Ludie is in the rear of the boat, her back to the shore. When Pa Pa, who is facing the shore, aee's the little mutt, he manages to distract Miss Ludie long enough to signal the little fella to come on. He begin's to casually fish as though he dosen't have a care in the world. Miss Ludie, who has a decided distrust of ole' man river, is trying to look as though she is enjoying herself. That is about to change.The dog approaches the boat from the the rear. When he reaches the boat, he proceeds to climb over into the back of the boat. Poor Miss Ludie almost went out of the front end of the boat. PaPa laughed so hard till he nearly cried. He DID drop his fishing pole into the river. For her part, Miss Ludie passed up a perfectly good chance to cuss that day. Nobody would have blamed her. And as near as I can tell, that was Miss Ludie's last boat ride. At least, I have never heard of another one. Hey, I know. When I get to Heaven I can ask her, right? You know, just for fun.

THE NIGHT OF THE 'HEADLESS' MAN

This is a rather short story. And it would probably make a good brain storm for some science fiction writer. My Mother got a good laugh any time she told this story. But she would tell you quick that she was not laughing the night that this event took place. She and a friend were on their way up Randolph Hill, on their way home from a movie at the Langdale Theater. It was very dark (can you say 'oooeeeeoooh'?). At some point they heard the sound of footsteps behind them. When they turned to see who their company was, they saw the figure of a man. He was wearing slacks. He had on a very long coat with the collar turned up. And he had............NO HEAD!!!!!!

My dear friend, do I really have to tell you that the girls reinvented the octave scale that night? Do you doubt that they covered the remaining distance to home in international track star time? And what of this practical jokester with the long coat and 'no head'? How many times across the ensuing decades do you suppose he repeated the story of the night he caused two girls such fright till they probably had to proceed directly to the bathroom when they got home.....to clean up? If we could know the truth, I would expect that his story has been handed down now to the second generation. His kids heard it, his grandchildren have heard it, and who knows how many other family and friends.

And I really wonder, my friend, how many stories like the ones I am sharing in my little book about those who came before me will fade into history because nobody thought enough, or cared enough, to write them down? I am convinced that there are many books out there that need to be written. And if I, a child of the mill village, a career 10th grader, and a perpetual student in the 'school of hard knocks' can do this, so can you, friend.

ME TOO⁇⁇

I have to share this little story Mother told me more than once across the years. It takes place at Valley High School. It has to do with Mothers home economics class. In her day teaching home economics was teaching a young lady how to function in the home she would someday run. This involved just about any area you want to name. The area that is germaine to our story concerns the making of bisquits. Apparently there was a young lady in Mothers home ec. class who came from a family of, lets say, above average means. She apparently was used to having someone else do 'servants duty' at her home. So on this particular day, the girls get to home ec. class and discover that this day they will be learning how to make biscuits.

Friend, if you are from the south you know what that means. Flower, and buttermilk, eggs, and whatever other ingredients you have to put in the pan. This is what rich folk, I suppose,would call a 'goo' that had to be brought out of the pan by the handfull, then formed with the palms of both hands, then placed on a baking pan for cooking. Understand now, my Mother is already amused that any girl in the community would have to be 'taught' how to make a biscuit. She had been doing that for a long time already. But this young lady in our story took one look into the dough pan, grimmaced, and exclaimed, "Do you mean to tell me I've got to put my hands in THAT???" Mother used to tell me that the teacher answered "Well, if you want to pass this little ole' class of mine you do". Friend, I`m sorry. But to this day, I'm tempted to think that rich folk really don`t have a clue.

THE AFTERMATH OF TRAGEDY: PART ONE

I decided to do this in two parts, because I want to talk about my Grand-Father. I am somewhat concerned that I may leave you with a negative impression of him. To me, that would be sad. I will begin by saying that life is about choices that we make. There are exceptions to this rule, of course. But for the most part, we get out of life exactly what we put into it. PaPa had sown alchohol, and had harvested personality changes that included anger, and hatefulness. He harvested separation from his wife. Now he was experiencing the bitterest harvest of all.... grief and regret.Yet thankfully, my friend, this sad time was not the end of the story for my Grand-Father. Years later, he would accept Jesus Christ as his personal Saviour. At that point he laid down that demon of alchohol forever. Many times he passed me on the way out the front door, his Bible in his hand. He would say to me "Hugh, PaPa's gonna go out here and argue with ole' Paul for a little while". He would sit in a chair under the oak tree at the corner of the house that Mother called home when she went Home. And he would read that Bible for hours. I still have that chair today.

PaPa struggled with some things in life that he did not understand. I'll never forget something he told me one day. It was one of those moments that for whatever reason stay with you for life. I had come home from wherever, and found him sitting in his chair under that tree with his Bible. In the course of that conversation he said, "Hugh, I've been in this world a long time. I think I must have done something right to stay here almost 80 years. But there are some things PaPa still don't understand. Hugh, in my day I've seen little babies, who I know couldn't know right from wrong, die tormented deaths. Then I've seen the wickedest people you ever saw die the most peaceful death. Why these things are, PaPa just don't know. Thats why I read my Bible, and argue with ole Paul like I do. Maybe some day I'll find out what the answer is". Friend, I think he knows now. I'm sure Paul was glad to explain, when PaPa got Home. Not only that, but PaPa spoke to me many times across the years about Miss Ludie. He always referred to her as "the only woman I ever loved". Indeed, I never heard him even speak of any other woman but Miss Ludie. Not even the hint of a date. And not only that, but let's consider what must have happened when PaPa got to Heaven. Do you think Miss Ludie was sorry to see her husband? I don't think so. I believe that she, along with other friends and family, rejoiced greatly that he made the choice to join them in a place where reunions are forever. Can you imagine the discussions that PaPa and Paul must have in the years since PaPa went Home? I can't imagine PaPa winning a debate with Paul. But I imagine he has had great fun in the attempt.

The fact is, Albert Corbet Yarbrough was very welcome in Heaven, especially by our Saviour. All past sins having been forgiven, all past mistakes irrelevant. Friend, the same thing is true of any person who has ever wronged you in any way. If that person belonged to Christ when he/she took their last breath on this fast declining earth, that person is just as with the Lord as you will be when you get there. So why not allow God to give you the healing that you need now? Why not experience that kind of peace while you can use your experience to help someone else who thinks that forgiving past wrongs is not possible? After all, there will be no thumb sucking in Heaven. That activity is now reserved for any of you who are going to be bull-headed and just refuse to let God do for you what you will not or can not do for yourself. It`s your choice, friend. I was a thumb sucker for a long time, a lot of wasted time. I'm enjoying peace a lot more these days. Try it. I dare you.

THE AFTERMATH: PART TWO

My Mother graduated high school on schedule. She finished with a 'B' average too. I really hope that this part of her story will bring some student who is going through painfull adversity these days some hope. In her senior year, my Mother went through the separation of her parents. She moved not once but twice. She was a student, still responsible for keeping her grades. She basically ran a home just like any house-wife would. Washing, drying, and putting away clothes, cooking meals and cleaning up after them, all the responsibility of an adult was hers. She had a bad case of the mumps during a critical time of her senior year. Then she lost her Mother suddenly. And even with the emotional pain she had to deal with, she was determined to finnish school and get her diploma. I'll say it again, friend. Brother Jerry had it right. If you want it bad enough......., you can suck it up, and you can DO IT!! Or you can spend your life living with thumb sucking regrets. It`s your choice.

Mother had to make some decisions after high school. Many of her friends had gone on to their four year colleges. Mother wanted to continue her education too. She knew that her Mother would have wanted that for her. But she had a house to run too. Her Mother and Dad had decided that the last of their kids left at home would inherit the home when the time came. That would now be my Mother. Of course, her Dad still lived there too. My Mother was now a young adult. She was fresh out of school and able to do with her life whatever she pleased. She would have been completely within her rights to wave her diploma in her Dads face and say; "O.K. Dad, the party is over now! You have caused me pain for the last time. You drank Mother and me right out of the house. The only reason I came back is to keep you from terrorizing us any more at Grannys house. I have washed your clothes, cooked your meals, and cleaned your house, all without so much as a 'thank you'. I have done those things for the last time! I'm out of here, buster! Now, who's gonna do everything for you?"

My Mother did not do that. 'Home' was precious to her. If this house was going to be a home now, it would fall her lot to see to it. But she also struggled with continuing her education. The plan she tried to make work would be the most difficult thing she had tried to do in her young life. Mother had begun to work at the Langdale Mill. Getting a job there was not hard at all. Both of her parents were known hard workers there. And again, Mother was an apple that did not fall far from the tree. But she also enrolled in a school called Opelika Tech in Opelika, a short bus ride from Langdale. Mother would get on a bus early each morning for the commute to school. In the afternoon the bus would let her off at the mill. She would work a full second shift. She would get home sometime after 11:00 P.M.,try to study a bit, then try to get enough sleep to do it all over again the next day. Do you understand friend, that there are times that our head and/ or our heart wants us to do things that our body just won't cooperate with? At some point our 'want to ' will be over-ruled by our 'can't do', and the answer to that equasion will be our 'get to'. So it was with my Mother. When she finally HAD to make a choice, she chose sacrifice over self. Instead of becoming the secretary she had hoped to become, she chose to take on the role of running a home and working to keep it functional. For the rest of her life, anyone who knew her will tell you hat she put others first, sometimes to a fault almost. Friend, you have only just begun to hear about that sacrifice.

A LESSON IN GRACE

I want to add this final observation about Mother's relationship with her Dad. Not only did she not read him a riot act and storm off after high school, but he lived with her and our family for the rest of his life. And as the end of his life drew near, she was right there for him, any time he needed her. At the end of the day, Albert Corbett Yarbrough was still her Daddy. I will testify that she never had a day where she did not love him. I didn't say there were not times when she was almost ready to "peench hiz noze awf". This was especially true when he still had a drinkin' habit. But she loved him even then. She was devoted to him. And she would tell you off proper if you wronged him. Maybe I'm being unfair to use Mothers grace for her Dad as a standard for all of us to try and live by. But I would submit to you that the grace she extended to her Dad is a picture of the grace that my Heavenly Father had for me on Sunday night, March 16, 1980 at Midway Baptist Church when Jesus agreed to come into the heart of an undeserving, low down, no good sinner by the name of Hubert B. Ogle Junior. I richly deserved hell. I did not merit, with the life I had lived to that point, the mercy of a Righteous God. But He extended that grace and mercy to me anyway. All I had to do was...ASK! And just like that, he took me just as I was. And my question is this. If He can do that for us, why is it that we can't seem to do that for one another? I don't get it, really. But I don't guess I'm supposed to. At any rate, my Mother modeled that kind of grace in her life with her Father. And she was so glad she did when it came time to lay his ole clay shell down at the Langdale Cemetary. She truly had, that day, something I hope to have when my turn comes to take that eternal walk we all must make at some point; no regrets.

Friend, I know I keep comming back to this thing about being willing and able to forgive. It has been a bit of a continuing theme in this little book of mine hasn't it? I just know what it is to live with the poison of anger and bitterness. I know the emotional cost as well as the mental duress it keeps the captive under. The most destructive thing I went through when I was dealing (or not dealing) with these destructive feelings was this; I became a master of disguise. I was able to convince other folk that I was "over it". I gave every appearance that I had "moved on". But I most decidedly had NOT moved on. Deep down in my innermost self, where only me and God can go, I retained poisonous and destructive feelings. And on two occaisions in my life, the resulting pity party almost caused me to take my own life. At the risk of sounding preachy, I was never able to deal with those feelings in and of myself. After all, I am a fallible human, subject to these type things. It is not in my personal ability to forgive even now some things that have been said about or done to me over the years. If we can all be honest with each other for a moment, none of us has any great love for being talked about, or made fun of, or ridiculed. I have had a broken heart from a 'love' gone wrong, and the aftermath of it. I know what it is to go from being fairly popular in my circle of friends, to being really sure that I didn't have even ONE friend left.

I have known the pain of feeling like an outcast even among my own family. I have been called a gold digger. I have been called a "Mama's boy" and/or a "Daddys favorite". It has been said of me in the past that I didn't care for anyone but myself. Believe me when I tell you that I have only just scratched the surface here. Not only that, but there were judgements or punishments made against me when I was growing up that I didn't always agree with. On and on it goes friend. Which of us can go through these things and get past them, fresh and able to get on with our lives, in and of our own selves ONLY? Most of the time going to others is not the answer, because 'other people' are just as human natured as we are. Many times they will take a side and actually enlarge the crisis, which does nothing to help you or me to 'get past the past'. No, it is ONLY when I have realized that my Saviour is the ONLY hope that I have in managing these emotions, ONLY when I make a decision to give HIM my pain, my hurt, my bitterness, that I have EVER been able to overcome some of the hatefull and hurtfull things that I have been put through at different times in my life. And friend, let me say with all the love of a person who has been there, you haven't been any more successfull than I have. Maybe it's time that you take a good, long look deep down inside you where only you and God can go. And once you find yourself alone with Him, really ALONE with Him, maybe you can give your demons to him as I did. The results of that simple yet powerfull act will be such that your own family won't know you at first. But beware of pride! It is the great killer of way too many 'new beginnings'. My heart and my love to you friend, as you ponder whether you want to stay the person you are, or become the person you were meant to be.

THE NEXT BIG THING

Well, Mother settled into a simple life with a regular routine. She worked a regular shift at the mill. She ran the home. She was a regular at her church. In spite of all she had been through, I have no information that she ever strayed from her faith in her Saviour. As I think of it now, I wish I had asked Mother about how she and her Dad coped in those days. He was no doubt dealing with all manner of feelings and emotions. She now had this great big hole in her heart. They both grieved. But somehow they moved on. One of the things that Mother enjoyed doing in her leisure time was sitting in the swing on the front porch and reading a good book. I suppose that is where I got my occaisional fits of reading from. My favorites are the Bible and anything to do with the Civil War, or World War Two, or the story of the Cherokee Indian. I don't know what Mothers favorite reads were back then. I do seem to remember her reading some of the Harlequin (probably not spelled correctly) Romance books in my lifetime. But whatever the case, she was sitting on that porch reading one day, just minding her own business,when a chance event took place that would change her life forever.

MOTHER AND DAD - THE LANGDALE YEARS

Friend, I have had a good deal of fun across the years piecing together the events that brought my parents together. For a good many years I was under the impression that Dad saw Mother for the first time the day he walked past her home and saw her sitting there reading a book. But as it turns out, it wasn't as much a chance meeting as I supposed. Dad had actually met Mother some years earlier....when he had dated her sister! He took Flossie to the movies a couple times.Miss Ludie would make Mother go with them. It would be hard to say who hated that the most, Mother or Flossie. Mother told me that she would sit all the way across the theater from them.

A few years earlier, as Dad told it to me more than once over time, he had actually seen Mother at a church service at the Johnson Chapel Baptist Church, which is located south of Fairfax on the Judge Brown road. You all can call the following fact a coincidence if you want. But it was the Johnson Chapel Baptist Church that would start a church planting project near this period of time. It was located about halfway between the mill village towns of Langdale and River View, on the Langdale- River View road. Hence the name that was chosen for the church...." Midway Baptist", the church that Mother and Dad would raise us in! Personally friend, I don't believe in 'coincidence' when it comes to our Saviour. At any rate, Mother and Dad knew one another before the day when Dad saw Mother with 'different eyes' and set his hat to ask her for a date. Only now she was no longer the little sister who was made to be a 'chapperone' for a flustered older sister. She was not a young lady at a church service. She was a young adult now. She was still very shy, but at the same time quietly sure of herself. And when my Dad walked by that house and saw Mother that day, he knew he would be calling her.

You know friend, as I began to put the pieces of this story together, it actually occured to me that maybe visiting friends a few houses beyond Mother and PaPa's home might not have been Dads only reason for being at the top of Randolph Hill that day. But I never asked him that question. I have no regrets about that as I look back on it all now. Sometimes it is best to just let a story speak for itself friend, ya know? And I wish I had thought at some point across the years to ask the names of the friends he was on his way to see. Because if they are truly the reason that Dad walked up the hill that day, they are part of the reason I am writing this story now, and they deserve to be remembered. Now, there are two or three people out there who might not see it that way. But you all know what you can do for me, don't you? That's right. Don't suck on that thumb too hard. You wouldn't want blood to start comming out the end of it now, would you?

Sorry 'bout that, friend. Sometimes I just can't help myself. At any rate, I do remember this. I know that Dad invested not one, or two, but three phone calls to my Mother trying to get a date. And three times she turned him down. Why is that, you say? Because he didn't tell her who he was. Now why do you suppose that is? I can only speculate, because Dad never really talked about that. But let's park right here for a short time, friend. Let me use my suspicions to have a teaching moment. Don't skip pages on me now friend. I may just have something usefull for you here, if you are able to hear it. Let's start by remembering that Dad was, well, let's say it this way ; he was a little rough around the edges. On his own from the age of 15, he had worked hard, he had played hard, he had fought in a war, he had the occaision to "sow a few wild oat's". His philosophy of life probably included some "foot loose and fancy free". His circle of friends at that particular time would definitely not have been the same as my Mothers. My Mother, for her part, had lived a much more conservative life by way of comparison. A child of the mill village, she had lived in Langdale all her life. She already had experienced the responsibility of running a home. She really didn't need that much to make her happy. She had a good home. She took care of her Father. She worked hard in the mill. Her life was as stable as Dads was foot loose and fancy free.

Yet both of these young adult's were ready, for many of the same reasons, to settle down with a lifes partner. When Dad walked by Mother's home that day and saw her with those 'different eyes', I feel like he knew, just because people who live in small towns usually do, what kind of young woman she had become. I feel like he was concerned that she would turn him down for a date based on the life he had lived. Now, some of you are saying at this point, "Wait a minute, Brother Hugh, I thought you said that your Dad was saved at an early age, that he led his first singing as a teenager. What gives?" Yes, I did say that. And would you, O self righteous one, like to tell me that you never made even one mistake after your salvation experience that you would not like to do over? Have you never "backslid" away from the cross and the life you promised God you would live, for the rest of your life, the moment you got saved? That's what I thought. Lets just stay on the same page here friend, you and I.

Now, lets have that teaching moment. I have found a truth in life. A persons real personality is not wrapped up in the best OR the worst that is said about them. The truth of who they really are is usually somewhere in the middle of all that. However, the people who are going to talk the most AND the loudest are the people who say the worst of you. The best that you can do is to make good choices about the friends that you make and the company that you keep. Too many times other peoples opinions of who you are, are based on a PERCEPTION they have of you based on the friends you have and / or the company you keep. Not only that, but the baser your friends / company, the more likely you are to fall into temptation that will leave you with a lifetime of regrets and stunt your opportunities to have the kind of career or life partner that you really want.This kind of truth is just as hard to teach to kids today as it was when I was growin' up. But you young folk, if you will hear the words of an old man who has learned a lot of life lessons the hard way, hear this. The choices that you make in all areas of your life, will follow you around for the rest of your life. There is no going back. Indeed, there are those who have overcome bad youthfull choices and gone on to live productive lives. But my guess is that they will all tell you that they wish they had made the right choices in their youth. Choices about their friends, choices about the company they kept, choices about their education, the list goes on.

Since we are talking about my Dads hesitancy to tell Mother who he was, let's apply this little lesson of ours to chosing a life partner. Young folk, we live in a world now that is anywhere from apologistic to downright permissive of all kinds of behaviour that is convenient, indeed even pleasurable temporarily. But down lifes road when you get ready to 'settle down', those behaviours will diminish the quality of life you will enjoy. The fact is, if you have a lot of baggage from your past weighing you down when you get to your settling down place in life, it is going to be so much harder to reach your goals. If you have a history of drug abuse, if you have over-used alchohol, if you have been a known "player" socially, if you don't take full advantage of educational opportunities, you will not be the first choice of any member of the opposite gender who is looking for his / her forever partner. Many times they will just look right by you. My Dad would have told you that in his youth he made some choices that he would like to have back. All of a sudden there he is, walking by the home of a young lady who is really worth getting to know. He is normally a fearless man. But now he is nervous about telling this young woman who he is. Of course, Dad did eventually tell Mother who he was. She agreed to go out with him. That date led to others. Out of those dates grew a relationship. And in time, Dad got up the nerve to ask Mother to marry him. And she said yes.

Mother missed her Mother greatly as her wedding day approached. It would have been a proud day for Miss Ludie. I expect she and Mother would have had great fun planning the big day. No doubt they would have laughed some, and cried some. But they would have walked to this day together. I realize there may be an opinion out there that says Miss Ludie might NOT have been excited about this comming union. I will say that my guesing is just that, guess work.

I never heard one word from my Mother that suggested to me that Miss Ludie would not have accepted Mothers choice of a mate. Besides, I am the one writing this book. So go write your own. You can type with one hand while you suck the thumb on your other one. Mother did have some help from a couple friends in the planning of her wedding. The only big worry that Mother seemed to have on her big day was to make sure that her Dad did not get into any alchohol before the service. Friend, I have wondered across the years how PaPa must have felt that day. He was hardly two years removed from losing his wife. Now his baby girl was getting married. I never heard him speak of it. But surely it was emotional for him. There was one thing he did not have to worry about though, and that was where he was going to call home. He would be right where my Mother was for the rest of his life, which was a little over 30 years, and with my Dads blessing. Home would be at the top of Randoloph Hill, at least for a while yet.

My parents were both Christians when they married. Dad would now be a head of household who would provide for his wife and the family to come. For her part, Mother would have someone to share life with, someone who would protect her and give her security. The newlyweds enjoyed a honeymoon trip to Birmingham, Al. They took in "Gone With The Wind" and saw 'The Vulcan'. Then they settled into a quiet life on Randolph Hill. Both worked at the Langdale Mill. Dad worked in the card room running what was called in that day 'pickers and slubbers'. Mother worked in the spooler room as a spooler tender. I remember something my PaPa related to me about the early part of my parents marriage. He had a good laugh with his friends when Mother and Dad had their first argument, two or three months after the wedding. He told them that he had started to worry about those two. But now that they had gotten through their first argument, he thought they would be o.k. I would to God that it had been thus for the duration of their marriage. I also remember Mother tellin' me how frustrated PaPa would get with her and Dad because they spent so much money on groceries. In 1955, you see, he felt it completely unnecessary to spend $10.00 per WEEK on groceries! Dear friend, how many groceries can you and I buy these day's for that amount of money?

HERE COME THE CHILDREN

I was born on February 24, 1956 at George H. Lanier Memorial Hospital in Langdale. It was still a fairly new hospital at that time. Mother and Dad were still living on Randoloph Hill. But before my second birthday they had moved to another mill village house across Moores Creek on Tallassee Street. This home was just a short walk from the Langdale Mill where both of them worked. I never asked Mother or Dad exactly why they made this move. One advantage was obvious. Now they could walk to and from work instead of driving or walking up and down Randolph Hill. Too, I think the house on Tallassee Street was just a little bit bigger. This young couple had started what would be a growin' family. Any extra room would come in handy.

But really, friend, if the truth could be known, I think there came a time when it was just time to move on. First of all, this is the home where Mothers Mamma had died. They had brought her home to lie in state before the going Home service. Not to mention all the memories of all the time my Mother spent with her Mother there. Imagine what it would be like to go through these rooms daily, with memories around every corner. Now here I was. I would have been the first grandchild that my Mother would have presented to her Mother. I'm sure they must have talked about it a time or two. By the time I was two years old, Miss Ludie would have fed me lots of candy or ice cream more than once, then given me back to my Mother, playfully telling her that she ought not let me get in such a mess. What fun those two would have had!

Yes, truly sometimes it's just time to move on. I suspect this was as much in my parents thinking as anything when they made the first of the four moves they would make during their marriage. Miss Ludie lived on, in two places where she would most want to be. One was a brand new home in Heaven, where she was enjoying the warm embrace of her Heavenly Father. The other was in my Mothers heart, where she enjoyed a special place until the very moment she made that journey from which none of us can return. What a time the two of them must have had these past 6 years! And how I long for the day that I will know the kind of rest they are now enjoying! In the meantime, both ladies hold a special place in the heart of your humble writer.

TALLASSEE STREET FAMILIES

Of all the places we lived in my growing up years, the little mill village house on Tallassee Street is the one that I am the most sentimental about. It is my link to another era, when Dr. Calhoun still made house calls, and you actually knew your neighbors, and were friends with most of them. The distance of 45 plus years causes some of the names to escape me now. But some are still with me. Standing on our screened in front porch and looking right, the first family were the Whites. I especially remember their daughter Drewcilla. She was older than us Ogle brats. Maybe even high school age. But she was always kind to us kids. That old home burned down many years ago. A double wide trailer sits there now. I'm sorry friend, but seeing a trailer sitting in the middle of a mill village surrounded by mill village houses is just a sore spot to me. It does the same thing to my eyes that my taste buds would go through if I bit into a buttered bisquit and found pickles instead of jelly or jam, if you know what I mean. It's just not the same.

Two houses below the Whites lived the Stevens Family. They had a son Tony, who I was pals with at that time in our lives. We used to think it great fun to go across the road to the railroad track and put different things on the track, just to see how flat the train would mash them. Coins and anything metal were the favorites of course. But they were by no means the only things we tried. Then one day the engineer of that little train almost caught us. That cured me right there, friend. If he had caught us, we would have been escorted to our parents. I can't speak for Tony, friend, but I KNOW what either of my parents reaction would have been. It would have been revival time in the bathroom for me. I decided there were other ways to have fun that were not nearly as hazardous as that.

On the other side of the street I remember the Creamers. There were two boys and a girl. One of the boys, I believe his name was L.C., became a motorcycle enthusiast some years later. Up from them a couple houses were the Piggs. Friend, let me say right here that Mr. Charles Pigg was one of the finest men I have known in my lifetime. He was a great husband and Father. He worked hard in his community. His son Byron, who I went to school with in my second stint at Valley High School (more on that later, much more), is still the fire chief at East Alabama Fire Protection as of this writing. Another son is in real estate. I've lost track of everybody else including another son, Nathan, who graduated high school when I was SUPPOSED to. This was, and I believe still is a good family. I still see Mr. Charles from time to time. I still consider him to be a friend, and one of my first role models, in the mill village on Tallassee Street all those years ago. His wife Patsy has been with the Lord now many year's.

There was a man who lived across the road on the corner, next to the road that went down to the railroad track. I really wish I had recorded his name at some point. But he had a small enterprise going with some of the Mothers on our end of the street. This fellow had a bunch of hogs over close to the river, see, just north of the mill. Several of the ladies had a bucket that they used to put their table scraps in. They would put the bucket on one end of their T-shaped clothes lines. This fellow would come around each day and take those scraps (or what we used to call 'slop') and use it to feed his hogs with. After I was grown, Mother and I would reminisce from time to time. The memory of that man and his slop buckets would come up every now and again. Is it not crazy, the things you do or do not remember? Anyway, I had a little fun with Mother a time or two. I would tease her about all that 'hawg feed' she sent over to the river without so much as a pork chop for her trouble. A ham would have been even better. Mother would laugh and say that it was a small price to pay for not having to smell the stuff till trash day.

Since I mentioned the 'T' shaped clothes line pipe's, let me say one small thing right here about laundry. Nowaday's there are all kind's of thing's available to keep your clothes 'smellin' fresh' after the washer and dryer get done with them. But it is all so useless when I remember the smell of fresh washed clothes that were dried on an outdoor clothes line. It ain't even close, friend. You see, this is just a very small part of the community I knew on Tallassee Street. Yet it is part of the fabric of the mill village I lived in for far too short a time. It was a way of life that is gone forever. It died right under our noses, a kind of sea change sucker punch. But before I wax too mushily nostalgic, let's have a few short stories about our life on Tallassee Street, shall we? We`ll call this little set.....

ADVENTURES ON TALLASSEE STREET

There was a china berry tree in the side yard of our home when we first moved there. It went down during a storm of some kind. Well, the berries on that tree dried out pretty quick. We found out, quite by 'accident' (heh-heh) that these little dried out berries could actually be shot from some kind of cap gun that was popular at the time. They produced an 'ouch!' type red place on the skin if a direct hit was scored, but nothing serious. Certainly they were a farrrrr cry from the danger my best friend and I exposed ourselves to in later years shooting b.b. guns at one another. You'll hear about that later. The china berries caused just enough mischief to keep us occupied and our parents on the verge of a bathroom revival. I know my Dad was only too glad to see the last of that tree hauled off. Even then it was some time before the last of the berries were taken off the ground and used as ammunition. That, friend, is just one of the ways that kids could 'invent' fun in my childhood.

WHO NEEDS SNOW ANYWAY???

We don't get a whole bunch of snow in south Chambers County. Or north Chambers County, for that matter. I could probably count all of the really BIG snows (for us, anything over two inches) that we had in my first 30 years without using all of my fingers. Or either of my thumbs. I realize that is going to cause waves of jealousy to come over any of my northern friends who might read this little book of mine. But hey, there is plenty of room here yet in the great state of Alabama. Feel free to retire here. Until then, just enjoy a leisurely suck of the ole' thumb, kiddo. Anyway, we used to do some major league sliding that would give you the same amount of thrill without the frostbite and runny noses you folk up north have to go through. We did it every fall, when most of the leaves and acorns had fallen from the oak trees at the top of the hill in our back yard. All we needed was a good sized piece of cardboard or trash can lid. The cardboard was preferable.

It was bigger and went faster. You see friend, the leaves and the acorns were always plentiful enough to almost 'carpet' the ground. You placed the biggest piece of cardboard you could find on the ground at the very top of the hill. You took turns watching the paved road to make sure no cars were comming. You started on the other side of the road. You got a good running start and jumped on to the cardboard, being sure to get your fingers to the front for holdin' on' purposes, and whoosh! It was off down the hill with you! As an extra bit of excitement, we would aim ourselves at the concrete steps that went down to the back yard. The trick was to drag your feet at just the right time so as to stop before getting to the steps. Failure to do so brought on one of two ends. Either you wiped out, or you 'enjoyed' an extremely bumpy ride down the steps, which could leave you with little skin left on your knuckles. OUCH!

Oh, all you kids today who love to complain that "We just ain't got nothin' ta doooooo!" Let me say one thing to you, bless your neglected little hearts. Wah, wah, wah. Y'all could have never kept up with younguns in my childhood, that's fer shore! We had many hours of fun with our 'invented' methods, and this was one of the best. In fact, if you ask me even now whether I would prefer that kind of fun or a great big snowfall to slide on today, I would pick.............the SNOW of course, doofy! Hey, I still got a little kid in me! There is still a little magic in the rare "snow storm" (all you Yankees can say heh-heh -heh right here) that we get to enjoy, even today.

HERO TO GOAT....?? - THE ACCIDENT

A small event that happened on that little hill behind our home on Tallassee Street has given me a lot of laughs over the years, not to mention a good reusable Sunday School lesson. I can assure you however, that I was most assuredly NOT laughing the day this incident took place. On the contrary, I hit notes that day that I have never been able to hit since. Here then is part one of 'Hero To Goat'. Here we will talk about the 'accident'. We spent a good bit of time on that hill, as you have gathered by now. We were playing up there one day when at some point I fell. Now friend, boys out playing fall all the time, right? No biggie, right? That is exactly the way I saw it...that is, until I looked down and saw all that blood comming out of my knee. Then it became an instant biggie. Then I did what any self respecting four or five year old would do. Or self preserving, in this particular case. I began to SCREAM!!!! Not for a doctor, nor for my Dad. This was a life threatening situation in the opinion of the child that I was. So the alarm sounded for MOOOOOMMMMMMEEEEEE!!!!

Friend, is it not amazing that we call on Dad when it's time to play ball, or go fishing, or even hunting, but when trouble comes, it's MOOOMMMEEE!!! And Mommies hear that call too.

I am convinced that they can hear that alarm a half mile away. And they become instant super heroes. I heard a man make a statement once, and I completely concur. He said that if you want to find out whether your insurance will do everything the salesman said it would do, just put yourself between a Mother and her hurting child. Even a devout woman of God will hurt you in Jesus' name, in that circumstance. She will pray for you after everything settles down. She will call 911 for you, IF her child is o.k. But make no mistake, when she is trying to get to a child of hers who has sounded the "I'm hurt/ scared/ terrified/ or all of the above" alarm, you are nothing but an impediment. And you WILL be moved!

My Mother was no exception. I'll never forget the sight of her comming out the back door of that mill village house and up that hill. I don't know how she kept from fallin', 'cause she didn't look down at all (that I can remember). She was looking right at me, sizing up the situation as she came. By the time she got to me she saw that we did indeed have a problem. She couldn't tell how bad it was yet because of the blood. But the situation did beg immediate attention. I don't think she even slowed down much. She just kind of scooped me up and back down that hill we went. You may think me daft friend, but I can still feel the bump, bump, bump of Mother carrying me down that hill. Amazing, the things we remember.

Mother took me in the back door of the house and made an immediate left turn into the bathroom. She sat me down on the toilet seat, and she went to work on that cut. To this day I don't know what it was that made the cut on my knee. It wasn't long before Mother had the bleeding just about stopped. The cut didn't look as bad as she was afraid it would. Eventually she put a washcloth in my hand. She said "Now Hugh, I want you to hold this wash rag down on that cut just as hard as you can. I'll be right back." Mother left the room, and presently returned with a bottle of clear liquid. It had a picture of a swan on it. Some of y'all know where this is headed, don't 'cha? Mother said, "Hugh, I'm gonna pour a little of this on that cut. Now, it's gonna sting just a little bit" (Heh-heh). But it is going to help keep your knee from getting infected." Friend, this is my Mother speaking. She's my hero. She just carried me down the hill, my knee a bloody mess, and stopped my knee from bleeding. If she say's that this clear liquid is going to sting "just a little bit", well, I'm a big boy now,right? I can take it, right? So I looked up at her and said "O.k., Mom. Go ahead on".

Friend, my Mother poured the cap of that bottle of clear liquid, ALCHOHOL, full. She poured it on my knee so that it could do nothing but fall over into that cut. And friend, when it got inside my cut, that alchohol started jumpin' up and down on every exposed nerve in there.And those nerves sent an angry message to my brain, in unison. And that message went something like this........"OWWWWEEEE!!! THAT LADY LIED!! THIS DOSEN'T STING!! IT HURTS!!!!!" And friend, the little Baptist boy that I was had a Pentecostal FIT all over that bathroom! Honestly, I bounced off every wall in there except the one where the bath tub was. And if it had been full of water, I believe I would have dove on in there, trying to get some relief. My knee was on fire!

Mother now, she had a maddening reaction to my plight (at least in the opinion of the boy that I was). She is leaned up against the bathroom door, a bemused look on her face. She said, "Aw, it don't hurt that bad!" Of course, the child that I was wanted to say to her,"Oh yeah? Then you won't mind swappin' knees with me for the next ten minutes, will ya!?" Of course, in my childhood, we didn't dare talk to one of our parent's in that tone (or any other tone that sounded disrespectful). I already had a pain in my knee. There was no use inviting a pain in my butt to go along with it, right? Poor Mother! She had gone from hero to goat in the space of only five or so minutes. Or did she? We shall see in part two of our story, 'The Lesson'.

HERO TO GOAT - THE LESSON

Friend, I told that story from the memory of the child that I was. I've told it many times across the years. It always gets a few laughs from my audience. Then I spring my lesson on them. You see friend, my Mother didn't stay a 'goat' very long at all. Rather than me trying to tell you in 'fresh words' why that was, I will now open another window to my past for you. When my Mother went to be with her Saviour in 2007, I found a letter I had written to her, in her home. Friend, that letter was better than 20 years old. But Mother had kept it all that time. Don't ever believe that Mothers don't relish praise from their children, or that they don't want to know that they made a difference in your lives. After I told her about using this story on Baptist Mens Day at the church I was attending at the time, I tried in what I still think was a feeble way to tell Mother why I used this story. For her to keep this letter as long as she did, maybe I did a better job than I thought at the time. I hope you will enjoy this little lesson, friend. I may never get to teach it again:

.....After I told this story to the church, I tried to draw a parallel between my experience that day and our spiritual experiences in the world we live in today. I, the child, represented folk in the world; sinners, backsliders, even Christians, and what I call "bucking Christians." At one time or another all of the above find themselves 'bloodied up' by the world we live in, just like my knee was that day. At one point or another we all cry out for help, just as I did that day. And when that cry comes from a sincere heart, our Heavenly Father, through his Son Jesus, is always faithful to reach down with His strong hand and help us, just as you did for me that day when you treated my knee Mom."

"Now I know, Mother, that I placed you in some pretty High Company. Being the person you are, you are probably embarrased by all that kind of attention, and wandering what all the fuss is about. But the fact is, you have always had that Christ-like approach to life and especially to your own family. Speaking from my own personal life, you have been an inspiration to me in more instances big and small than I have paper to write them on. I remember quitting school after three very successful years in the tenth grade. Some said "Hugh will do this," or "Hugh will do that". But you never stopped believing or saying "Hugh will go back and finnish high school some day". And I did, too. You never stopped believing in me, even when I did not believe in myself. I'll never forget that. And I love you for it."

"You were with me when I bought a brand new suit for my first date. And Mother, you are the ONLY person who could have gotten away with telling me that I had bad breath and I needed to do something about it before my date (heh-heh). You knew, and still know, how to give that kind of advice to someone in a tactfull way, and in my case a loving way. That is not a widely held talent in the world we live in today. I love you for having it. I could go on and on. But one thing I know. I would not be the man I am, or be enjoying the things in life that I enjoy today, had it not been for a Christian Mother who knows the real meaning of love, and who lives and has modeled it every day of her life for over fifty years now (note- Mother went home at the age of 73. So she had kept this letter for over 20 years. It's still in good condition now).

I have been blessed above and beyond all that I could ever have hoped to deserve in this life. I know that I have let you down more than once. At one time or another I have been the worst possible brother to all of my siblings. I have a beautiful Christian wife who I take for granted too often. I have a handsome son who I lose patience with all too quickly. If there was one thing I could borrow from you from time to time, I think it would be your ability to handle and bounce back from adversity. You probably don't think that you do that too well. But I can make a fairly strong argument that you have passed both Adversity 101 and Advanced Adversity in the School of Hard Knocks with a grade point average of 4.0."

"Mother, I love you very much, for countless reasons. It is love that makes a nag out of me when I stay after you to go see a doctor when something might be wrong. It is love that motivates me to try and see to it that you have as many of lifes basic necessities as possible. To me you are a national treasure. You are not replaceable. You are one of a kind. You are well worth the time I spend on you, little though it is sometimes. I hope this letter has been an encouragement to you. And I hope you understand now at least some of the motives that cause me to be such a pain in the butt when it comes to your health."

I love you

Hugh

Dear friend, do I need to tell you that I had to pause just now and get my eyes under controll? I didn't think so. Listen, Mother knew that day, that it was necessary for me to go through some short term pain for my long term gain. That alchohol burned, now. And at the time, the child that I was would probably have gladly swapped legs with Mother or any other willing soul. But the alchohol started the healing that my knee had to have. So friend, I will tell you like I told my captive church audience all those years ago. At the time we are going through the pain, we can't see where our Saviour is taking us. Only later, through the 20/20 hindsight we always find in the rear view mirror of life, can we see God's purpose in the things we have to endure. The important thing is that we not take a judgemental attitude with the only One who can see us through our pain. Healing can only be given if we are willing to receive it. And you can't receive ANYTHING from God if you are eaten up with bitterness and rebellion. Please believe me friend when I tell you that I learned that particular lesson the hard, hard way.

DISCIPLINE BY ACADAMY AWARD PERFORMANCE

In these early years of their marriage, Mother and Dad would take us little ones blackberry pickin' from time to time. You have heard that my Dad picked berries to sell as a boy. What might surprise you is that Mother could pick berries with the best of 'em. Long after I became a teenager, Mother could still out walk most folk even younger than her. Till her health became an increasing issue, she loved to go for outdoor walks with us. One day my parent's decided to go berry pickin'. I want to say there were three of us kids by then. Due to disobedience of some kind or another (I really wish I could remember what it was), Mother made me stay home with PaPa. As you can imagine, this more or less ruined my day, and my attitude. So it should come as no surprise to you friend that while they were gone, I found a way to get on my PaPa's bad side. Don't believe for a moment that he had forgotten how to spank. And he decided that a spankin' was in order. I decided that I didn't WANT no spankin'. Then I proceeded to run from him. As you will see, before this incident was over, I had ample reason to remember, NEVER do that again! Obviously the child that I was did not think as clearly as the old guy who types these words for you now, friend. I don't have a clue what possesed me to think I could avoid the long arm of discipline with the short run that ensued. I first ran up Tallassee Street, away from the mill area. PaPa started right in behind me. I was amused at this obviously futile (so I thought) exercise at first. Then I was surprised that PaPa actually moved pretty fast for an 'old guy'. Oh, he wasn't gonna catch me. But he was staying close enough to me for a change in tactics in the middle of my run.

About half way up the street I decided to cut around and go back the way I had come, but behind the mill village houses. This way PaPa would have to dodge clothes lines, childrens toys, and other assorted obstacles. This, I reasoned, would give me the edge I needed to get far away from him. Think about this friend. Exactly WHERE did I think I was going to go? How long was I going to stay? Eventually night would come, even in a best case scenario. I would HAVE to go home then. But at that moment, I was caught up in the thrill of the race, and the desire to avoid what was most likely a very deserved spankin'. Anyway, imagine my surprise to see, half way back down the hill, that I was not gaining the amount of room that I had planned for. This would bring cause for yet another tactic change. When I arrived at the back yard of our home, I turned hard right and went up the hill all the way to the oak trees. There I paused and took a cautious look back. PaPa had started up the hill. Then he did something curious. He stopped, and sat down on a stump about half way up the hill. He appeared to be breathing hard. And he motioned for me to come down. Friend, I weren't havin' none of that.

But the more I watched him, I slowly became concerned. He was sweating a good bit. And he did appear to be having a hard time getting his breath. Then he spoke. "H-H-Hugh, c-come on d-d-d-down h-h-here. Ah c-c-cuden whoop y-you now if m-m-m-mah life d-d-depended on it". At this point I actually began to be a little concerned about him. Still.......Cautiously I eased down the hill towards him. All the way, he courted my sympathy. "Aw, c-c-come on down heah! You d-done run me to d-d-death. What c-can 'ah d-do to you in th-this shape?" Can you see the trap closing, friend? I aske PaPa whether he was o.k. He said, "Oh, ah'll b-be alr-r-ight in a m-minute or t-two. I said, "you shore are sweatin' a lot. We done been on a good little run, ain`t we...." BAM"!!! He reached out and grabbed me as quick as a cat. In one fluid move I was across his lap and friend, revival time had arrived! "Run from me will ya?", the preacher exclaimed. "You ever gonna do that again?", he asked. "NO,NO,NO" the VERY repentant sinner said. "You sure?" Sure? How sure did I have to be? I was repentin' as hard as I could between squalls, which were at a fever pitch by now. In the end, friend, how dumb is it to try and out run sure punishment? Whether you are a young'un or grown, most of the time you just make the punishment harsher. Take this day I'm talkin' about for instance. Do you think it was enough for my PaPa that he outsmarted me in the end? Or that he heated up my end? Noooo, he felt obligated to tell my parent's when they got back. Which caused a second revival meetin, this time in the bathroom. Different preacher. Same message. Same result. Ask me. Go ahead and ask me, friend, if I ever again from that day forward ran from someone who was about to discipline me.

THE ULTIMATE HOT FOOT

This story I don't tell from a personal remembrance. I was only about 2 years old at the time. Mother told me this story a few times over the years. It seems that my PaPa was burning trash in the side yard. I was out there with him. Mother used to tell me that I was his shadow, or at least in it, all the time. This day, he got just far enough away from me till I felt the need to catch up. Before he could reach and grab me, I managed to toddle right into the hot ashes on the outer edge of the burn pile. Mother said that both of my feet got it, and good. Big water blisters came up on both feet. In the end I had to learn how to walk all over again. As a two year old, I was traumatized to the point where I went back on the bottle for a time. My PaPa, of course, felt badly about the whole thing. But Mother would not allow him to beat himself up over it. The way she saw it, this was just the first of what she imagined would be many "boys will be boys" injuries. In fact, I don't ever remember hearing of even one time when Mother was punitive verbally to her Father about this thing. She didn't accuse him of being irresponsible. She didn't yell at him. Apparently, we all got over it in time.

Friend, in my lifetime I have watched some folk hold mistakes over an offenders head with impunity. I mean just hang them over hell like a weenie at a hot dog cookout and watch them burn. Sadly, I have to say that I have been guilty of this kind of conduct more than once. It is, of course, un-Christlike conduct. The really sad thing is, many times it is the people who we are supposed to love the most that we end up hurting the worst. In the end, the person we really end up hurting the most is the person who looks back at us in the mirror. Think about it friend.

CARING FOR THE SICK

I wasn't the only one who had a physical challenge in our time on Tallassee Street. Mother told me of a time when my middle sister became ill. She was so unable to keep food down that she began to dehydrate. As a young Mother, Mom could hardly bear to have one of us in that kind of shape. She remembered saying to Dad, "I don't want her to die". There were tears that only a Mother can understand. But she eventually helped get her child through that sickness. My Dad? He worked. As many hours as he needed to, so that Mother could stay home with one of us when we needed her, especially in the early years. If that meant double shifts in the cotton mill, so be it. If that meant working a second or even a third job, so be it. His whole training as the son of a sharecropper was to do what he had to do to support his family. My Father did that, and he did it consistantly. Dad gets precious little credit for the long hours and the multiple jobs he worked most of our growing up years. But he answered the bell. ALWAYS. We never did without a roof over our heads, or something to eat, or clothes to wear. We did not have things "as nice as the next door neighbors", as the saying goes. But we had the best that Mother and Dad could provide for us. Looking back on it all now, I am so grateful for that. I will NEVER be ashamed of the parents who raised me. Or of the mill villages we lived in. And I have little use for anybody who forgets, or denies, or fail's to honor the people of their birth-right. I am a child of the mill village. And I'm %$#@* proud of it. For those of you who have gotten too big for your britches when it comes to the village of your raisin' or the people who made it possible for you to be who you are today, you all can suck your thumb till Jesus comes!!!

A WASTED TALENT

I remember carefree days when I was allowed to walk to Mrs. Masons house, alone, to take piano lessons. I had to walk all the way to the end of Tallassee Street, turn left, and Mrs. Masons house was about six houses up that road oln the right, up a small hill. What are the chances, friend, that you would allow your five or six year old to walk alone that far today? As for me, there are two chances; slim and none. Mrs. Mason was always kind to me. We 'butted heads' from time to time. Mrs. Mason was trying to teach me music, how to read and play notes. I had a bit of an independent streak in me though. Sometimes I would want to play a song a little bit differently "just because it sounds better". But Mrs. Mason was very patient with me. Her patience, along with occaisional 'encouragement' from my Mother, if you know what I mean, kept me on task most of the time.

The first piano recital I ever participated in was also my last. It was a disaster. I was fine with doing my part till we got to the church that was hosting the recital. It was packed! I was terrified of doing anything in front of a crowd. Mrs. Mason, bless her heart, finally had to come forward and sit on the piano bench with me in order for me to get my number done. My poor Mother was under a church pew somewhere. My Dads face was as candy apple red. People were stifling chuckles all over the church. Well, some of them were able to anyway. I have wandered, friend, just where I might be today if I had continued to take piano and advance my talent. The story of why I quit will be told when our walk down this life road of mine takes us to a little town called River View. For now let's just say that the quitting itself was a sad mistake. It was a waste of what could have been a life changing talent.

Mrs. Mason has been with the Lord many years now. I just wander whether she and Mother have met up in Heaven yet. If they have, I am sure they have already shared a laugh about a bony, buck toothed, bald headed little boy who once brought down the house, in a very unconventional way, at a piano recital all those many years ago. Right around 48 years ago, now that I think about it. WOW......

A RIGHT WAY AND A WRONG WAY

I pause now for a lesson in the right way and the wrong way to teach your son or daughter to stand up for themselves. As I have said, my Dad came up 'on the rough side of the mountain', as the old song say's. This son of a share-cropper was raised being disciplined by a horse strap. He left home as a 15 year old boy because of that. He finnished his teen year's living the life of an adult. At times he had to fight. He never went looking for the fight. But he was not going to back down from anyone. And that's the way he raised us, beginning at a very early age as you are about to see. I could not have been more than five or six year's old when this took place. One day I got the worst end of some disagreement with a neighborhood kid up the street. I was a "runt of the litter" type for my entire growing up experience. In addition, I had a dangerous mix of genes. I had my Daddy's brashness where my mouth was, and my Mothers meekness where my backbone was. Not good.

So on this particular day, I came down the street, beaten and crying. My Dad had a firm two part rule about fighting. Don't get yourself into anything you can't fight your way out of, and don't you dare come home from a fight cryin'. On this day I was in violation of both part's of that rule. I was treated to the sight of my Dad comming out the front door of our mill village house, his belt already wrapped in his hand. He met me in the street, friend. He whipped me all the way into the house, and then he whipped me some more. I got whipped at both ends that day. There would be no discussion with my Dad on this. You come home from a fight crying, you get another reason to cry. Period.

Now, friend, your eyes have narrowed at this point. Your ears are twitching. Your nostrils are flaring. The hair on the back of your neck is standing straight up, and you want to go and see if Dad can take what he dishes out, right? Easy now, easy. First of all, you can't. Dad is in Heaven these day's, completely out of your reach. Secondly, if you were going to face the Dad I knew as a boy, you wouldn't like the experience too much. Seriously, on that particular day, I probably would have applauded you in your effort. I speak now with 45 plus years of memory of that day, and as the father of two myself. I will say three thing's. One, I fully understand what my Dad was trying to teach me. Two, I think that his methodology, while well suited for the day's of his youth, was ill suited at best for the time we were raised in. Finally, Dad acknowleged this year's later when we settled all account's between us. He knew very well that there were thing's he could have and should have done differently. I chose not to condemn him forever for these type thing's. He was a different man in later year's. He allowed hindsight to reveal some thing's to him that needed fixing. And when he was ALLOWED to, he fixed every one of them, too. When my Dad left this world in December of 2008, one week before Christmas Day, he didn't owe me even the hint of any further apology. And he did not owe one to anyone else in this life either. Are you listening, friend?

Look, I have taught my boy's certain principles when it comes to this thing of 'fighting'. One, a fight is to be avoided if at all possible. It should always be a last resort. Second, you need to make sure that the thing you are gettin' ready to fight about is worth that big ole' knot you stand to be carrying on your head when it's over. Third, pick your fights carefully. In other words, you might want to have some idea that you can actually WIN the fight you are so fired up about havin'. Also, if there is an adult nearby, let the adult sort through the thing and rule on the problem (teacher,coach,etc). BUT...(a) if you are backed up in a corner,and (b) if there is no adult around, and(c) if your choices are to tote a whoopin' or come out swingin', well now. Sometimes a kid's gotta do whut a kid's gotta do. At that point you come out of that corner swingin'. You swing with what God gave you, and anything else you can get your hands on. And you keep right on swingin' till an adult does intervene. If you follow that plan, and you get booted out of school because of it, you won't hear one word from your Dad. And that is all I've got to say about that.

GOING TO SCHOOL AT LANGDALE

I did not know whether I would be able to have much to say about Langdale School. I only went there two years. I will say that I don't have enough memory of the kindergarten there to say anything at all. The building is still there now. It look's the same. Exactly the same, in fact. But it is used now for social functions of all sort's. But the school, now, that is another story. When I think of the Langdale School, the child that I was sit's straight up and begins to flood my brain with memories. The first memory is that I did not want to go there. To the child that I was that school looked like a huge prison house. Remember, this had been a K-12 school when my Uncle Pep was in school. When I started attending there, it still went through the eighth grade. I was intimidated by the sheer size of the school. I was intimidated by the size of the older students. I just wanted no part of that school at all. Of course that impressed my parent's so much till they let me home school, right? Now youre catchin' on, friend. It was off to school with me. For the most part, I'm not really proud of my first year in school. I had a wonderful teacher. Her name was Mrs. Sides. Bless her heart, she earned her pay that year on me alone. I kept my poor Mother busy comming to the school for one reason or another. I well remember sitting in the principal's office one day. His name was Mr. Pennington. I was crying. I said to him that I wanted to go home. Poor Mr. Pennington said "Son, right about now I wish I could go home too."

I would ask to go to the bathroom. If given permission to go, I would stand outside the door and refuse to go in as long as even ONE of the older student's were in there. This would bring Mrs. Sides or some school staff person looking for me. And off to the office it was for me. Well, in time the school had enough of that and stopped letting me go to the bathroom during class. Only then I had an accident in my drawers one day. Now I had to be sent home. So my Mother comes to pick me up, and finds out that I have to go home because my drawers were......not in good shape. "Son, why did you not go to the bathroom?" "' Cause they wouldn't let me". "Did you ask to go?" "Yes M'am". Remember, Mother once had the same thing happen to her at this same school (Tho I must admit she had a much better argument than I in this case). Now SHE is upset. But she did not yet have all the fact's. When she get's them, she is still upset. At me!! Now going home isn't going to be such a smooth event after all. Can you say "bathroom revival?"

It was that kind of year. I had a brand new winter coat that year. One day I took it off to play in a game of kickball. I laid it across one of the big floodlight's in front of the school. And forgot about it. And went home without it. "Hugh, where is your coat?" Uh-oh. "Did you leave it at school?" "Which room did you leave it in?" "You left it WHERE?!?" "Get in the car right NOW!!!" This wasn`t my Mother, friend. It was my Father! We went back to the school pronto. Happy ending? I wish. The coat was gone. You can guess what kind of meeting took place in the bathroom soon after, right? Yes, it was that kind of year, friend.

There was some fun to be had from time to time. We had this little race thing that we would do at recess. In those days there were several huge oak trees lining that death trap called highway 29. They were inside the fence, of course, and ran from one end of the school to the other. In this race you ran from the first tree to the second. Then you walked from the second tree to the third, and so on, from one end of the school to the other, and even back sometimes. Kick-ball was a favorite game with us. It was essentially a softball game without bats and gloves. Someone would roll a big rubber ball to the batter,er...kicker, who would kick it as hard as he / she could. The only way to be 'put out ' was to be hit with the ball by someone 'in the field'. This was probably our favorite recess game. The old oak trees were taken down some years ago. That was sad to me. You would never know that children once did run / walk races between towering oak trees on the grounds of that grand ole' school. The story was that the trees had become diseased, and therefore a safety risk. I yield to the knowledge of folk who were trained to know such things.

But they didn't look diseased to me. Their removal left another ugly scar on the landscape of the Valley I was raised up in.

It was somewhere during this time that Mother Nature took a personal interest in blowin' up the only birthday party I had in my early years. Mother sent out invitations and everything. She and Dad had reserved the bottom room at the Langdale Gym (Sears Memorial Hall) for the occaision. That was a year when Mother Nature decided to send in a good portion of our spring rains a couple months early. The gyms front door is only about thirty feet from Moores Creek. It rained torrents most of that week, and especially the day of the party. Nobody came. Not a soul. Mother did what only a Mother can do. She made it a 'family' birthday party, and she made it fun too. It would be decades later, when I was grown and married, before I would be surprised by a birthday party thrown for me by my wife. As for this rain-out, it turned out about as good as it could. Mr. Moore stayed within his banks (barely), and we still filled up on cake and ice cream.

By my second grade year, I had settled down a bit. Mrs. Campbell was my teacher. I did have a noticeable improvement in my reading ability that year. Mrs. Campbell had to be patient with me too. But my memories of her, though they have grown somewhat dimmer with the passage of time, are fond ones. I remembered something we did as a class one day. I'm going to put it in here, but it might have happened in my first grade year. A classmate of ours had been sick. It was either measles or chicken pox. Her family lived just a short walk from the school. One day as a surprise to her, our teacher led us on a walk to her house. No, we did not go into the house, of course. We stood on the side of the road,in fact. Her parents let her come to a window, and we waved to her and shouted our 'get well's ' to her. Then we just walked back down the hill to school.

You see friend, this is another example of my living in the last days of the simple mill village way of life. Langdale School, and all the mill village schools for that matter, was serving it's last years as a true 'village school'. It was almost exclusively Langdale kids who went to Langdale school. Granted, it was only through the eighth grade (since the opening of Valley High School some years before), but it was OUR school. The child that I was had no clue that events would come not too many years later that would once again bring drastic change to the way these grand old school buildings would function, if at all. When I look back on it now, I'm so glad that I had those two years at Langdale School. I was the second generation of my Mothers family to attend there. And the last.

A very sad thing happened during my second grade year. One day we were interrupted in class by a shocking announcement on the school intercom. President John F. Kennedy had been shot in a far off Texas city called Dallas. Someone led the school in prayer, and we tried to get back to our studies. But a short time later, there was a second announcement. President Kennedy had died. There was another prayer, followed by Mrs. Campbell leading us in the pledge of allegiance to our nations flag. I still remember watching on a black and white t.v. as our nation mourned the passing of the leader of the free world. I saw John Jr. wave a small American flag and salute his fathers hearse. The idea that a President of the United States should be felled by an assassins gun left boys and girls like us as well as our parents in shock. Little did we know that this was just the opening scene in what would be one of the bloodiest decades in our nations history. Indeed, we would grieve again.

THE FABLE OF LABELS

Friend, from time to time in this little book of mine, I come to a place where I just have to get something off my chest. At the risk of having you scold me for 'chasing yet another rabbit', my friend, could I make an observation right here? Of course I can. After all, I`m the one doing the writing. You, patient friend, are doing the reading. I have already done some ribbing of folk who I call 'liberals' or'new age thinkers' in these pages. But I'm real close to swearin' off any name calling like that. See, I'm evolving right before your eyes.

Make no mistake that hate killed President Kenedy. Rage, in turn, took that mans life. Vengeance like this never bears any good fruit. It only bears bad fruit like misery, confusion, and more violence, to name just a few. Be sure that this kind of hate was seeded first in hateful rhetoric. I make that point now, in 2012, because we are going through a national election that is as mean and nasty as any I have ever seen in my lifetime. The contenders for whatever office is being contested, be it local, state, or national are spending more time dissing and accusing one another than they are talking about what specific things or talents they bring to the table in helping to govern,that makes them more qualified to serve than their opponent. This is bad enough in a state or national race. Amazingly though, it gets even nastier when you get to the local level in many cases. It almost becomes a political fight to the death that has too much to do with butchering the other party and not near enough to do with putting concrete ideas before the voters for them to chose from. Good men and women, who have committed the high crime of being a member of the 'other party', have their character assassinated, their motives questioned, and their records distorted.

Look, America, we used to be a nation of good ideas and great thinkers. There was a time when we could have a meaningful debate that pitted one persons ideas against anothers. And the voters had a clear choice about what a man / woman stood for in terms of specific issues. The world we live in now has devolved into a political mud wrestling tournament. The winner is the person who can make his / her opponent look like the biggest liar, or traitor, or the least qualified, often because of some transgression that happened years, even decades ago. If we voters made a hard decision not to vote for ANY candidate who stoops to that kind of politickin', we would literally have to stay home from many elections.

Listen, I don't give a three legged grass-hoppers crooked jump WHAT a man / woman did 20 years ago. I want to know how he/she stands on issues that affect me and my family TODAY. What direction does he/she want to see the country go with health-care? What about helping our economy recover; what about immigration policy?; what about keeping us safe from mad men who actually believe they are doing (their)gods will when they kill us just because we are American? Those are the things I want a candidate to tell me about. As a voter I prefer a candidate to give me their best solutions to these issues so that I can compare them to those of his/her opponent. I am well able to make up my own mind which of the two will be the best person to represent my community, or county, or state, or nation. Enough of this political blood-letting that too often characterizes elections in our country.

ANYWAY...... I'll make one last statement on this sad state of affairs and move on. A label, in most cases, is nothing more than a fable. A label is one thing and one thing only. It is what someone else WANTS you to believe about a person. And usually, that involves a fable, especially in politics. If you really want to get to know a person, and especially a candidate for public office, don't form your opinions based on the slick attack dog ads you see or hear anywhere in the media. YOU go to that candidates rally. Or YOU go down to their campaign head-quarters. And YOU meet that candidate or his/her rep., and form YOUR opinion "from the horses mouth" as much as you can. Then YOU can be an informed voter and cast an untainted ballot. Now friends, THAT is what true democracy is all about. Not just fabled labels. And thats all I have to say about that.

LEAVING TALLASSEE STREET

There came a time when Mother and Dad made a decision to leave Tallassee Street. I think it was during my second grade year. Friend, at this moment I am 56 years old. Since we lived on Tallassee Street I have lived in nine homes if you want to count the two trailers I lived in before I married and the homes my wife and I have lived in together. I have lived in five communities. Tallassee Street is the most sentimental to me of them all. I did not say the most important, just the most sentimental. When my parents moved there, they only had me. By the time they made this move they had four kids. My baby sister would not be born till we moved to River View some time later. I still remember fondly the little hill behind that ole' mill village house, where the slidin' was always good in the fall, and where a fall took my dear Mother from hero to goat to hero again. I can still call back the experience of sitting on the screened in front porch singin' to the drumbeat of rain falling in the street. The people who were both neighbors and friends in our part of the village I still remember fondly. The Whites, the Stevens', the Creamers, the Piggs, good families all.

And I can never forget Mrs. Mason, who tried mightily to get me to stay within my music book and not try to create my own version of the songs she was trying to teach me to play. All the ladies helping that fellow to slop his hogs, Dr. Calhoun comming to our house to see us, so many memories! I was in front of this house playing one Sunday morning before we went to church. For some reason I'll never be able to justify, I decided it would be fun to stick a rock up my nose. Only when I tried to get it out, It just moved further up the nasal passage. I went crying to, say it with me class, MOOOOMMMIIIEEE, again. For this we had to go to the doctors office. He had to use a looooooong contraption to get that rock out. And he told my parents that if that rock had gotten the slightest bit further up my nose I would have suffocated.

I remember being in the storm drain next to the house, and peering out to watch my Uncle James walk down the street in his army dress uniform. I held him in awe for his service to our country. The flag that draped his coffin when cancer took him from us sits in a special place now above my mantle. For the record friend, I couldn't get my LEG in that storm drain today. I walked down this street to meet my PaPa when he came home from the mill, just before he retired, many times.

I'm remembering that there was a small room next to the bathroom where PaPa kept his tools and a big tool box with all his smaller tools in it. I had great fun using various nails, screws and the like to play imaginary games of 'army'. As a child I came in onto the front porch of this old house one afternoon, so my Mother used to tell me. Uncle Pep and Aunt Margaret had just left the house to go to her Mothers house in Lanett. Mother said she called me over to the swing and said to me "Uncle Pep tried to speak to you a while ago, and you just kept right on walking. I think you hurt his feelings". Mother said I got a real concerned look on my face and asked "Is that why he's got all them wrinkles on his face?" Who can fathom the thought process of a child, friend?

You know, it's really hard to leave this place. I've told you that my PaPa still drank at this point in his life. Too much sometimes. One day I was on my way into the house, and I passed by PaPa and Mr. Henry Yarbrough. They were working on a car. And they were arguing over who could drink the most. I heard PaPa say, "Henry, I can drink you 'under this car' right now." Of course, Mr. Henry disputed that. I went on in the house. I was in the little 'tool room' playing army a while later when I heard a commotion of some sort. I walked out just in time to see Mr. Henry and someone else, I can't remember who, helping PaPa to his bedroom. He didn't know me from 'Adams house-cat', but he had the biggest smile on his face I ever saw. PaPa had done found out whether or not he could out-drink Mr. Henry. I'll never forget, Mr. Henry looked around at me,winked, and said, "When your PaPa wakes up, tell him he can just wait till next week to pay me."

The part of the mill village I grew up in is in a sad state of affairs today, at least by the standards of the people who lived there when I was a boy. If the adults of my childhood were able to walk up and down Tallassee Street today, they would be shocked and angry. Our Mothers would cry. Our Fathers would go silent, their eyes narrowed and their jaws set. These adults would either begin trying to buy up all of these homes and restore them to proper health, or they would move their families far away so that they would not have to be around for the slow crumbling of a happy, proud community they once called home. Lets make a deal friend, you and me. You help me sell a million copies of this little book of mine. And I'll tell you what I'll do. I will immediately buy this little mill village home that I love, and I will immediately restore it to what I remember. I will restore the front porch and screen it in. I will restore the two rooms in the back that had to be removed because of termites. I will clear off the bank behind the house and reseed it with grass. I will do my own archaeological dig to uncover the steps that my Mother used to come to the rescue of me and my bloody knee that day so long ago. Maybe this would cause others to do the same for their old mill village homes. And we could create the "bed-room community" that current leaders have envisioned. Well friend, this could go on all day. Tallassee Street, we must take leave of you for now. But my heart has never taken leave of you all these years, not once. And it never will. But for now, the sand's of time are shifting in this story. And I must move on.

THE FORGOTTEN MOVE

I seriously doubt that any of my siblings remember the house we moved to when we left Tallassee Street. It wouldn't rank on any of their lists as a memorable home that we lived in. And yet there are some things that I have retained in my memory, that are worth noting in this little book of mine. To be honest, I don't even remember the name of this street, pre or post 911 addresses. But if you go north on that death trap called highway 29, you will pass Hoods Drugs on your right. Just past that you will see a health spa on the right. You would turn left directly across from that spa, and that is the street we lived on, first house on the left. It still sits there today. It's a little white frame house, built much like the mill village houses. Maybe it will not fall victim to the kind of neglect that so many of the mill village houses have.

Our neighbors directly across the street were the Jones'. I don't remember first names, but there was a Mom and a son. I seem to remember that he played football for Valley High School. He couldn't be all bad then, could he? He was very kind to spend time with us kids from time to time. I don't remember names at all for our neighbors just past our house on the right. But I am quite sure they remembered us long after we moved away. These dear people had the neatest little "cement pond" in their front yard. It was very small, almost like an overgrown bird feeder without legs. And in that little cement pond they had some of the prettiest 'gold fish' looking fish I ever saw. I seem to remember orange being their dominant color. Friend, I had never seen anything quite as pretty as those fish. Of course, once I had found out about them, it was only fair that I show them to my siblings. They becaqme just as enthralled with the fish as I.

We loved to slip over there to watch them. Or feed them. Or harass them. This began to cause no small consternation for the neighbors. Finally, the man of the house was compelled to ban us from his yard. Friend, you know how kids are. Once we were 'hooked' (no pun intended) on how pretty those fish were, we were going to find a way to have our visits with our new 'adopted' little friends, even if it meant risking sure and swift discipline. We would be outside our home playing. We would see this couple leave. We would just wave at one another like neighbors do. And just as soon as they were out of sight, we were off to their yard. Good plan too, till one day this man figured out our little plan. He and his wife came out of their house. They got in their car. They drove by our house as on many other occaisions. We all waved like neighbors do. As soon as they were out of sight, here we go over to their yard as we had many other times before. We had hardly got down on our knees and started to look, when there was the sudden blaring of a car horn. Behind us! This man had merely gone around the block. He had sneaked up on us from behind!

Pity us friend, would you? All we wanted to do was visit with the goldfish. And feed them. And look at them. And harass them. Instead, we got escorted back to our home, presented to our parent's, and 'told on'. Friend, please believe me when I say that my parents solved our neighbors problem for him that day. Permanently. We never saw those goldfish again. Didn't want to. You know what I mean, don't you, friend?

THE "OOP'S" MELON EATIN'

We were living here whe we came back from a particular vacation to Florida with three or four watermelon in the trunk. Friend, you won't believe this one at all. But there was a time when you could buy watermelon at a farmers market at the rate of something like 4 for 5.00. Thats less than a dollar a piece. Tell me friend, tell me what ONE dollar will buy you these days? Anyway, on this day I had harassed my Dad into the notion that I was plenty big enough to carry one of those huge watermelons into the house. You have already figured out what happened, haven't you friend? Dad relented. I carried. I dropped. We ate. What do you mean,'did I drop it on purpose'? Really, friend, I am deeply disappointed that you would think that of me. Of COURSE it was an acciddent! Heh- heh, heh-heh. No, really. It was!

THE REAL GIVERS IN LIFE

There was a big 'crawl space' under this house, especially in the rear of it. It made for a really great (and cool) place for a kid to play on a hot summer day, at least to the child that I was. It was also a place where my PaPa could retreat with friends for some occaisional, how can we say this,'sippin' fellowship'. Mother made Dad go out there one day and break up one of these 'fellowships'. They had finally got on Mothers last nerve drinkin' under there. Dad was to instruct them not to come back to our place with their alchohol.

Later that year, we had one of those spells where sickness ran through the family, especially with Mother. But Dad got a dose of it too this time. Both my parent's lost time out of work. Money got short. We were in a bad way financially. We had a caring group of church family, extended family, and friends who "passed the hat", and made up a 'love offering' for us. Someone bought a card, and everyone signed it. Back then folk would sign a card like that and put in parentheses how much they gave. Well friend, who do you reckon gave the most at this time? Why, it was the very people who were run out from under Mother and Dads house that day. Now theres an attitude for ya, friend. "Take that lady!. Run me out from under your house just 'cause I'm usin' the space for a bar! The next time they pass the hat for you in hard times, I'll jes' haul off and put a hundred dollars in the hat. That'll fix 'ya! "Actually, it did. Friend, you find out who your REAL friends are when you're down. I know that for a fact. I've had times when I had friends I did not know I had, and I've had times when I did not know I had a friend. In fact, friend, right now you are one of the best friends I have, because at least you have stayed with me this long on our journey through this life I have lived. And I thank you for it.

LOSING GRANDMA

My Mother lost her Grand-Mother during our stay here. I was 7 years old. I'll never forget it. We had gotten home from church on a Sunday night. I forget whether we informed by a phone call or someone comming by the house. But I can still see and FEEL my Mothers grief. She was not even 10 years removed from the death of her Mother. And now her beloved Grand-Mother was gone too. She had been sick for a while, but had taken a turn for the worse that weekend. Mother and Dad had debated staying out of church that night and going to her Grand-Mothers house. But Dad was music director, and Mother was our piano player at our church, Midway. In the end, we went on to church.

My Mother was tender about her Mother and her Grand-Mother all of my life, as you have seen through her letters. I remember, one day while we lived here I asked Mother a question about her Mother. I don't even remember what it was now. But it was around the time of Miss Ludies birthday. Mother started to cry, and had to go in and wake my Dad, who was on the third shift then. She cried for a while. Friend, I went under the house and did a little cryin' myself. Of course, presently Mother came out to me. She gave me the kind of hug that only a Mother can give, and assured me that I had done nothing wrong.

A SLIMY SACK OF SNOT

I have debated whether to tell this story or not. It is not one of my favorites. Nor will it be easy to tell. But for some reason I feel compelled to tell it. Hold on to your drawers, friend. It's not often that you read a story like this. My Dad was on the third shift in those days (12:00 till 8:00 a.m.). Mother was home with us. One night Dad went to work, the phone rang. When Mother answered, she was met with a few seconds of silence, then a 'click' sound as someone hung up on her. This became a nightly thing. At first Mother was more aggravated than anything else. But then the mischief became more serious. After Dad left for work, a car would go by the house, someone blowing the horn over and over. Then, Mother started hearing a voice when she answered the phone. Ladies, what if you heard stuff like this on a nightly basis: "Hazel, I'm going to get you. Sooner or later, I'm going to get you. Not tonight. Maybe tomorrow night. But one of these day's I'm gonna get you. One day you will open your door thinking I'm the mailman, and it's going to be all over for you. One way or the other, Hazel, I WILL get you!" What about it, ladies? How would you react? Husbands,what would you do?

My Dad was beside himself. Mother was almost to the point of a nervous breakdown. Dad would stay home from work. Nothing would happen. He would try to fool the jackass by hiding his car and slipping back into the house through the back door. Nothing. It seemed like this piece of trash knew every step Dad made. Dad could not concentrate at work for worrying about what might be happening at home. Finally, one night at the mill, Dads supervisor had him in the office. He said to my Dad," Hubert, I'm not going to tell you which one,'cause I don't want nobody gettin' killed down here. But look over there around that smokin' booth". Dad looked, and there were three of his co-workers in and around that smoking booth. His supervisor said," One of those three men is the cause of your problem at home". Now friend, in todays world, a man armed with that kind of info might well just bring a gun to work and kill all three men, just to make sure he got the right one. Shootings are as common as spring rains, anymore.

The way my Dad handled this situation was about as good as could be expected. Friend, you may well say that he let it go too easy. What he did was this. He walked up to that smoking booth as though it was just another night at the office. And he said this; "Fellas, I have it on pretty good authority that one of you three is the one that has been scaring the hell out of my wife for the past couple weeks. Phone calls, car horns, threats, you know. This has got to stop. So I tell you what I'm goin' to do. If my wife hears a horn or a threat, or ANY kind of communication like that again, I'm goin' to come back to you three. And I'm goin' to pick out one of you, just at random. Me and that man are goin' out back of the mill. And either you are goin' to beat the hell out of me, or I'm goin' to beat the hell out of you. And if you wind up beating me, you will be sore from the effort for several day's. Now, if she hears anything the next night, I'll come back and pick a different one of you, and we'll do the same thing. Now fellas, we can do that every night for as long as you like. But let's understand something. This nonsense is GOING to STOP!!!." Mother was not bothered again after that night.

Well.

Friend,that has been over 45 years ago. Many times across the years I all but begged Mother or Dad to tell me who it was who did this. They would not budge. It's just as well, I suppose. I would now be telling the whole world who this 'south end of a north bound mule' was. He richly deserves to be known for the low down, egg sucking dog that he was. But I know this. 'People' (and I use that word in this case loosely) who commit this kind of cowardly practice seldom keep it to themselves. Sometimes this kind of heartless ruthlessness gets handed down through a family as though it was just a bit of good clean fun at the expense of folk who did not know how to take a joke.

So parden me for just a moment, friend. I won't be here long, I promise. But on the off chance that this monster is still alive, or that he passed the story of his utter ignorance off to sons who still repeat it now, give me just a moment with them, if you please: First, it's not much of a man who who has to get his excitement at the expense of a precious lady who never did anything but love her God, her church, her family, and her friends. This person was nothing but a slithering snake, a slimy sack of snot, and a coward of the first order. He had enough yellow in his back to paint a two story colonial style house. The ONLY way I could ever hold that man in anything other than total contempt would be to find that somewhere in his miserable little life he came to a heart changing, mind renewing, soul saving knowlege of the Saviour I have known since 1980. With a heart washed as white as snow, and a new 'sheet of paper' as it were to write a different life story, I could embrace him. Failing that, I can only say that he richly deserved the toasty spot in the hottest corner of hell that was waiting for him when he slipped out of this world and into eternity. And if you are a son or a grandson who heard this pitiful tale and repeat it with a smile today, you deserve a spot right next to him. You putrid bum. And that's all I have to say about that. Anyone who thinks I went a little overboard here, do me a favor won't you? Go suck your thumb. Not hard, because I understand what you are sayin'. All the same, go suck your thumb.

WHO IS IN THE BED???

Now, lets end our time in Langdale on a much lighter note, if that will be o.k. with you, friend. Trust me when I tell you that it was YEARS after the fact, but my Dad laughed with me a few times over this story. I know already that there will be a few folk who will say that I might not be doing the 'right thing' by tellin' it. But my Dad and I got some mileage out of it while he was with us. And I don't think he would be one bit embarased by it now. So don't waste your time commin' to me, or writin' to me, or e-mailin' me. Just suck your thumb and enjoy the story.

One night my Dad was workin' at the mill. By now Mother worked some nights too. But on this night she was not well, and sent him word that she would not be going in that night. However, she got to feeling good enough to go in later. She tried to contact Dad to let him know about her change of heart. But they missed connections somehow. Mother called in a lady who worked for her and Dad when both of them were going to be working. The maid has permission to use Mother and Dads bed when both of them are working at night, once she knows that all of us kids are asleep. On this night, all of us kids are already asleep when the maid gets to our house. SO, there is nothing for her to do but look in on us, then pile up in the bed and go to sleep. This she does, knowin' she will be up before Dad gets home in the mornin'. Are you with me, friend?

Meanwhile, Dad decides to come home early to check on Mother. Dad has no idea that Mother has gone to work, much less that she has called in the maid. Dad arrives home. He enters the house. It is very quiet. The house is dark. Mother and Dads bedroom is especially dark. Dad has no intention of waking Mother if he can get out of it. He quietly slips into his pajamas. He VERY quietly slips into the bed. "" Won't Hazel be surprised to see me?", he thinks to himself. There's goin' to be a surprise alright. Dad eases up to the warm body in the bed. He gently slips his arm around that body. And he whisper's, "Hi, honey". There was an earthquake in our community that night. They say it was felt all the way to River View. Dad and the maid both had a pentecostal fit trying to beat each other out of that bed. Mother and Dad almost had to remodel their bedroom. Ask me friend. Go ahead and ask me if we ever had a maid at night after that night. Or do you really need to?

Well, there came a time when Mother and Dad decided to leave this little street. It was quite the "never a dull moment" home, was it not? This move would take us out of Langdale for good. We never lived there again. But friend, I will forever have a big ole' soft spot for the little mill village town where I was born. I have been out of the Valley area almost 20 years at this writing. On the rare occaision when I get home, I still like to ride down Tallassee Street and look at that precious little house that is still so close to my heart. I have to drive or walk by the old mill. The city of Valley rescued this grand building from certain destruction a few years ago. God bless 'em. As for textiles, they died a slow painfull death that was, in my humble and obviously biased opinion, unnecessary. I have not forgotten you, William Farley. I'll be dealing with you soon enough. But for now, I have to move on to the next mill village we would live in. Actually, we lived on the fringe of the town of River View, or as I have enjoyed sayin' over the year's," in the suburb's" of River View. But our lives would be centered in that village. And we would finnish our growin' up there.

But you know, I am still drawn back to a certain sloping hill that looks out over the Chattahoochie River. In fact, I can stand on a little bluff there and see the exact place where once there was a boat landin' from which Miss Ludie launched out on the only boat ride she ever took with PaPa. I stand there from time to time. I can get the cam- corder of my imagination to conjure up what that scene must have looked like. And it can still make me laugh. My fondest dream would be for me to be able to be laid to rest on this little hill when you all have to lay down my old clay shell some day. Then again, friend, I have found that the only thing necessary for a dream to not come true is for me to be the one who is dreamin' it. Oh, ' hesh yore mouf',self pity. You have no 'bizz-ness' in this here book! Ahhh, Langdale,Langdale, you will always have a piece of my heart. I feel as though I have not done you proper justice. But the sand's of time stand still for no man. And they are shifting again in this little story of mine. Come, friend. Sadly, we must be going now.

MOVING TO MARS, AND ETERNAL GRATITUDE

Friend, I have told you how that each mill village was like a small city unto itself. So it was, to the extent that even though our move could not have been more than six miles, for me we may as well have been moving to Mars. But looking back on it now, I know this move was all a part of Gods plan for our family. Before we get to River View itself though, I think it important to stop here and talk about the 'bridge' our family used to get from one mill village to the other. It was a little place called Midway Baptist Church. And friend, it was there that God would put people in front of me who would plant the spiritual seeds in my life that would some day bring me to the Old Rugged Cross, where my life would be changed forever. I owe my beginning in life to the people of the Langdale Mill village. I owe my raising to the people of the River View mill village. But I owe my Eternel Destination to the people of Midway Baptist Church. Friend I think you are goin' to really enjoy seeing this little country church and meetin' it's people. Let me introduce you to them.

THE MIDWAY STORY

Midway Baptist Church is the church that my siblings and I were raised in. Mother use to say that it was the first place she and Dad took me, outside the home, after I was born. When my mind wanders back through this life that I have lived, I think I can say this truthfully. The people of Midway are more responsible than any others (outside of my parent's) for the fact that I am not in hell today. What this church family meant to me goes so much further than the feeble words that I will now use to tell you about them. I could never repay them for what they have neant to me in my life. My biggest regret is that most of them are in heaven now and will not read my humble attempt to thank them for their witness and the testimony all of them were to me.

Mother and Dad started attending Midway early on in their marriage. At that time, Mother had been attending what I like to call a "First Church of the Frigidaire". You know the type, friend. People smile at you. They will shake your hand during 'greetin' time'. They are quite glad to have you and your tithe check in their midst. But you don't get to enjoy the intimate 'church family' relationship that is so important to have. Somehow you are held at arm's length, and never feel like you are a member of a 'family' of believers. Down the road just a ways', between the two mill villages that shaped my life, a new church was forming. It was called 'Midway' for obvious reason's. It was a 'church plantin' mission taken on by the people of the Johnson Chapel Baptist Church (you will remember, I spoke of this church earlier in these pages.). Plantin' a church is not the easiest thing in the world. Nor is it possible to do outside the involvement of the Holy Spirit of God,which moves on the hearts of the 'planters' to do the hard work and make the sacrifices that are necessary to bring a new church into being.

These planters first would do a survey to determine a need for a proposed church in the community. The next thing would be to find a building to begin meeting in. A man of God (preacher) to be the spiritual 'undersheppard' of this new flock of believers would have to be searched out, prayed about, then 'called' to accept this new ministry. Now some really important work would begin. There was much door knocking to be done, introducing this new ministry to the community. Some 'out of the church house' meetins' would start being held in any willing home.These were called 'cottage prayer meetins'. Friend, even when I was a child these meetins' were still fairly common. I have seen folk come to the Lord before they even attended their first church service. By the time they got to the church house, they were ready to be trained for service.

AN HUMBLE BEGINNING

In the case of Midway, the church got it's start in an old store buildin'. That buildin' has been gone for many years now. I have seen a picture of it though. Friend, it was not much to look at. But my, my, what a ministry came out of it! There were charter members of that church who were full of zest in tryin' to make this new ministry a true soul filling station. By the way friend, Let's get this in. 'The church' is NOT the buildin' that we meet in. 'The church' is folk like me and you. Friend, I have not done much scripture quoting in this little book of mine, for a reason. I would rather have you read the words I write and be provoked to go and look in your Bible to see if what I'm saying is on target. But on this thing about 'the church', let's do a little study, you and me. Go get your Bible. Make sure it's a good old fashioned King James Bible, now. Turn it to Matthew, chapter 16, verses 13-18. Jesus has just finnished teachin' his disciples about steerin' clear of the "leaven" (or the doctrine) of the pharisees and the sadducees. Then he asks a question of them. Lets follow that conversation:

(13) When Jesus came to the coasts of Caesarea Phillippi, he asked his disciples, saying,"who do men say that I am?"

(14) And they said, "Some say that thou art John the Baptist: some, Elias; and others Jeremias,or one of the prophets".

(15) He sayeth to them, "But whom say ye that I am?"

(16) And Simon Peter answered and said, "Thou art the Christ, the Son of the living God".

(17) Then Jesus answered and said unto him, "Blessed art thou, Simon Barjona; for flesh and blood hath not revealed it unto thee, but my father which is in Heaven."

(18)"And I say unto thee, that thou art Peter, and upon this rock I will build my church; and the gates of hell will not prevail against it."

Friend, in my small, career 10th grade student mind, I can't find that Jesus had any 'physical' building in mind when he talked about building his church. The 'rock' that He talked about was Himself, of course. And on that truth, folk like Peter, and in our day you and I, who accept by faith that Jesus is the ONLY son of the ONLY true and living God that there ever has been, or ever will be. WE are the church. And among the church planters and charter members who started the Midway Baptist Church, there were people of faith who were determined to live out the command to take the Gospel to EVERY creature, to everyone in that community who they could get to listen to the Gospel story. They invested many hours where they could have been at home restin' from a hard day of cotton mill work. They spent many hours in prayer seekin' God's direction. They did a whole lot of plannin', and not just for that present day. God did not give them that old store buildin' for a permanent home. It was just a place to START their mission. These folk spent a whole lot of time doin' a bunch of door knockin' in this community. They went out and met people where they were. They shared their vision for establishing a house of worship in that community. And at the slightest chance, they shared the good news of a risen Saviour who could make all the difference in their lives, now and in eternity, if they would only call on his Holy Name.

TO THE WORK!!

The early Midway church was able to move to it's present location at least in part due to the generosity of West Point Pepperell. The company donated the land for the new building. Then, there began a whole bunch of 'sweat equity' on the part of the members. All accounts I have described this group of folk as the very picture of a "family" of believers. The first Thanksgiving they shared was right in the middle of a work day. They used saw horses and plywood for tables and broke bread together. They thanked God for the building that would soon house the ministry of their church. They shared what must have been a Jim-dandy of a meal. And they went right back to work. Try that one today, church pastor. That is, if you think God may be leading you to your next assignment. You could certainly speed up the process by callin' a workday on a holiday. But in this case it was actually the Midway PEOPLE who had a zeal for the work at hand. The basement of the building,where the Sunday School room's would be, was finnished. The floor to the sanctuary had been laid. Excitement built as they got closer and closer to the day when they would hold service in their new building for the first time. You know, I have a copy of a picture of this bunch. I believe it was taken during a break in one of these work day's. Many of their faces are very familiar to me even now.

There's Mr. Will Henry Frazier and his dear wife. He was a supervisor at the Langdale Mill. But once he got on the church yard, business was on hold and worship was on. And there is Brother Luther Birchfield, a man who could flat out preach the corn slap off the cobb friend, then suck on the cobb for a while. Well, feed me a big ole' bowl of banana puddin' and call me satisfied, there's Mr. Olin De Loach and his wife Christine. We called these two MaMa and

PaPa De Loach all our lives. PaPa would later shame me out of bird huntin' forever, and talk me out of changin' my name legally when I was on the outs with my Dad. And there's their daughter Betty. Not far away is Billy Joe Coker, who would one day ask Betty to be his wife. They would spend more than 50 years together and raise two kids, a boy and a girl. One of the highlights of my life was the night Mother and I went with them to their 50 year high school reunion. Mother and Betty were in the same graduating class together. What a blast we had that night! On and on the faces and the memories go. You know what friend? There is not one unhappy face in the picture. These are faces that show a combination of joy, determination, and purpose. On a mission, they are truly one big, happy family.These are the people Mother and Dad met when Mr. Carl Yarbrough crossed their life path. Midway was about to go into revival, and Brother Carl invited them to come one night. They accepted that invitation. Well, they found Midway to be a mix of mill management and working class people. They found that once they got into the church house, no-one considered themself to be any better than the person that he or she sat next to. Social or economic stature in life made no difference to any of them. They truly acted like family. They made Mother and Dad feel welcome from the start. They never went back to the First Church of the Frigidaire again.

Friend, let me make an observation here. We have already determined that the 'church' is the people IN the building, not the building itself. A visitor to your church may LOVE your facilities. But if "the church" does not make that visitor feel welcome, loved, and needed, chances are that he/she will be a one time visitor. For my Mother and Dad, the way they were made to feel on that first visit was far removed from what they were used to. Yet it was everything they had been missing. Another important thing is to be willing to avail the church of the talent's any new member bring's into that ministry. I know that there has to be a period of time for acclimation to the church family. There might even be some necessary training that has to happen. New members to your church, in most cases, will be gung-ho to get started doing their part within the church family. The surest way to deflate a willing member is to put off allowing them to be active, with impunity.

Mother was an accomplished piano player already. Dad had already led music in various gospel meetings. In time Mother became the regular church pianist. Dad became the music director. They and their talent's were openly welcomed and utilized in their new church home. And they helped to build a music program that once sported choir for children, and youth, and adults. Midway was blessed with some of the best soloist's around, too. Mother played piano at Midway for almost 40 years. Dad spent 20 years or so as the music director. The first song I ever sang in public was right here at Midway. I was standing just to the right of the communion table, next to the piano. My Mother played for me that day. The name of the song was "Saviour

Gently Take Me Home". It was her favorite song. She deserved to go out that way too. Alas, it would not meant to be.

THE MIDWAY I KNEW

At it's zenith, Midway Baptist Church had 199 enrolled in Sunday School. There were 99 enrolled in what we used to call Training Union. Those may seem like small numbers to you, friend. But consider; it was located halfway between two small mill village towns. Too, in my neck of the woods there tend to be twice the number of churches in small towns like these than there are in other places in this great country of our's. And remember, this little church was started by 'church planters', from scratch. They literally started without so much as a building to meet in. From an humble beginning like that, in an area that was still fairly small at the time, the number this church grew to is impressive indeed.

One of the hallmarks of the Midway I grew up in was how busy it stayed around there. I remember Vacation Bible Schools in the summer that even had young adult classes. There were organizations that were specific to all areas of children/youth. There was "Sunbeams" for the smaller children. There was "Royal Ambassadors" for the boys. There was "Girls In Action" for the girls. There were Acteens for the older girls. All of these programs spotlighted things like missions and service in the community. Of course all of this was taught from Bible principles by people who not only taught the walk but walked it as well. Friend, there is no substitute for a teacher, of ANY kind, who is willing to go where he/she is teaching the boy/girl to go. I will testify that this was never a problem as I grew up at Midway Baptist Church. I'm not sure I have adequate words to express how thankfull I realy am for the Godly leadership that the child I was received in those years. And right about now, I find myself wishing I had told more of them how I feel before they got off to Heaven on me.

We had a thing called "Study Course" once a year. It was a one week concentrated study of one book of the Bible. Friend, do you know of a church anywhere today that spends an entire week in the study of Gods Word? We had classes for every age group, including adults. Let's be honest, friend, we don't even do this kind of Bible study in our own homes anymore. How in the world would we be able to do it in our churches? Foot, we don't do week long revivals in our churches anymore. We either go from Sunday night to Wednesday, or the other way around. And we fuss about that. Cottage prayer meetings? Say those three words to folk these day's, and they will give you a blank stare and ask, "what's that?" I will testify to seein' a time when there would be a week of cottage prayer meetin's in the week BEFORE our week long revival's. I have seen salvation come to the sinner, repentance come to the backslider, broken heart's mended, friendship's restored, all in the cottage prayer meetin's prior to the revival! More than once the evangelist arrived at the church to find that revival was already well underway. Show me a modern pastor / preacher / evangelist who would not LOVE to walk into a situation like that, friend!

CHURCH FAMILY GET TOGETHERS- FELLOWSHIP AND FUN

We had recreation at Midway Baptist Church. In fact, my Dad coached a men's softball team that so dominated the church league of that day that they had to start playing in the industrial league with the mill teams. Their first year in that league, they came in second. The second year, they won the thing. This was a team made up of Cokers, Williams', Pitts', and Yarbroughs who could flat out play some softball. It was not a team to be trifled with once the umpire called out "play ball!" They would love you and pray for you before and after a game, and even between innings. But once the first pitch was tossed, look out! Heck, as I remember it, there were almost enough Coker's on this team to form their own team! And every single one of them were ball player's, buddy!

HOMECOMING DAY

Once a year we did an all day service at the church. A former Pastor would be invited to come back and preach the morning service. There would be 'special music' after the choir music. Most of the time this music would be provided by a soloist or group who would spend the day with us. They would do a concert in the afternoon after the 'dinner on the grounds'. Ah, friend, that 'dinner on the grounds'! I've seen a many a diet busted at a church homecomming. All the ladies of the church would fix their favorite dishes, and bring them to the church, where they were stored in the kitchen. All manner of tables would be moved out behind the church, and table cloths spread across them. When the pastor started his closing prayer, the ladies would begin to slip out the door and down to the kitchen. All the food was taken to the tables outside. By the time the congregation got to the back of the church, there was a feast before them that any king would salivate over.

The paper plates, plastic utinsels, etc. were on the front end of the first table. Usually you would get to the greens first. Cole slaw, cabbage any way you could cook it, all manner of peas and beans, enough to satisfy any vegetarian. There was 'tater salad, boiled 'tater's, baked

SWEET 'tater's, sweet 'tater casserole,and anything else you could think to make out of a 'tater of any kind. Then you came to the meats. Pork chops, meat loaf, baked chicken, fried chicken, chicken casserole, bar-b-que chicken (hey, it WAS a Baptist church!), B.B.Q. ribs, ham, roast beef, and hush mah' mowf! Then, you got to the breads. There was anything from dinner rolls to cornbread, and all breads between the two. Homemade bisquits were coveted for the cubed steak with gravy. Is your tounge hangin' out yet, friend? Then you got to the REALLY good stuff, desert!! Where to start? Any kind of chocolate cake known to man. Strawberry shortcake, red velvet cake, pineapple upside down cake, fried apple pies, and the absolute 'must' desert for any homecomming meal (especially at a Baptist church), banana pudding!! Friend, you DO know, don't you, that there is a mandatory club that all Baptist churches are required to have, right? If you go to a Baptist church, and if that church does NOT have a chapter of this club active, then you could be called before the convention to explain your obviously backslidden state. This club is called the "Baptist Bible Believers Banana Puddin' Brigade". And friend, at Midway Baptist Church we had SEVERAL world class banana puddin' maker's, my Mother being among them. Of course, there was plenty of iced tea, or lemonade, and soft drinks available to wash all these calories down with. The art of making really good, home-made, sweet iced tea is going away fast, friend. Everything these days, anymore, is 'instant this, instant that'. It's palatable, friend. But it will never match the old fashioned, made from scratch stuff I was raised on.

I have a copy of an old video made at a church home-comming when I was a child. My favorite little snippet in that video is a brief shot of my Mother, fixing a plate of that good ole' home-comin' food. Every time I see that video, and see all of the people who were so special to me then, and even more special to me now, I get just a wee bit home-sick, friend. You know what I mean, don't you? These were, and in my heart still are, MY people. I loved them then. I love them now. By the way friend, in the world we live in today, folk like to pretend they can take 'short-cuts ' and still have the same quality of food you and I were raised on. For example, some will make their banana puddin' with jello gelatin, and without the white stuff on top, and sometimes they will even cheat on the vanilla wafers. I have never offended anyone by refusing to eat this stuff. But neighbor, that stuff is in the same category as those 'wop-wop' biscuits Jerry Clower use to talk about. It is most decidedly NOT banana puddin'. It dont even qualify for 'banana puddin' LIGHT, neighbor. No offense intended. Jes' sayin'.....

GOOD TIMES AT SHARPES LAKE

From time to time our church family would plan a family day away from the immediate churh area. One of our favorite places to go was a place called Sharpes Lake. It was located a few miles outside of the county seat of LaFayette. This was a family owned complex that had a little something for everybody. It was one of the prettiest places I ever saw. There were two or three lakes on the property. The biggest one was down a dirt road and toward the rear of the property. I'm sure there was some fishing that went on at this lake. But I remember it for the 'swimmin' hole' that it was, where the dirt road ended. The boy that I was remembers that there were two outhouse looking buildings that were used for 'changing room's,' one for each gender. We enjoyed many a cool dip on a hot summer day in that water.

As you drove into Sharpes lake you could see straight ahead a series of pic-nic tables in a neat row. They were covered by a tin roof but no sides. Each table had a "Lazy Susan". This was a turn table that you would put your meal on. Instead of having to pass the food around by hand, all you had to do was turn the Lazy Susan to get before you the dish you wanted. The boy that I was marveled at this, and more than once got into a spot of trouble for turning this piece around without really needing anything.To the right of the dirt road and across the road from the pic-nic tables, the boy that I was remembers a small lake to the left and a softball field of sorts on the right. And then there was the most poignant place at Sharpes Lake. It was an outdoor church. By that I mean that it looked like a church facility was built except for the sides. The sides were open. It was a beautiful, rustic old building that gave you a real flavor of how church might have been conducted in a different time.

The pulpit was made of a huge old oaken stump. There were pianos on either side of the pulpit, and a place where I would imagine a choir might have sat at one time. On the far side there was a well, no longer in use, where no doubt church goers quenched their thirst with cool well water. If you found a quiet moment to stand behind that pulpit and close your eyes, you could almost hear the choir, the congregation, and the pianos. It wasn't hard to imagine hearing an old fashioned Bible believing preacher 'breaking the bread of life', in no small voice, to any ear within a quarter mile of the place. Can you imagine what it must have been like to participate in an Easter sunrise service at this grand place!? Ahhh, to watch the first pale colors in the sky in the morning; to watch them explode into brilliant sunshine as the moon respectfully retreated; to hear the woods around that grand ole' place come alive as God's creatures celebrated another sunrise, just as God's people celebrated when they knew their Saviour had arisen on that first Easter morning! It must have been a sight to see!

There was another feature to this sprawling place that I enjoyed very much as a boy. If you walked down the sloping little hill to the left of the pic- nic tables, you would find a spring at the edge of the woods. Someone had built a bridge, a dirt one, across this spring. But they first put down a pipe across the road bed where the spring was. This had the effect of making the spring look like a spicket that had been left on, since the pipe stuck out on the other side of the road, and about a foot or so off the ground. Not far away, there were what we called "mus-kee-dime" vines. Now, you city folk, bless yo' hahts, if you even know what I'm talking about, call this a "muscadine vine". And that's o.k., too. 'Jes' y'all 'member, ah'm a cun'try keeid, an' you all 'noe how uneducated we is, raght? Oh, there you go again, Hugh. Leave them city folk be, you hear? They don't mean no harm (tee-hee).

I went back to Sharpes Lake last year. They still do a festival on the ground's each year for a whole weekend. But friend, it wasn't even a shadow of it's former self from the perspective of the boy that I ws. The church is gone. Only the building where the pulpit is has survived. The pianos are gone. The pulpit, thank God, has survived. The pic-nic area where the tables with the 'Lazy Susan's' were is a thing of the past. All tables are gone. They were using the building for booths for the festival. No-one uses the dirt roads any more. They are marked as private now. I have to confess that me and my boy's took a little walk down there anyway. I wanted them to see the old swimming hole. The lakes are still there. But to me, having spent more than a few days watching great fun being had on those waters, they looked lonely. And I was sad at the sight. The saddest of all however was the spring area. Long abandoned and left to natures devices, it is a grown up weed infested place now. And can you believe it friend? I could not find even ONE mus-kee-dime vine anywhere around. I really wish I had me a picture or two of the way Sharpes Lake looked in my childhood. My boy's had heard me speak of this place so often. I'm afraid I set them up without knowing it.

Please, my friend, don't see this as my throwing off on whoever the owners of this property now are. Only in a rare case does a private family owned recreational place like this last for multiple generations. Also, in the world we live in today there are sooooo many government regulations that would have to be adhered to in order to keep a place like this up and ensure public safety, till the cost would be prohibitively high. Just another reason why places like Sharpes Lake must be remembered for their beauty and their service to the public, through the stories told by folk like you and I, in thing's like this little book of mine. I probably wont be going back though. The people of that community do an outstanding job with this festival. You can hear good music and eat good food. But for an old dinosaur like me, the sight of a place me and my family revere for the memories it gave us is just a bit too sad. Better to remember it through the lens of the boy that I was. Sharpes Lake was, indeed, a very special place.

ANYWAY, I will testify that a good three or four hands-full of mus-kee-dimes, washed down by as much spring water as you can stand, beat's anything you can get at a pic-nic table anyway. That is, unless somebody brought a banana puddin'. My last memory of going to Sharpe's Lake was not with the church family, howeever. It was at a Yarbrough family reunion. In my childhood, they met there every year for that reunion. On this day, I was with my Mother and my Aunt Flossie. We went down to the spring and had a good drink of that cool spring water. I remember that my Mother had a brief "spell" when some of that spring water "went down the wrong hole", as we used to say. But you should ask my dear Mother, friend, when you get to Heaven. Ask her if that "spell" caused her to regret that drink of spring water. You ARE going to be there, aren't you friend? In Heaven, I mean. It just wouldn't be the same without you.

WHATS A FAMILY REUNION?

That is what many of the younger generation will ask you today if you start to discuss that subject. In my early childhood, we had the Yarbrough reunion, not at Sharpe's Lake, but at different homes within the family. Believe it or not, friend, there was a time when families actually looked forward to that one day each year when the extended family would spend a whole day together. Us kids could roam free and play. From time to time you would be called over and presented to an uncle or an aunt. The aunt's especially could be counted on to make a fuss over you. "My, but haven't you grown since I saw you last!?" That's a line I have heard more than a few times. Sometimes they would take your cheek between their thumb and their pointer finger as they said that and just "squeeze the tar out of it" as they said that, too. The Yarbrough family would lay out a food spread that would cause a king to blush. After grace, we scattered to the four winds to put down what was usually an overpacked plate. Afterward, you had your choice. You could explore the expanse of Sharpes Lake. Or you could stick around for the concert. Anybody who could play a "gee tah" usually had one on hand. Before the day was done you could hear the best of gospel music, with a sprinkling of country to spice thing's up. I'll tell you something else. Nobody was in any hurry to leave our family reunion either. As a boy, I have seen tears shed when it was time to go. After all, when it was time for the next family reunion, there was every chance that someone would not be back. The Yarbrough family treasured their time together. But sadly, when my grand-fathers generation died out, interest slowly waned, and in time our yearly reunion became a thing of the past. Sad that is, friend. Very sad indeed.

You don't hear of family reunions much anymore, friend. When you do, they meet at this hotel, or that city park, and they seldom last a whole day. Part of the reason is that the world we live in now is just too fast, and we have so much goin' on. Family, especially extended family, have been relegated to the bottom of our collective priority list's. Already, I see in the Yarbrough family the reality that I probably have cousins who I would not be able to pick out of a photo album. Reunions are just too much trouble, anymore. And that is a crying shame, friend. There also arises another problem in this matter of family reunions, and that is having the wrong person in charge. More to the point, having any ONE person in charge. Many years after the Yarbrough family reunion died out, some folk in the Colley family worked hard to create a reunion of that family. We had some great times together. The generation of the Colley family that started and nurtured that reunion is almost gone now. The year after my Mother went to Heaven, I was asked to (the technical term is, 'elected') to be the president of the Colley reunion. The first year I did a tolerable job, but nothing special. The second year I just absolutely 'dropped the ball' in every way that a person can drop one. I can make every excuse in the book, but the bottom line is that I let an entire family down. I will take that to the grave with me. So in this little book of mine, let me make the most public apology possible for the lack of leadership. If this little book of mine does anything at all, maybe I can yet sponsor someday a Colley reunion that nobody will ever forget.

One last thing I need to get off my chest about family reunions. That would be the question of why people stop going to their family reunions. I have watched one family reunion die (the Yarbrough's) because one generation died out. I know I need to be carefull with my words here. But do you think, friend, that this is what the 'older generation' had in mind when they started their reunion? Did they want their reunion to peter out because it is 'inconvenient'? Did they want it to stop once they moved on to Heaven? I am the only one of a nine strong sibling/cousin group that has been to a reunion since Mother's generation of the Colley family all went Home. Painful? Sure. Memories? Plenty. Regret's? Not a one. My dear Mother would have had a 'hissie fit' if she knew I stopped going to her reunion just because she wasn't going to be there. No, the only regret I have is that I did such a poor job of trying to lead that reunion. It was a very humbling, humiliating experience, and nobodies fault but my own. And then there are those who will not go to a family reunion because some family member that he / she can't get along with might be there. Those are people who need to go suck their childish, immature thumb's. To not go to a family reunion for such selfish reason's as that is the very height of disrespect and dishonor to your forbears.

Well, I could go on and on. But I will end my comments about the 'family reunion' by saying that there is one reunion that I am REALLY looking forward to. It is one that will take place one sweet day when the eastern sky breaks wide open, and Gabriel blow's his trumpet, and Jesus himself descends from Heaven with a shout, and the dead in Christ rise up first, and then we who remain are caught up to meet him in the air, changed "in a moment, in the twinkling of an eye", and we are with our Saviour forever!! Well, bless the name of Jesus, and thank Him for his grace, his provision, and the victory he made possible for us when He vollunteerd for (temporary) death duty for us on the Cross!! In THAT reunion, friend, there will not be any of the silly, stupid, political games we play with one another in this world. So get it out of your system now if you are planning on being there. In the meantime I want ALL of my family to know (Ogle's, Yarbrough's, Colley's, Grizzle's) this; I love all of you, and I'm going to do my best to honor as many of you as I can in this little book of mine. Please forgive me for my faults and failures.

A LITTLE PLACE CALLED RIPVILLE

Sorry 'bout that, friend. Sometimes I just get caught up in the moment, ya know? Let's get back to Midway and the 'family time' we shared, shall we? Sharpes Lake, as good as it was, was not the only place that our church family enjoyed getting away to from time to time. There was a smaller place located a little further north in the county. It was called Ripville. I have no idea how this place got it's name. But it was a place not soon forgotten by anyone who visited there. Ripville was a quaint little place by today's standard's in recreation, especially by my urban buddies. It was "off the beaten path" as we used to say. Basically, it was a swimmin' hole that Mother Nature spent many year's carvin' out. The swimmin' hole was fed by a creek that ran down through the wood's there. It came to a natural rock formation, where it tumbled steeply down into what became a natural swimmin' hole. If the memory of the child that I was is still good, the swimmin' hole was about 20 feet around, and about 7-10 feet deep. That sound's fairly basic, dosen't it, friend? Ah, but not so fast, my patient reading buddy! Mother Nature had added a "scratchin' off "feature to this recreational wonder. The child that I was can't be sure, but he thinks it was moss that had covered the rock, just under the water, all along the top of the 'slide'. He will tell you this, however. You had a very small margin for error if you did not want the rushing water of this creek to wash you down into the swimmin' hole below. That rock was slicker than a mushy banana peel, and it took no prisoners. The child that I was saw many a brave soul try to negotiate the top of this slide on foot, only to be dropped on his / her tailbone (ouch!), then swept into the swimmin' hole below. He dosen't remember even one soul making it all the way across.

The best thing for you to do was this; just sit down on your tush, ease out onto the slimy rock, and enjoy the ride. If you were just goin' to be bull headed about it and try to walk across the top (everyone want's to be the 'first' to do something, right?), and your tush would soon have a violent collision with that wet, slimy rock. When you got through losing that fight (which would take all of 5-10 second's in most cases), the water was going to grab you, then throw you down the slide and into the swimmin' hole below. You would not enjoy the ride though, because you would have this great big knot commin' up on your very sore tailbone. And if you had tried to brace your fall with your hand's, there was a good chance that you could have at least one sprained wrist. So, just sit down on the rock and slide, already! Now, the child that I was had the same disposition as the man that I am now. He never got near the deep water, for one very good reason. If he jumped in, he would have done the "drop like a rock boogie", as it were. To this day, I can't even 'doggie paddle', friend.

There were some grillin' places back near where folk parked their car's. The child that I was seem's to remember some pic- nic tables,too. Friend, there aren't many smells that out-rank the smell of hot-dogs or burgers being grilled, especially outdoor's. While that was goin' on, other's were probably busy hand cranking the world's greatest desert, home-made ice-cream! Friend, even as a child I could put together a hamburger that would make Dagwood Bumstead proud. That comic page character had nothing on me! When I was really 'on my game', my burger would include ketchup, mayo, mustard, cheese, tomato, onion,cheese and lettuce on the bun before the beef pattie joined them. I was the object of many a joke about where I was puttin' all that food. That's because I was so skinny till I made a broomstick look like a sumo wrestler on steroid's. The child that I was could eat anything he wanted, and as much of it as he wanted, and never gain an ounce.The man that I am today is quite jealous of that child. Looking back, I have no idea how he did it. If I did, I would find a way to market it, using this vast middle age spread of mine (that jumped on me, I swear, when I was not lookin'!) as the guinea pig. Friend, it used to be that my eating ability PRE-ceded me. Now, many year's removed from the excesses of my youth, my eating reputation EX-ceed's me!

There was a small house there at Ripville. I suppose the folk who owned or managed the place lived there. I was in that house once, with my Mother. We got to look through a window in what I think was an upstairs room. The view was an overlook of the creek. The window pane was some kind of stained glass. It gave the creek below the look of a liquid rainbow. Beautiful. The child that I was had never seen anything like it. Well, any time you have a place like Ripville, where group's of people go for fun and recreation, it is a fairly sure thing that many folk will have a favorite story to tell about something that happened at that place. It should come as no surprise, faithful reading friend, that the child I was has a story he would like to tell before we leave this special place to the ages. He hope's you will enjoy it. He calls it.......

WATERMELONS ON PARADE

There was another food related ritual that our Midway family would take part in from time to time. It was called a water-melon cuttin'. Now, the water in this little creek at Ripville was the coldest I ever felt in the outdoor's. We all know that a good sweet watermelon is even better when it has been chilled for a time before it is eaten. So the Mom's-n- Dad's would take advantage of the cold water in the creek. They would take the water-melons up the creek a way's. They would lay them in the shallow water next to the bank of the creek. They would surround them with 'deadwood' so that they would not 'get away'. By the time swimmin' and eatin' were done, the melon's would be just right for cuttin' and eatin'. This little idea worked perfectly. That is, except for this one time I remember. Once, someone (or some PEOPLE, we never knew which) with a warped sense of humor and an obvious dislike for water-melon sneaked up the creek. This person / people pushed away the deadwood around the melon's, and pushed them out into the creek. Since the creek moved slowly till it reached the slide area, the perpetrator(s) had plenty of time to get back to the party and pick a good place to watch the fun. I am convinced that this is exactly what he, she, or they did.

Friend, you have to picture this. It is absolutely classic. Some folk are slidin'. Some are tossin' a ball around in the swimmin' hole below. All is well. Suddenly a girl scream's. Everyone look's to her. She's lookin' up the slide. Everyone look's up the slide. And here they come. Watermelon's, everywhere. Instant chaos ensues. Some are at the top of the slide tryin' to nab a melon 'fore it goes down the slide, completely forgettin' about that big ole' knot they are about to grow on their tailbone. Some are reachin' up the slide as best they can, tryin' to "break the fall", as it were, of a melon. There is no thought for any hurtling comrads with swellin' tailbone's who are all around. Some of the melon's survive. Other's become instant snack food as they burst on the rock's. Now someone get's the idea to hit a comrad in the face with a piece of melon. Now we have a melon fight! A real free for all too. And somewhere in the middle of all this madness, with what I have no doubt was a good degree of satisfaction, was the person / people who made all of this possible. Heck, they probably joined in! Us kid's got to do something that day that we rarely got to do. We had desert before lunch!

I am sad to say, friend, that the Ripville so loved by the child that I was has faded through time. I was by there recently, for the first time in over 40 year's. The old mill building burned down many year's ago. There is not even a trace of the cook out spot's or the area we would park our car's. All have been reclaimed by Mother Nature. The creek / slide area is still as pretty as a post card, however. There is a lesson there, friend. Man build's a mill house. It burn's down. Man puts up cook out places. They get torn up. God makes a creek, a water slide, and a swimmin' hole, and they all stay as pretty as a post card decades after the man made stuff is destroyed. I don't mean no harm, friend. I'm just sayin'. There's God, and there's man. God wins every time. Any question's? Well, at any rate, the happy care-free days when a church family could go there and enjoy a day with one another are a mere memory. At one time several years ago I was told that this peaceful place had digressed to a place where all kind's of ill repute went on. This was confirmed to me on my recent visit there by a couple who happened by as I stood there rememberin'. The land is posted now. How sad. But my memory is secure. And I will never forget the day that mischief caused watermelon's to go on parade, and completely change the focus and the scope of a church swimmin' party.

WHEN IT IS A HEART STORY

Friend, you have been very patient with me on this journey through the life I have lived. I know it seem's to you as though I tarry a bit long at certain places. And certainly I have tarried at Midway Baptist church in this little book of mine. But when it's a heart story that draws you back to a time or a people who occupy that kind of place in your heart, to where you feel it in your gut also just by remembering, that will happen. And I could go on and on about the little church I love even now. Almost all of the men and women who took a heart and soul interest in a little bony, buck toothed, bald headed boy and planted seeds that sprung up into salvation in my life are in Heaven now. If not for them, my salvation decision, which was made on March 16, 1980 on a Sunday night, may never have been made. I could well be in hell today. As the years have passed, and as I have gotten older, and as I have watched these old heart love driven warriors of the Cross pass from this life to an Eternal one, I must confess this one thing friend. I find myself longing, from time to time, for the day when I will rejoin them in a reunion that will have no end. Theres an old gospel song entitled "Heavens Sounding Sweeter All The Time." Amen, my traveling partner. Amen.

I am sad to say that the Midway oy my childhood dosent have the faintest resemblance to the Midway of today.The last time I ws privileged to visit there the Sunday School board showed a membership of 25. The Discipleship Training membership was half that or less. This did not happen overnight. When the decline had started in earnest life had moved me away from the Valley I called home. I'm glad I wasn't there to see it happen. There is nothing to be gained by repeating here the events that contributed to the Midway decline. It would be second hand information. More importantly, here is one place in this little book of mine where I will strictly enforce on myself the goal of telling my readers about the good and the Godly things about the

Godly people I left behind. But I will speak in general to what causes this kind of degeneration to happen in any church, and to what can prevent it.

Scripture teaches us that "Where there is no vision, the people perish." So first of all, The founders of Midway Baptist church had a vision for reaching our community for Christ. In my childhood that vision was advanced in every conceivable way. Secondly, they had a plan to make that vision come to pass. From doing an initial survey, identifying need, establishing a meeting place, to hours upon unending hours of door knocking and meeting the people in the community, on and on it went. They had a plan. Thirdly, they were willing to sacrifice to make the plan work. No doubt there were many, many days where folk got off work in the mill and went straight to the work in the field. Fourth, they maintained, both in the good times and through any adversity, a sense of family. They were yoked together in a work that would transform a community, dedicated and determined together in their task. There were no big I's and little U's. They were all soldiers who answered only to their General. A fifth thing, if you please. They were very careful to utilize ALL the talent's God sent their way. Sure, there were times when some traing was needed. Yes, some mentoring was in order when for example a spiritually ditch dwelling no 'count sinner came to Christ. But be sure of this. If a talent was known of, it was put to good use. And here is the most important thing friend. They never, ever forgot Who the church belonged to. It was God who birthed that ministry through the obedience of the church planters from Johnson Chapel Church. It was God who provided the little store building they started meeting in. It was God Who provided the land to build the church building when that time came. It was God who burdened the hearts of the search committee during their search for their first pastor. Do you see a common thread here friend? It's God, God, God; not man, man, man. Scripture tells us that house not built by God is built in vain, does it not?

A common acceptance that God, and God alone, was directing their paths created a unity among the congregation that is so necessary in ANY ministry. Any time unity amongst a local family of believers is compromised,it can become a festering sore within the local body of believers. If that sore is not dealt with using spiritual balm, the entire body can be made to suffer. Maybe you doubt me on that point, my friend. Let me ask you a question. Have you ever had a really terrible toothache? Is there any part of your body that felt relief as long as that tooth was protesting? Don't even get me started on kidneystones. I have had some personal experience with those. I can GUARANTEE you that NO PART of your body feels relief till that kidney stone is dealt with. The same principle is true with the local body of believers. If there is one part, or member, of that body that is out of kilter, the whole body potentially, can suffer as a result. Think about that friend. And take note; 'Dealing with' an out of kilter member does NOT mean ostracizing them, ignoring them, shaming them. There is a need that needs to be met there. The way you deal with that need will determine the outcome of the matter, and potentially the future of the local church.

Reverance for the church house is something that was drilled into us at Midway also. A quick story. No, really...quick, I promse. There was a huge pine tree behind the Midway church. A muscadine vine had grown up into that tree. It produced HUGE muscadines every year. Us kids loved to go out there between Sunday School and church and eat as many as we could before church. A problem developed however. Muscadine hulls started comming up into the song book racks on the back of the pews. This would not be tolerated. We were warned more than once. But someone, or two, or three, were determined to 'push the envelope', and hulls continued to make their appearance in the song book racks. One Sunday we went out to get our usual quota of muscadines. To our shock, the entire vine ws GONE. As we stood there gawking, one of the men of the church came up to where we stood. He said, "From now on when we tell you young'uns not to bring anything into the sanctuary, maybe you'll listen!" Not only that, but when I was a child you better not be caught chewing gum in church, or writing notes, or any other thing except listening, or at a minimum pretending to listen, to the man of God preach the Word of God to the people of God. Anything less, and you might just have a revival in the bathroom when you got home. And it might not wait till then. I well remember MaMa DeLoach meeting my Mother in the hall as she took me towards the bathroom. She asked "Whats the matter with Hugh?" Mother said, "I wipped him. And I'm fixin' to whip him again!" Go ahead and ask me friend. Ask me whether Mother had to whip me the third time. Respect for the Lord's house was both taught and demanded. And enforced with discipline that spoke louder than the "now sweetieeee, we don't need ta deewwww that in church, now.." that we hear these days. Geeeez, and we wander.......awwww, I aint gonna start right now.....you know what I mean, don't you friend? Now look at me. I done went and started our new agers to start suckin' their thumbs again. Is your skin getting wrinkled yet?

One other thing right here, and I'm done. We have already established that WE are the church and the church buiulding is where the church MEETS. The God we serve is the owner of that building, and we are to serve Him. He provides us with an under shepard, our PASTOR, to lead the local flock. Thats the order, period. Sooooo, you folk who think you are especially entitled because your family has been going to your local church since the doors first opened, or because you put more money in the offering plate than anyone else, or because you are the chairman of deacons, or because you're the only REAL piano player the church has.......or anything else I left out, let me cause you all to start sucking your thumbs in unison. You are NOT the answer. You are the PROBLEM. Check church histories anywhere you want friend. Show me a church that went through a major decline, and you will also show me mortal wounds in the fabric of that church called envy, self inflation, coveting, probably a big mess'a pride, all cancers that were provided to satan deceived members as legitimate concerns. And if they're not careful, they will have a satan sponsored reward in eternity. Be cautious, my dear friend. Beware the slyness of the enemy.

At any rate, I have to believe that there will come a day when Midway Baptist Church will once again regain it's spiritual footing, reclaim the vision of those early years, and be a force for eternal change in the lives of hurting people. God never plants a churchfor the purpose of dying or becomming dormant, devoid of energy or purpose.He want's very much for the church to succeed. The question is, do we want success by Gods definition, or by our own? There is a difference, my friend. A really big one at that.

THE PEOPLE OF MIDWAY

I know we need to get on down to River View, my new friend. And you are being very patient, you really are. I just had one idea after sleeping on the Midway story I just shared with you and our other friends. One of my goals in the writing of this littlre book of mine is to provoke other folk, maybe even you friend, to remember the time, the people, and the town or city you were raised in. Some of the best stories from any community come from the people in the local church. These are often the people who were the strongest fabric in the local community. I know that was true in the villages where I was raised. So I thought I would spend some time telling you and our other new friends about some of the people I remember the most, and what they meant to me. I promise you, my friend, these will not be boring stories at all. I hope you will have your memory provoked to remember special people in your life also. Friend, I'm gonna talk you into writin' a book yet. You just watch. I tell these stories now as my way of saying thank you and to express my love for the people you will be meeting. They deserve to be remembered. The first person I would like you to meet lived the very definition of what a friend, a REAL friend, truly is. I have entitled it...

WHAT IS A FRIEND ANYWAY???

In my early and young adult years I was very fortunate to have people like Carl and Eleanor Yarbrough who thought I was worth investing time in. Eleanor was a nursery worker at Midway for years and years. More notably, she was the first alto in the adult choir when it was formed. When new Mom's began to leave their babies in the nursery, there would come a time when they would hear their nchild fussing from right down the hall, in their Sunday School class. More than one Mom, including my own Mother, so I've been told, would excuse herself from class and go to the nursery to 'check on' her baby'. Elleanor meet them at the door with, "Now Hazel, you just go on back to class. Me and Hugh will be just fine." Try that in todays world, neighbor. That kind of thing will cost you a visitor, maybe even start a verbal confrontation. It might even cost you a church member. But you know what? I've never heard anything to suggest that me and Eleanor didnt get along just fine when I was that age. She was a gem of a lady.

Mr. Carl now, he came into the picture during my boyhood years. He remained a major influence in my life until the day he went Home. I think of him, and his influence in my life often, and I smile. I picked black-berries as a boy and sold them for fifty cents a gallon. I would pick them into just any gallon container I could get my hand on. Mr. Carl taught me how to cut a hole in the top of a gallon milk jug opposite the handle and strap one to each hip. That way I could pick 'two fisted' and get done quicker, and with more berries to boot. We loved to find berry bushes that grew in low lying wet places, along a stream or even along the Chattahoochie River near our homes. In those kinds of places you could find what we called 'swamp berries'. Those type berries could be as long as the first knuckle on your finger. Friend, it didnt take long to pick a gallon of those type black-berries. You just had to remember to give brother snake his due diligence. You know what I mean, dont you friend?

However, as good as this activity was, our favorite thing to do, Mr. Carl and me, was to go fishin'. And we LOVED to go to cat fish lakes to do our serious fishin' too. Neighbor, if Mr. Carl Yarbrough could not catch a fish, you and I may as well stay at home. This man could think like a fish, so it seemed. It use to confound me to no end that he could use one reel and rod, and I could use SEVERAL, and he would still out fish me. Once, Mr. Carl had a little good natured fun with me. He was out fishing me, AGAIN. He must have seen my frustration. He was about to loosen me up a tad. He could keep the straightest face you ever saw, and pull you into a practical joke right up to the punch line. He said to me on this day, "Hugh, I can tell you what you're doing wrong if you want me to." Dear friend, I wanted to hear ANYTHING my frind / mentor said, especially if it would improve my fishin'. I said any advice would be welcome. And he said this; "What you're doing is, you're putting the wrong end of the worm on your hook first. What you want to do is to put his FRONT end on first." Well friend, I started going over my next worm. I looked at one end up close. I looked at the other end just as close. I looked the entire length of that worm looking for clues. Now neighbor, if you can watch this kind of thing and not laugh, I'll buy your lunch. So it was for Mr. Carl on this day. After a couple minutes of watching me, he said, "Awwww, Hugh, go ahead on and cast your line. I was just kiddin'." What's that? Nawww, friend, I did NOT get angry with Mr. Carl. Geeez, I laughed just as hard as he did. You see, where I was raised friends could have that kind of fun without becoming enemies. That's not always the case in our present world, is it friend?

You want to hear a story that will show you just how close to God Mr. Carl was friend? Listen to this. There was a place near Opelika in Lee County where Mr. Carl and I especially enjoyed fishing at. If my life depended on it I couldnt get back there today. This man had a big place, see. He had a really large lake on the front side of this place. But you could take a small dirt road to the back of his place, and he had a smaller lake that we prefered. You could drive your truck to within twenty feet or so of the water and almost fish out of the truck. This is where Mr. Carl was fishin' early one Saturday morning when God gave him a bonus. Beyond where he parked was a wooded area. A powerline cut right through the middle of it. On this day Mr. Carl had gone fishin' rather early. When he got out of his truck he took mental note that dogs were runnin' some distance to his rear and left. He checked to make sure he had his gun in the truck and started fishin'. It was some time later that morning when Mr. Carl got his bonus. He had already caught a fair stringer of cat-fish. He needed to go to the truck for something. As he raised up to go, his eyes caught something on the power line. It was a great big ole buck. Mr. Carl was down wind from it too. The dear was looking back over it's shoulder in the direction of the soon coming dogs. It was a fatal error. It should have kept on moving friend. Mr. Carl got down and eased up to his truck. He quietly eased his gun out. He eased to the back of his truck crouching. And he eeeaaassseeed that gun up and drew down on that dear......BAM!! The deer dropped in it's tracks. Mr. Carl went home that day with enough fish for a good fish fry, and enough deer meat for the whole winter. But thats not the best part friend. Mr. Carl was sharing this story with us at church the next day. I got to laughing. I asked him, only partially in jest, "Mr. Carl, are you sure that's even legal?" Mr. Carl looked at me, and with that dry sense of humor voice that was telling the gospel truth said, "Well, I reckon so. The assistant game warden helped me dress it out." Now tell me friend, was this man living right, or not?

We pause right here for the chasing of a small rabbit. Friend, I never had any use for 'huntin' with dogs'. To me that was no hunt at all. I mean, anybody can put six or seven guys off at a ridge, then drive around to the far side of the hunting land, put out twenty dogs, and have them chase the poor deer into a waiting ambush. To me that aint huntin' at all. A hunt is where you go out into the woods, into the deers turf, and track it, and out wit it, and take it down by skill. Heck, I dont even take no pity sake on the huntin' done today, where it is fashionable to have a 'shootin' house', and you sit in there in your warm clothes, and maybe even with a small heater goin', and wait on the deer to walk out of the woods. I dont mean no harm here neighbor, but lets be honest. There are a number of things you can call this kind of activity, but a 'hunt' is not one of them. It's an ambush, and an ambush alone.

A FRIENDLY WITNESS

I wish I had been there to see Mr.Carl take down that big buck. And yes friend, I will concede that you can make an argument that Mr. Carl engaged in ambush of a fashion that day. At any rate, a trip I took with him another day involved some seed planting that was beneficial to me later on. It was another lake at another place. We were on one of our 'all day' fishin' trips. On a day like that we took a sack lunch. About the middle of the day the fish always seemed to take a siesta or something. We would leave our rod's 'set out' and retreat under the pine trees to put down our lunch. That's what we were doing on this day. We had finnished eating. Mr. Carl still smoked a pipe back then. He had lit him up a smoke. We were sitting there just solving all the world's problems, Mr. Carl and me.

All of a sudden Mr. Carl said to me, "Hugh, I know what I'm doing wrong." He emptied his pipe, stuck it in his shirt pocket, and took off to the waterside. Well friend, if Mr. Carl was goin' to correct a mistake, you can believe I wanted to be there so I could learn from him again. What happened next is the gospel truth. I'll place my hand on a good sized stack of King James Bibles and swear to it. Mr. Carl reeled in his line. he took the old bait off. He put on new bait. Then he looked around at me. He winked. Then he dipped his reel into the lake and said, "I baptize you in the name of the Father, the Son, and the Holy Ghost." He then cast his line as far out onto the lake as he could. We were using 'slip corks' friend. What that means is we only hooked one end of the cork to the fishin' line. That way, when your bait and sinker hit the water they went all the way to the bottom. The cork stayed top side. When Mr. Carls cork hit the water, I noticed that it hardly settled before it sunk out of sight. I got tickled. I opened my mouth to tell Mr. Carl that he was gonna have to replace that cork 'coz it had a hole in it. Before I could do that his rod jerked and bent waaaay over friend. Mr. Carl siad "Whoaaa Nellie, come back heah!" Friend, if he didnt pull in a gooood eating sized cat- fish, then I ain't typin' this story right now.

I was incredulous. I jokingly, but with a realistic sounding voice, said to Mr. carl, "O.K., Mr. Carl, thats it. I gotta quit now." I made as though I would walk back to the pines. Mr. Carl asked me why. I said to him, "You deacons use help I cant compete with." Mr. Carl called me back. He had something to say. He said "Hugh, you have access to the same power I have. All you got to do is ask." Friend, it was well known that I had never known Christ as my Saviour. I usually had any number of come-backs for anyone who tried to talk to me about it. But that day, on the bank of that lake, I could not come up with anything to say. Mr. Carl had gotten a friendly witness to me without bangin' me over the head with 90 pound a Schofield reference edition Bible. He went right back to fishin'. So did I. But Mr. Carl had forced me, not in a judgemental tone, but with the soft voice of a friend who loved me and cared for my eternity, to consider my fate. I did not get saved that day friend. But be assured, seeds were planted in my life. I never forgot that day. I still think of it from time to time. And I miss my friend.

THE ART OF 'BEING THERE'

Friend, when my PaPa Ogle went Home, it just about beat me down. Dont ever let anyone tell you that the Home-going of someone you love is easier when you have time to 'prepare'. That is a lie. I was a young adult by then. I had grown up goin' to the fields with PaPa. I had stayed many a night in his home. I had heard his stories, seen him at his mischievous best. In many ways I considered him to be more of a 'best friend'. There were some who did not understand the open grief I felt and showed. But I'll tell you this friend. I still feel his loss today, more than 30 years later.I remember being at the funeral home. I remember being a bit indignant in a silent way to see that PaPa was dressed in a suit. Why, he never wore anything but over-alls all my life. I wandered what his reaction would be could he somehow wake up long enough to see how they had him dressed (though I think I know,friend). I was sitting in one of those ladder back chairs at one point, just crying my heart out. Other people were in the room, but I dont think I remember anyone trying to comfort me for a while. Then I noticed someone sit down next to me and quietly slip their arm around my shoulder. I looked up, and there sat Mr. Carl. Friend, he didnt say one word to me. He just let me cry. He stayed by my side for a good thirty minutes. We did eventually talk a bit. Then at some point he leaned in and said to me, "I got to go now Hugh. But I'll see you at the service tomorrow." I can't tell you what that meant to me friend. You see, a true friend understands that the 'being there' is sometimes more valuable than all the words of comfort you can think up to say. Mr. Carl was good at that.

Friend, I have a saying that has evolved for me over the years as I try to comfort someone who is dealing with grief. That little passage goes like this; "I'm not going to tell you that I know how you feel. That would be a lie. Only you and God know that. I'm not going to tell you that you know what this loved one would want you to do. That is redundant. Of course you do. What I will say is this. I can't walk through this fire FOR you. But I can, by God's grace, and with your permission, walk through this fire WITH you, even if only by prayer. And I'll do this for as many tomorrows as it takes."

That about covers it friend, don't you think?

UNCONDITIONAL PRAYER

It was a Sunday afternoon, an hour or so before the evening service. I was in our little church, Midway Baptist. I was at the alter just crying my eyes out. Friend, I don't even remember what my problem was. I know that it was not what I call a 'holy prayer'. You know, the kind you hear 'Brother Hot Air' pray over the offering. Nope, I was in OHHHHH GOOOOD mode. Funny how, across the years, I have forgotten why I was so upset. I do remember feeling alone, so very alone. Suddenly, as I kneeled there, I felt a hand on my shoulder. Friend, can I tell you this? When you are in prayer, regardless of where it is, and you KNOW you are alone, and you suddenly feel a hand on your shoulder, it WILL separate your head from your shoulders. I wanted to say "Yes Lord?" I did not dare look up. After what could not have been more than three minutes, the hand left my shoulder. I heard footsteps walking softly down the carpeted aisle of the church. I timidly looked up just in time to see Mr. Carl going out the double doors. You know what? For the rest of his life, he never asked me what I was so upset about. He did not need to. He knew that his friend needed prayer. And he wanted to be there. I never forgot that.

You know friend, what ever happened to that kind of friendship? That old fashioned "I don't need to know, I just want to be there" type of unconditional prayer that true friends could share? We live in a 'give me the details' type of world now. Even amongst Christians sometimes, 'enquiring minds want to know'. I am so grateful that I had the example of men like Mr. Carl Yarbrough who knew how to be, and to model, true unconditional friendship. Would to God that I be seen in eternity as even half of what this man was to me, in at least one persons life. I would dare say that he is one of the bigger reasons I am not in hell today. To be remembered in that way, friend, is about the greatest testimony a person of faith can leave behind.

I remember when Mrs. Eleanor went Home. As Mr. Carl related it to me, she was in the hospital. They had taken her to the emergency room. She knew it was time to go Home. She said to Mr. Carl, "Well, I'm gone. Take care of the kids." And she went Home, just like that. I wish it could have been so for Mr. Carl. He fought a running battle with prostate cancer. For a time he had it beat too. I remember sitting on his front porch with him one day. He said that his doctors had told him they got all of the cancer in a recent operation, and that he would live a normal life. It was not to be. The cancer came back in time, and with a vengeance. Mr. Carl, a warrior for the Lord these many years, went into the hospital for the last time. I stopped by to visit with him one day after work. He had several family members in the room with him, so I kept my visit fairly short. But before I left I went to his bedside. I said to him, "Mr. Carl, I'm gonna go home for now. But I'll be back again tomorrow after work." Mr. Carl was too weak to speak, but he looked at me with tired eyes, and he slowly shook his head no. He knew his goin' Home time was near. You know friend, even when you KNOW the end is near in this life for someone you love, you are never prepared for it. I got word the next day after work that Mr. Carl had left this world during the day. I went way out into the woods, almost to the Chattahoochie River, all by myself. And I cried like a baby. My friend, my berry pickin' partner, my fishin' partner, my mentor, and one of my chief role models was gone. I still miss him today. You know what I mean, don't you friend?

DYNOMITE COMES IN SMALL PACKAGES

That was one of my friends favorite things to say when she was playfully, or in all seriousness, telling someone not to misjudge her because of her size. Friend, if she was over five feet tall, it's a wander. Francis Bailey was a member of the Midway church where our families attended. My Mother and I worked with her at the Fairfax Mill on the first shift, in the spooler room. She wasn't as big as a minute, but she was as spunky as they come, tough as nails. She was tougher than a lot of fellas I knew in that day. Frances once told me that in her teenie years she wanted to become a professional wrestler. Her Mother, however, would have none of it. I have no doubt that Frances could have made a go of it though.

All of us at Fairfax Mill enjoyed having a bit of good natured fun at one anothers expense from time to time. Frances and I kept a runnin' game of 'gotcha!' going most of the time. Neither of us stayed one up on the other for very long. At the time I was running the elevator. Frances was a warper creeler. Her warper was right in front of the elevator door. One Friday I stepped off the elevator to find Frances all leaned over into a box of yarn. She was half in, half out of that box. I could not resist. I eased up behind her and just tipped her on over into the box. I then made it my business to skeet back onto that elevator and get gone. I did not see Frances again till time to go that afternoon. I was walking down what we called the 'big alley' on my way out. I could not resist looking over towards the warpers. There sat Frances, on a stool in front of her warper. She was waiting for me to look. She was smiling her very best 'I WILL get you back no longer how long it takes' smile. She had her finger pointed at me, nodding her head. I had no doubt that come Monday I would have to have eyes in the back of my head, as it were. But first there was the matter of a trip to Six Flags over Georgia on Saturday. My sister and I,with some friends, had been looking forward to that trip for a while. We spent the whole day there. I think we even stayed for the fire works show.It was a great day. We had tons of fun.It was late when we got home, tired and ready to hit the sack. That is, till my Dad met us at the door with the news that Frances was killed that day. I'm not even going to dignify the events or circumstances surrounding her death. I will say that alchohol abuse was the culprit. And it was NOT Frances who abused the alchohol either. Please forgive me, but I must pause here for an impassioned plea. Young folk, I'm begging you. Don't buy the lie that alchohol is recreational, or that there is no danger if you will 'drink responsibly'. At best consumption of alchohol is a game of Russian roullette. No alchoholic is born an alchoholic. Nor did they become an alchoholic after their first drink. Or their second. But the process of becoming one STARTED with that first drink. Ask anyone who has ever caused an accident, or woke up in jail because of bad behaviour, or lost their family, if they wouldnt give all they had to go back to the day they took that very first drink, and erase that day from their lives.

People say the Bible dose not speak against alchohol. Why, they say, even Jesus turned water into wine. They won't tell you that Jesus turned the water into NEW, or UNFERMENTED wine. In Bible days good drinking water was sometimes hard to come by. Wine became a water substitute from time to time. They won't point you to the book of Proverbs either where these words are spoken; "Wine is a mocker, and strong drink raging. And whosoever is decieved thereby is not wise." The bottom line, whether young or adult, is that alchohol is NOT a necessity in life. It is not something you can't do without. You have read in this little book of mine how that my Dads Dad almost got caught by the revenoors, making 'shine whiskey' at his still. You have read about hw drastically alchohol changed my Mothers Dad and his personality. His wife eventually felt compelled to leave him. In my lifetime I have seen any number of people come to untimely ends by any number of tragedies. And none of it had to happen. What happened to my friend did not have to happen either. These things happen because people make some very poor life changing decisions, some poor choices. I submit that their FIRST bad choice was to take that first drink.

I woke up the following Monday. I went to work. I was walking down the 'big alley' towards the break room. Without even thinking of it, I looked over to the warpers to see whether Frances was still of a mind to get even. And she wasnt there. I went into the bathroom, friend. And I had myself a good cry. And I had to keep close charge over my emotions that day, every time I opened that elevator door and saw my friends warper, now attended by someone else. For God's sake friend, give it some thought, won't ya? There are better ways to have 'recreation'. You know what I mean, don't you friend?

GIVE TILL IT HURT'S

As a small boy Mr. Clifford Hamer was one of my favorite people. He always had a smile or a kind word for me. Years later Mr. Clifford and hid son Pete would build the home Mother was living in when she went Home. Mr. Clifford was very passionate about Midway. He loved his church. One thing he just could not tolerate was to see the finances of the church get low. He was not bashful one bit about asking God's people in the local church to do whatever it took to keep the church financially sound. It's worse now than then friend, but isn't it sad that anyone, lay person or pastor, would have to resort to impassioned plea to the church family to do what they are supposed to do on their own? Think about it. God only ask's us for ten cents of every dollar we make. I mean, He gave us the whole dollar, did He not? He could require, and truth be known, TAKE, much more. But he ask's us for only a dime. And too many times we begrudge Him even that. I thank God that I knew people like Mr. Clifford Hamer who were not afaid to call the attention of the church familyto the basic things that are still so important for us to do. Like so many of my early role models, Mr. Clifford was not one to just demand of everyone else. He was one of God's best at MODELING what he asked others to do. Let me share a story friend, about how he 'stood in the gap' for our family during a potentially tragic time.

My Mother wasin the hospital. She was recovering from a surgery. Dad took us there to see her on a Saturday afternoon. In those days friend, children under 12, if the memory of the child I was is correct, had to wait in the waiting room. If the patient was well enough, they could come down for a brief visit. So it was on this day. My Dad, as it was for him for ost of my life, sang with a quartet. They were scheduled to sing just outside of nearby West Point Georgia the following day. Dad told Mother he thought he might just cancel the date so he and us kids could see her at the hospital after church. Mother would have none of it. She said we could come see her after the singing. After all, she was doing well with her recovery, and it's not like she was going anywhere, right? So that was that. So dad took us kid's with him and went on to the singing. All went well until someone interupted Dad in the middle of a song to say that they had put a critical sign over Mothes door at the hospital. He needed to get there as soon as possible. Friend, that was the fastest trip down Highway 29 I ever took. Even with all those infernal red lights along the front of Lanett Mill. We did not have I-85 then friend. So '29 was it. But Dad wasn't messin' around. He had to take us by the house and backtrack to the hospital. He told me to call MaMa DeLoach and tell her what was goin' on. And off he went to the hospital.And there we were, us kids, to wait for word from the hospital. I called MaMa as I was told, and then we waited.

After a while the phone rang. It was Mr. Clifford. "You kids, y'all had any lunch yet?" I told him "No sir, we're waiting for a call from the hospital about Momma." Mr. Clifford said, "Well you all come on over to my house, and we'll feed you a little something before chrch." He only lived a short walk from our house, just below the church in fact. So here we went, us Little Ogle's, all in a row, walking to Mr. Clifford's house. My baby sister wasn't much more than a toddler, so I'm sure we took turns either holding her or holding her hand. We thought we would have a sandwich and a glass of milk, something like that. Friend, what we saw when we stepped into Mr. Cliffords house boggled our minds. And our taste buds. You would have thought the church moved the home-coming meal to Mr. Cliffords house on a rainy day! The boy that I was seems to remember there was even a banana puddin' on the table. Honestly, they sat us down at that table, and we were able to eat till if we ate another bite, we would lose some at the other end. Even then, the folk there encouraged us to eat more.

Not only that, but I well remember the day when Mr. George Will Monks delivery truck pulled into our driveway. The back of that truck, I promise you, was FULL of groceries. Groceries given to us by our church family. I dont have proof of it, but I am quite sure that Mr. Clifford was right in the middle of that too. As to that Sunday afternoon, I will never forget that day. And I will never forget Mr. Clifford Hamer nor his wife Wilma. These were 'salt of the earth' people. These are the type people who are, at best, 'missing in action' too often in todays churches and communities. If we still took care of one another like the Midway family did, a social program here or there may never have needed to be started. But we are digressing too quickly into a country of communities with an 'entitlement' complex. We want to recieve without the giving,anymore. And we are diminnished by the digression. Was it not Jesus who said, "Inasmuch as ye have done it unto one of the least of these, my brethren, ye have done it also unto me"?

FAITHFUL

I really wish I knew more about Mr. and Mrs. Thompson. They were an elderly couple in our Midway family. But I wanted to mention them because of their faithfulness. When I'm at a place where I think I can not go another step in this life, I still think, from time to time, about Mr. and Mrs. Thompson. Mrs Thompson, you see, was in a wheel chair. It was that way the whole time I knew them. Being a 'senior saint' couple, they had earned their rest. It would have been proper for us to start a 'shut in' ministry and take church to them. But every Sunday they were able, here they would come. Mr. Thompson would get out of his car, help his bride into her chair, and push her right on up into the church.They sat four pews from the front of the church, on the left. Friend, I never heard a complaining word out of them. There was very little they could do physically,but you would find them in their place on Sunday mornings. If they were not there, something was wrong.

Such was the case one day when one of their grand-daughters, who lived just up the road from them, went to their house to check on them. They had not spoken with any of the family for a day or two. And they did not answer their phone. She found that both of them had moved on to

Glory. Mrs. Thompson was found in her bed. Mr. Thompson was found sitting in a chair near the heater. We can only speculate. But the scene seems to speak to me that Mr. Thompson found at some point that his wife had moved Home. And he decided to just sit down in his chair and await his turn. And a merciful God saw his broken heart, and decided to mend it for good. Can't you just see Mr. Thompson walkin' up behind his wife in Heaven, tapping her on the shoulder, and sayin' to her, "Did you really think I would let you come here without me?" And I can see our Saviour looking on this scene, and smiling approvingly.

THE BIGGEST FISHIN' LAUGH I EVER HAD

Mr. Henry Yarbrough and his dear wife Leila Mae were another of my favorite senior couples as I grew up. Henry was Mr. Carl's brother. I never knew Mrs. Leila Mae not to be up to her ears in anything that was going on in church. Over the years she taught Sunday School, Training Union, Sunday School, Study Course, and she was always active in the Womens Missionary Union organization. Revivals, home-comings, you name it. Mrs. Leilea Mae was the example of a 'hands on' Christian. Mr. Henry now, he was a little different. He worked for the county till he retired. The boy that I was seems to remember that he drove heavy equipment, bull dozers and the like. He worked hard. He loved his family, and provided for them always. But when it came to church, he rarely attended. The story I'm about to tell you is about one Sunday when he did. Or more accurately, what caused him to attend. It's a story that makes me laugh even now friend, when I remember it.

As you might imagine, Mrs. Leila Mae would try time and again to talk her husband into a notion of goin' to church with her. Her successes were limited, according to the boy that I was. But one time we had Home Coming nearing. And Mrs. Leila Mae was trying to talk Mr. Henry into going. She said, "Henry, you don't have to go to Sunday School. Just come to preachin'. There will be plenty of good food to eat. Everybody always asks about you. So, if you'll go with me I'll leave you be about it for a while. Mr. Henry thought he had a good idea in response. You see, he and my PaPa were fisher men. they loved the outdoor things. Mrs. Leila mae, apart from her plants in the yard, not so much. And to get her to go to the river, well now. That was mite near impossible. So Mr. Henry says to her, "Tell you what. You go fishin' with me Saturday, and I'll go to church with you on Sunday." Friend, he never dreaned that she would say "DONE!" But she did. I don't remember, nor does the boy that I was, how I got invited on this trip. But I am so thankful that I did. I'm not sure I can name a fishin' trip, even with Mr. carl, where I laughed as hard as I would on this day.

There was a curve in the Langdale-River View Road just below Mr. Henrys house. he went to the hollow down from that road many times squirrel huntin'. There was a drive way of sorts right in the middle of that curve on the right. We parked here. From this place it was a fair walk to get to the river. Mr. Henry is in the lead. He's wearin' one of his tan looking work shirts and britches. He's carrying a couple reel and rods. He's wearin' boots. Mrs. Leila Mae has on one of those wide brimmed sun hats. She's wearin' one of her every day dresses. Folk nowadays call these a 'moo-moo' dress for some odd reason. I never saw her in pants, not once. She's also carrying one of those old timey fold up chairs. You know, they were aluminum armed and had this polyester type ribbon lookin' stuff for the seat part. I'm bringin' up the rear with my bony, buck toothed, bald headed self. I'm carrying a rod and reel and the bait, which would be red worms this day. I was wearin' knee knocker shorts, made from some old blue jeans, and a t-shirt. I have on flip-flops, which I intend to flop onto the ground as soon as we start fishin'. What a sight we must have looked! There we go, navigating the trail, Mr. Henry pushin' aside the brush in places for his bride, her probably thinkin' to herself, "What in the world have I gotten myself into?" And me, day dreaming about all them big catfish I would be eatin' this night.

We got to the river, then turned right and walked down the 'fishermans trail' along the banks of the Chattahoochie. Mr. Henry and I had a favorite place we enjoyed fishin' at. It was always good for a channel cat, or a speckled cat, even bream and crappie from time to time. It was about four and a half feet from water to the top of the bank. When the water was low, as it was this day, there was two or three feet of sand, or mud, depending on how long the water had been down. There was an old tree that had grown outwardly towards the river, close by. I liked to cast my line out and sit with my back against that old tree. Mr. Henry was more of a 'crouch and stand' fisherman. He stood to cast, crouched till he had a hit, then stood for the contest that would provide him with a fish fry. Mrs. Leila Mae, for her part, found an open place, set her foldin' chair up, and settled in for the action. Our fishin' hole was well shaded, so the heat was not as bad. With all of this said, here comes the fun.

We had caught a few fish after a while. A fish fry was not gong to be a problem. But friend, you know how it is when you go fishin'. You always anticipate that great BIG'UN that you just KNOW is out there. And suddenly Mr. Henrys rod bent almost double. He yanked on the line, then began to reel. "I got ya now, big boy!" he almost hollered. I said "Mr. Henry, looks like that one might feed both of us!" Mrs. Leila Mae even got into the spirit of the moment. "Henry, bring it on in! Don't lose it now!" He says "Dont you worry none. He's commin' outta here tday!" Finally he gets that fish out of the water and onto the sand below the bank. Indeed, this one is a catfish that can be de-boned and supply more than one plate with fish! Then, just as Mr. Henry was about to bring the fish up the bank and put it on a stringer, it flopped off the hook and onto the sand. Just a triple flop from freedom.

Mr. Henry said, "Oh, no you don't!" And down that bank he went, just'a scoopin' with his hands, tryin' to toss that fish up the bank. Mrs. Leila Mae was aghast. "Henry, Henry you come on up outta there! You gonna drown yo fool self!" She's waving that wide brimmed hat around like she's shooin' flies off a pic-nic meal. Mr. Henry is still scoopin'. He said, "Well, if I do, you stuff this fish and mount him on the wall, coz he's comin' out of this river!" About that time he finally got enough of his hands under that fish to scoop it out almost on a line drive. It sailed right past Mrs. Leila Maes shoulder. She did some more shoutin' then friend! Mr. Henry, for his part, is tryin' to get to that fish as fast as he can before it flops back down the bank. Mrs. Leila Mae is sayin' as to how that's about the most tom-fool thing she ever saw, and he's just glad for the meal the fish will provide. Whats that friend? Where was I? Well, let me say that if that tree had not been there to support my back, I would have been floatin' off down the Chattahoochie River. I think I lost my rod. I laughed till I had tears in my eyes. And you friend may cry a bit too if your imagination will allow youto picture the scene I just told you of.

Well friend, as you might imagine, the fishin' trip ended shortly after this adventure. There had been plenty enough excitement for on day. We had a good mess of fish for a fry. And I had a story that has made me smile on a many a sad day. By the way, Mr. Henry went to church the next day, good as his word. I'll never forget seeing him walk in.

A CONTRITE SERVANT

One Sunday morning the pastor stood to preach. For some reason he could not out of the starting gate as it were. After he stumbled through a short sermon, he said words to this effect; "The time is at hand for a happening. I dont know whats making me feel the way I feel today. But I do know this. Next week I'll be standing here reminding you that I said this. I dont know what it is God has in mind. But I know we will be different when we meet together next week." His message had been about salvation and the importance of knowing your eternal destination for sure, and trying to make sure someone else gets to Heaven because you passed by in their life.

The whole thing had only consumed about twenty minutes. Then he gave an altar call. At the first note my Mother played during that altar call, none other than Mrs. Leila Mae Yarbrough stepped from her place. She sat the end of a pew about seven pews back from the front of the church nearest the wall, on the left. She went to the altar to pray. She was very emoyional. After she prayed she asked the pastor if she could say something to the congregation. He readily agreed.

This precious lady asserted to the church that she had not been 'pulling her weight' at the church recently. She apologized. She asked forgiveness. She said she was going to try really hard to do better. I was a young adult by now. I grew up watching this dear lady lead and be a first class example of a Christian witness and example. She long ago had earned the right to have some rest. Yet there she stood, a contrite servant, feeling convicted in her own spirit that she was not doing enough. At that time we had a Bible study on Wednesday nights. Our pastor let us take turns leading a study of one chapter of whatever book of the Bible we were in. On this Sunday, Mrs. Leila Mae asked if she could lead the Bible study the following Wednesday night. The pastor, tears in his eyes, said that would be just fine. Friend, I could not wait for Wednesday night. I knew we were in for a good lesson indeed.

Mrs. Leila Mae Yarbrough went home to be with the Lord the next day, Monday morning. She woke up with chest pains. She told Mr. Henry that she needed to get to the hospital as quickly as she could. He told me that story one day as we sat on the couch in my Mothers home. He remembered fumbling around trying to get dressed and get his shoes on. She said, "Henry, you're the slowest thing I ever saw." He said, "Leila Mae I'm going as fast as I can honey." He got her to George H. Lanier Hospital as soon as he could. But God had already decided that this day was Home-coming day for Leila Mae. A little bit of Midway died that day too. Friend, I was talking with Mr. Henry another day in Mothers home. I remember his words as though they were spoken yesterday. "Hugh, sometimes I come in the house and go into the kitchen, and I call her name. Then I realize she's not there. I sit in the yard sometimes, and I'm thinking she will be home from church in just a while. Then I realize she's never comming back home again...." and his voiced trailed off.

Ohhh, dear friend, who is the person you love the most in this world? Did you tell them today? When was the last time you said I love you to them face to face? Was your voice softly full of firm conviction? Were your eyes full of compassionate love? When you look at the old, cold clay shell that loved one use to live in for the last time, there at the funeral home or the church, will you have regrets about things left unsaid? The last words my Mother or my Father ever heard me say to them were "I love you". In this I am forever thankful to God. I count Mr. Henry and Mrs. Leila Mae Yarbrough as two people I loved both as role models and as family. You are loved friend, really loved, when those you leave behind think of you years later, and feel the hurt of your passing as though it was just the other day. Much like I still get wet eyed, even as I type these words and tell you all this story. I just wander if I will ever be remembered in this way........

"I'M A WINNER EITHER WAY"

Friend, those word's are the title of an old gospel song. They are also the exact words that Brother Charlie Bohannon spoke to me as I sat on the couch with him in his living room one day. He was about to go to the hospital. We did not know it, but but he was going there for the last time. His kidneys had been failing him for some time. He was tired, and deep down I think he was ready to go Home. As we sat there in that living room, he said to me, "Hugh, there is no worry for me. If I get to come home from the hospital, I have a good home to come back to. If I don't, I have a better home to go to. I'm a winner either way."

The day God gently called him Home, my Mother was at the hospital with Brother Charlie and his dear wife Louise. They knew Brother Charlies time was short. He was in sort of a coma, resting peacefully. I've heard it said that at times people who are in a coma can still hear what's going on around them even if they can't respond. Mother mentioned this to Louise. Louise leaned over the bed. She held one of Brother Charles hands, my Mother held the other. Louise softly said to him, "Charlie, you go on Home now. I'll be on in a little while." A few moment's later, one of God's most spirited warriors, a man who faithfully preached the Gospel of Jesus Christ for more than 40 years, slipped the bonds of mortality and fell into the warm embrace of his Saviour. My Mother took note that on what had otherwise been an overcast day, the sun broke through the clouds soon after Charlie started his new life in Heaven. I like to think of it as Charlies last smile.

You know friend, after many, many years, I will now make a statement now about a part of my faith life that I have been loathe to make. Not only did I love Brother Charlie and Louise as brother and sister in the Lord, and even as family, not only were they two of my closest friends, but I am ready to say that he was my favorite pastor of all time. I hope that won't offend any of the other pastors whose preaching I have sat under in my life. I have served under some good ones. I have only served under one that I would rethink if I had the opportunity. I'm sure I will write about some of them too, before I'm done. In fact, in future writings I can almost GUARANTEE that I will. But I have come to realize that Brother Charlie and Louise have a special place in my heart. I'm not just speaking as a man reliving fond memories. I speak also through the eyes of the boy that I was. The teenie I became agrees. And the young adult I became makes it unanimous.

AT THE POINT OF NEED

Brother Charlie and Louise' involvement with our family when we rented the little green house on the Farfax short-cut road from Mr. John McCullough. You will hear much of this hallowed ground as we continue our journey friend. If you had not known it, you would not have picked Brother Charlie out to be a preacher. He did not see the need to be all dignified all the tme. He use to say that church pastors were only regular church members with a Higher calling. He never placed himself above his church members in any way. He said that it is very hard to lead God's people if you are OVER them. Better it was, he said, to be AMONG them. He would not allow himself to be treated any differently from anyone else. He firmly believed in meeting people at their point of need, especially if they were in need of a Saviour.

In our community there was a place where there was a store on either side. One store was a regular 'watering hole' for many people in the community. The other, not so much. Those folk were known to drink and cuss. Every now and again they would fight amongst themselves. Not a place where a lot of folk wanted their kid's for instance to hang around. Not long after Brother Charlie became our pastor, he and my Dad were driving around the community. They passed by this place of business. There were a group of men sitting outside playin' dominos. Brother Charlie asked about this store and the people there. Dad was honest in telling him both the good and the bad that he knew of them. Brother Charlie said, "Hubert, I've always enjoyed a good game of dominos, haven't you?" To my Dad that was just like asking whether a Baptist liked banana puddin' or not. So, they stopped that day. They joined right in the domino playin'. And they went back from time to time. Friend, I'm not going to tell you that everybody affiliated with that store got saved over tme. Some did, some did not. But without the time Brother Charlie was willing to invest in folk many would have nothing to do with, in getting to know them, to make friends of them, NONE would have.

A lot of folk don't like me to say this. But they have the option to go suck their thumb if they want to. Friend, how many churches do you know of that are more than ready to engage in outreach, as long as they don't reach out of their comfort zone, or outside the social class that dominates the church rolls? Brother Charlie was determined that Midway would NOT be bound by social and economic status or the lack thereof in regards to church outreach. And we weren't either. Brother Charlie was particular about who he called 'friend'. Once he called you his friend, you were his friend for life. He and Louise were in our home for Christmas Eve supper every year for over 30 years. More than once he would do something like shake my Dad's hand, saying "Hubert, hang in there. God is going to get you all through this." And as he shook Dad's hand he would slip him a 20 dollar bill. I am convinced he did that for others as well. Neither man ever said anything about it publicly. People who do the most good in this life friend, are the people who say the least about it. There is a concept of 'not letting one hand know what the other is doing'. To this day I'm a bit leary of folk who like to talk about the people they have helped.

Brother Charlies preaching was always timely, pointed, and scripture based. I went to a church some time back that had one of these new fangled 'contemporary services'. The pastor had in his hand as he spoke to the people a 'People Magazine'! Not a Bible. I did finally notice a big screen back behind the stage where scripture was posted. But he never called the scripture to the congregations attention. If you saw it, good. If you did not see it, you heard the gospel of 'People' magazine. Brother Charlie would have had a fit. Friend, if you are in a church that does not preach THE word of God from a BIBLE, with all due respect you are not in a church. You are in a meetin' house, and nothing more.

GOOD CLEAN FUN

I wanted to relate to you friend, how Brother Charlie enjoyed a bit of good clean fun at a brothers expense, and how he laughed as hard as anyone else when the expense was his. Brother Charlie and my Dad kept something going between them all the time. My Dad, remember was the music director. One Sunday night Dad got through th music part of the service and started to go take a seat. Brother Charlie quickly got up from his seat and said, "Hubert, come back here for just a moment, would ya? Dad, with a leery look about him, turned and walked back to Brother Charlies side. Brother Charlie put his arm around Dad and eyed at him with a look that said, "GOTCHA SUCKER....AGAIN!" Brother Charlie looked out at the congregation and said, "I want everybody under the sound of my voice to stop what you're doing right now and take a good look at your music director. You haven't done it in a while. Take a GOOOOD long look at him." Friend, even the note writers and the paperairplane makers on the back row looked up for this. Everybody wanted to hear this. When Brother Charlie had everybodies undivided attention, he said this: "Y'all ever notice this fellas ears? You know, his ears make his head look like a big cadillac car goin' down the middle of Highway 29, with both front doors wide open, Don't they? Don't they?" Friend, we almost had to do away with the preachin' that night. First time I ever saw a church full of Baptist folk....rollin' around on the church carpet....just SQUALLIN! Why, you'da thought a pentecostal meetin' done broke out in there! My Dads reaction? A sheepish look, with a smile, and a look to Brother Charlie that said "I'll get ya...just wait...I'll get ya" We could have fun like that back then friend. We didn't wear our feelings on our shirt sleeve like so many of todays pious folk who think you're suppose to go into church, sit down, cross your legs, and sit up straight and tall like you got a crowbar for a neck.

The next story finds Brother Charlie as the butt of the joke. Every Christmas my Aunt Flossie use to send my Mother a great big fruit cake. It was always made in a pan that had this doo-ma-flitchie in the middle that left a round hole in the cake when you took it out of the pan. You ladies know what I'm talkin' about. You fellas, just stay with me here :)! Well, my PaPa would go to the store and get a very small bottle of rum and pour it all into the hole in the middle of that cake. Weeeelll, one year PaPa went to get his rum, and they were all out. So what he did was, he got a like sized bottle of....100 proof Kentucky whiskey! Ohhh, yes he did friend. He poured every drop of it into that round hole. The cake soaked it up. Are you with me, friend?

So here comes Christmas Eve. Brother Charlie and Louise are in our home again, along with a few other friends. Dinner is had, and it's time for desert. The fruit cake has always been popular at Christmas Eve. We got to noticing PaPa laughing to himself as that cake disappeared piece by piece. He seemed quite tickled with himself for some reason. The next day after all the gifts were opened we thought to ask him what had him so tickled the night before. He told us about that 100 proof Kentucky whiskey he poured into that cake. And he said, "I got to noticing, the more cake that preacher ate, the more yap-yap-yappin' he did". And he just roared, again. We had a good laugh too. Nobody had a clue about PaPa's 'secret ingredient' that was in the cake that night! And here's a lesson for ya. Of course Brother Charlie had to be told about this story. And of course the 'secret ingredient' didn't cause him to become more loose tongued than any other Baptist preacher at a supper fit for a king. Only in my PaPas eyes did that happen. But I remember Brother Charlie laughing just as hard as anyone else when he heard the story. See? We had FUN in those days friend! These days, why, you can lose a friend over such as that. I mean, why don't we just get off our cotton pickin' high horses and stow our vanity in a deep dark hole for a season already!?

ANYWHO...nobody preached like Brother Charlie. Nobody LIVED it like Brother Charlie. He was another of my role models, another of my mentors, and a dear friend besides. I miss him so much, to this day. When he went Home, it was another of those times when I found myself a quiet, private place. And I emptied my tear ducts one more again....And that's all I got to say about that.

MOVING ON

Friend, I suppose there could be an entire book written about the people of Midway. In no way have I scratched the surface here. Perhaps I'll writ that book some day, if I live long enough. But let me say this before I take my leave of Midway, for now. I owe everything I am, and everything I will ever be, to my parents and to the people of Midway, who I still think of as an extension of my own family. My parents would later divorce after 33 years of marriage. But they kept us kid's in church at every opening of the church door. We heard enough good preachin', good teachin', had enough Godly examples around us, that none of us have an excuse not to belong the Christ, to live for Him, and to witness for Him.

In those days we always planned our lives around church. Church was first, always. If we had out of town company on a Sunday, or Wednesday, or during revival, they could go with us or relax at our home till we got back. Now'a'days, sadly, too many times church has become more of a social or recreational function that has no more importance than any other event in our lives. We'll go because a friend goes there, or because there is a gym there, or because it makes us look good in the community, or because the church sponsors lots of trips to Six Flags or the mountains. Family reunions, once almost always held on Saturdays so as not to interfere with church, take us from church now, After all, it's only once a year, right? Out of town company? Well, they dont get to come often. God understands. And you BETTER! Friend, in the day we live in, a pastor can be dismissed from church for having the temerity to suggest that church, service to the King of Kings, should come FIRST. The fact is, when I was commin' up we were still taught that our commitment to Christ was a 24/7 thing, a constant life of service and sacrifce.

Let me REALLY offend some people. We planned our entire life around church. Heck, the COMMUNITY, to a vast degree, did the same. For us, to play softball or baseball on a Wednesday night was just unheard of. Today, some coach will look you in the eye and demand to know where the scripture is that says you have to go to church on Wednesday. We never thought to entertain stupid questions like that. I heard about a baseball coach who was going to coach an all star baseball team some years ago. At their first practice he gathered the players around him and asked for a show of hands as to who thought they might miss some practice time because of church camp and so forth. Two or three of his players raised their hands. He said, "Well guys, I appreciate very much you being good enough to be voted onto this team. But I'm not going to be able to use you." They were dismissed from the team. Their parents, of course, were ludicrous. They instantly complained to their local board of directors. Their answer? "Hey, it's his team. He has a right to conduct it any way he sees fit." REALLY?!?

Not only that, but I watched this debate rage in a town once. A public event was sponsored by this town each year. It was a very successful event that drew thousands. There was a move to allow the consumption of alchoholic beverages at this event. The city council voted it down. Neighbor, it was not a month until the issue was reintroduced to the council. Word was that some business interests had objected to the previous vote. The local ministerial association attended the council meeting to lobby for the previous vote to be the final word. A local businessman stood up in the council chamber that night and said to the ministers, "I would never force my religeon onto YOU. Don't YOU force YOURS on ME!" The issue was revoted and alchohol was allowed.

Further, I know of a bowling league that was called the 'Christian Fellowship League.' Christian music was allowed to be played in this league. But some started slippin' in secular music with it, and some of it quite raunchy too. Believers complained about that, and the debate that ensued was one of the saddest things I ever witnessed. Even a few who espoused Christ in their lives loudly supported SECULAR music being played during a CHRISTIAN bowling league. Anyone who spoke in favor of retaining Christian music only was shouted down.

I know I need to get on down to River View friend. But this needs to be said. What if every family of faith in every community got together and organized themselves? What if they went to their parks and recreation department and said this; "This is the way it's going to be from now on. We are not going to support the playing of any sport on a Wednesday or a Sunday. Don't ask us about Bible books, chapters, or verses. We're just not going to do it. Since our kids make up half to as much as two thirds of your players, you're not going to have much to play with. And you all star coaches, you travel league coaches. You have one more time to penalize one of our kids, or dismissing them from your team, for having the good sense to put the God Who gave them their ability tp play sports, over the sport itself. The next time that happens you, your parks and recreation board, and your city will be playing defense in a court of law against charges of religeous prejudice. Maybe we'll make it a class action event too, if other cities are putting up with the same tom foolery we are.

Further, let me say this to people who accuse people of faith of 'forcing our religeon down you throat'. We live in the same community you do. We love our community just as much as you do. We pay our taxes there just like you do. If a tornado or a hurricane comes through our city we will be the FIRST ones out in the street helping to clean debris. We will be the FIRST to search and rescue homes before the fire department or paramedics get there. We will be the FIRST to open our houses of worship to be used as shelters or soup lines. You expect as much, and we gladly serve. But let us dare to take a faith stand on a public issue that is contrary to your high and mighty compromising attitude, and all of a sudden we done quit preachin' and went to meddlin'! But you dare to say we are 'FORCING' our way of life on YOU?

We have as much right to sit down at the table of ideas and have our thoughts added to any civic discussion as any one of you do. We are a little weary of being painted as 'brutes'. In fact it is WE who are constantly being forced to back down. It is WE who are shouted down when people of material or financial influence want to take the morals of our communities down another half notch. We are weary of politicians and civic leaders who constantly bow down to that kind of pressure. They show a complete lack of moral or political backbone. And I, for one, think it is time, it is high time, and it is PAST time that people of faith get MORE, not less involved in the affairs of our communities. I think it is vital that people of faith run for public office on a pro life, pro family, moralistic platform that embraces simple rules like not spending more than you take in. Let people of faith band together and create a voting bloc that can not be ignored. We will take some lumps, no doubt. Every mistake we make will make the evening news and the front page of the morning paper. But my, my, if Gods people just stood together. What changes might we affect, if we just stand together? And thats all I got to say about that.

THE BIGGEST LITTLE TOWN GOD EVER MADE

We moved to River View before I entered the third grade. As I said before, it was only about five miles or less from our home in Langdale. But for the child that I was it might as well have been a move to Mars. I never asked Dad or Mother about the why of this move. But I believe there were two primary reasons. One, we would now live within a half mile of our church. More importantly, dad had transferred to the River View recreation department. He had to come out of the mill. A combination of what radicals of the day called 'brown lung' disease and his being a 'chain smoker' had caused emphysema to surface in his lungs. West Point Pepperel was kind enough to find him the job in the recreation department. He would now have a job that required being out doors most of the time. No more breathing cotton dust for him.

As I have noted elsewhere in this little book of mine, Dad spent some 25 years in Langdale Mill. It was towards the end of that time when an issue that went 'viral' cropped it's ugly head up. It came to be known as the 'brown lung' disease. The proposition was that the breathing of cotton dust over a long period of time caused emphysema and more to pollute the lungs of the worker. Textile companies were accused of deliberately exposing their employees to cotton dust without protecting them in any way. At some point, 'advocacy groups' sprang up and got traction with the national media on this issue.

In the beginning the textile industry asserted that this 'disease' only affected smokers. I could line up any number of ex-employees or their families who would testify to being in meetings where 'company doctors' made this claim to employees. I'm sad to say this includes West Point Pepperel. That argument died however when people who did not smoke and never had smoked started coming up with the 'disease'. Over time the national government got involved, threatening sanctions against any textile operation that refused to 'protect' their employees with any nimber of masks. I well remember working at the Fairfax Mill when these battles were playing out in the legal arena. I remember West Point Pepperel eventually beginning to measure the amount of cotton dust in the air in any given department of the mills. Some departments had to wear masks for half their shift, others for the entire shift. I remember hating the things. I thought and said that if those government 'agents' had to work just one shift with those masks on, and work as hard as we worked in the spooler room at Fairfax, most of them would die of a stroke. I remember once when the textile industry won a temporary reprieve, our plant manager was in the mill near to midnight telling his people they could take off those masks. And neighbor, we were glad too!

I must describe my perspective too, about a television show that got involved in this story. You remember the program '60 Minutes', don't you friend? It was announced that they would be comming to our Valley to do a story on the whole 'brown lung' issue. The story surrounded a gentleman from nearby Opelika who they chose to be their 'poster child' for the program. Pro-mos for the show never failed to show him coughing and coughing. It's not my purpose to diminish this mans sickness friend. But if you are going to be fair and present two sides of an issue, you start with the pro-mo spots that air. We pretty much knew that fairness was out the window when the promotional stuff that ran only showed, or at a minimum gave priority to, a fella coughing over and over. For our Valley it was a big deal for a big time television show to come to our area to do a story for a prime time show. I remember our local paper saying that the reporter and crew were 'closeted' with West Point Pepperel presedent Joseph Lanier Jr. for the story. When the time for the show came, what I feared came to pass. They ripped into West Point Pepperel every way they knew how. Mr. Lanier was presented to be a textile executive presiding over an attempted cover-up. He bent over backwards to accomodate them. He pulled the medical records of the gentleman from Opelika for discussion. He gave the reporter and crew a tour of the Lanier-Carter Mills along Interstate 85. Everything they asked for he gave them to the best of his ability.

The television program of course took a very one sided view of the 'brown lung' issue. For example they made sure to note that Mr. Lanier took them to the most modern facility the company had, at a minimum insinuating that the company avoided on purpose giving them a tour of the older mills. I mean, for Heavens sake people, by this time the company had already begun to fully integrate a protection program for ALL it's employees. Any industry that is under the type scrutiny that textiles was under is going to want to put their best foot forward in any report that is going to be shown on national television. It was almost as though the company was still 'hiding something' by chosing to use the best they had to show how they were trying to make a difference for their employees. There was a fleeting comment and picture of the protection methods being used, and I DO mean fleeting. But the story, in the main, was a mutilation of West Point Pepperel. Never doubt that. All you have to do is pull the program out of the vault and show it. What I have shared with you is my opinion and perception of what was done in this story. And I am NOT going to back down either.

Listen, it's not as if I give West Point Pepperel a free pass here. They did NOT always meet this challenge the way they should have. They DID resist, at least initially, the need for breathing protection at all. They DID pass what turned out to be prejudiced and unsubstantiated information to their employees initially. They WERE held accountable, Lord knows, for these actions. Now a question, if you please. Does this preclude the responsibility of the media to present both sides of an issue? Should they only have presented the wrongs of the industry, and especially in this case West point Pepperel, without presenting their efforts to comply with the safety needs of their employees, however hard they had to be pressed? Basic fairness dictated yes. But this report, and the cannibal style reporting that was done in that day, was about as one sided as it gets.

As a restitution, employees who were found to have been affected by the 'brown lung' malady were given lump sum settlements. There was no mention of this in any report I am aware of. Certainly not Sixty Minutes. My Dad had his settlement calculated by the company, and then halved. The reasoning was that his heavy smoking habit was half his problem, and cotton dust half. My Dad never voiced any displeasure of his settlement. After all, he was retained at a job where cotton dust would not be a problem. And he got a financial settlement. He thought that fair enough. He went to his new job with thankful appreciation that he could still provide for his family.

Friend, there is enough blame here to go around for everybody. The government was overbearing to the point of bullying at times. The industry had to be dragged into the age of protection against their will. And the media was as one sided as it has ever been in the way they handled this issue. They were correct in pointing out wrong where it existed. They were wrong to the core in not giving equal credit to any company that tried to do the right thing or to comply with directives after losing political or legal arguments. Parents, when you discipline your children, and see them make the changes you require of them, do you still beat them up with their mistake ad nauseum, or do you acknowlege their compliance with encouragement and give them a fresh sheet of paper to start over with? I have never watched another episode of 60 Minutes from that time to now, over 30 years later. And I never will. And thats all I got to say about that....

THE LITTLE GREEN HOUSE

Friend, let's get our readers to see the new life my family started by allowing them to see the lay of the land through the eyes of the boy that I was. Can you see what we see, dear readers? There it is, a little dirt road that turns to the right off the Langdale-River View road, just down from Midway Baptist Church. The pretty brick home on one corner belongs to Mr. Ralph Frazier, the principal of River View School. I remember his youngest daughter Amelia. She was a twirler in Valley High Schools band. She was several years my senior. And most importantly she took a little bald headed, buck toothed, bony little boy under her wing. She made sure I was not bothered on the bus when we moved to River View. That someone as pretty as her would even notice a kid like me,well...I never forgot that. The older looking home on the left as you turn onto the Fairfax short-cut road belongs to Mr. John McCullough, who is our landlord. He is as honest as the day is long. He will be the best land-lord we ever had. He and his wife were Godly people. They treated everybody fairly. Just past this house you see right there, on the same side of the road, a white frame house built in the same basic style of the mill village homes. Mr. Rudolph Cannon and his wife Edna live here. I still have a ceramic swan she made for my Mother many years ago. It's in my home in a place I keep knick-knacs. Can you see that beautiful plum tree on the other side of the house near the road? Mr. Rudolph is a soft heart who will let us Ogle brats have plums from this tree anytime we wanted. But the boy that I was remembers Mrs. Edna runnin' us off once, sayin' "I don't care WHAT Mr. Rudolph said. I want to make some jelly out of some of these plums if I can keep enough of them!"

Can you see the small pond just beyond the Cannons home? There it is, just before you go around a curve in the road. That's Mr. Johns pond. When he drained it, he let me and my brother wade into the mud and get the last of the bream and catfish that were there. We had ouselves a big fish fry the Saturday after. Before we get around that curve, look to your left. There is a huge pipe that was put under that road to accomodate drain water from two lakes upstream. Over time it has dug out o huge hole about fifteen feet wide, about the same long, and believe it or not about six feet deep. The boy that I was used this hole as a secret fishin' spot till he was found out. This little hole could be a sight to see after a hard rain. Just up the road as you come out of the curve, look to your right. Can you see the small pasture there? There are a few cows there and one ole bad tempered bull. The kids we were had to be careful not to go into this pasture when the bull was near. Whats that? Why would we go inside the fence? Well, start with the small barn you see there. Always a magnet for enquiring little minds. Then theres the pig sty, which always had five or six big porkers inside. Those rascals could be a hoot when feedin' time came. Too, Mr. John had a 'worm bed' he would let us get fish bait from every now and again.

Just barely past that pasture and barn, on the same side of the road, there is another larger lake belonging to Mr. John. The kids we were will spend many a day fishin' here, and pickin' blackberries along the bank next to the pasture. There is a small place, across from the lake, too small to be called a field, where my Dad made ONE attempt one year to have us kids learn about how his family made their living in his childhood. It was an experiment that he did not repeat. See that little hollow just beyond the garden spot? This was a favorite berry pickin' place for the kids we were. And just past there, there it is. The little green house that has my heart yet. As we stand by the dirt road in front of this little house, you can see that the small front porch is screened in. The door to this porch is a side door, just down from where Mother and Dad would park their car. Lets go in and have a look.

There is a swing on the porch in front of you there as you enter the porch door. The front door entering the house is a hard right hand turn. You look surprised friend, at how small the living room is. And by the size of the small gas heater in the far right hand corner. Whats that? Is that the only heat in the house? Ohhh, no friend. There is another heater in the bath room about half that size. You look as though you disapprove, friend. Why is that? Anyway, let's look to our left, and we'll walk into a bedroom. This is the largest bedroom in the little house. What? You dont want to see the smallest? Sorry friend. You're already hooked on my story now. You cant help yourself. This was also my baby sisters bedroom when God blessed us with her during our stay here. Not what you expected, is it? Lets see the rest of the house anyway, since we're already here and all. We leave Mother and Dads bedroom, and I call your attention to a book shelf that doubles as a counter. It divides the living room from the eating area. It opens on the opposite side. On the top row you will see a set of Britanica Encyclopedias. Then other assorted books and nick knacks. Dad was a fan of westerns written by Zane Grey, an author of some note. Mother enjoyed romance type books, though the boy I was cant tell me anymore who her favorite author was.

As we stand next to the end of the book case we see just to the right the little area where our family took their meals. The refridgerator sits in the far right hand corner of this room. Whats that? Why did I just chuckle? I'm sorry friend. I was remembering when we moved from this home to our new home where Mother still lived when she went Home. When they moved that fridge, they found about a pound or so of fossilized butter beans, black eyed peas and so forth. Mother then knew why her children always jockeyed to be the one that sat at the corner seat at the table. Had she discovered this when the beans were fresh, Dr. Green (a switch, for my northern friends who forgot) would have made an immediate house call. We walk about three steps and turn left to see the kitchen area. I'm smiling again, aren't I? It's just because I was remembering a really important lesson my Mother taught me one time about sneaking food before the meal was served. She loved to make a fresh batch of corn bread for lunch or supper. Whats that?

There is a difference? Well yes, there is. We had breakfast, then lunch, then supper. THREE meals a day, friend. I know, there are many others to whom this is a strange idea these days. We would do well to go back to some of the 'old ways' friend. We would be much healthier. Anyway, Mother would slice up a fresh bell pepper to go with the corn bread. Friend, that was some tasty stuff indeed! Mother would set the corn bread in the window to cool, and the bowl of sliced bell pepper next to the sink. I had a bad habit of sneaking a slice of corn bread and a slice or two of the bell pepper before lunch. At some point Mother decided to teach me a lesson. Or as the old folk use to say, to 'break me from suckin' eggs' for good! She sliced up some bell pepper that was hot as a fire cracker. She left it right where she usually did. Sure enough, watch friend. See that little bald headed, bony, buck toothed rascal? He just took a piece of that pepper and some corn bread. Watch him sneak out the back door. If we follow him he will go under the house. Theres a huge crawl space there. He'll take a big bite of that corn bread, then a big bite of that bell pepper. That bell pepper is going to burn through the corn bread and savagely attack his taste buds. Those taste buds are going to frantically demand that he get into the house PRONTO and get SOMETHING cool...no, COLD on them IMMEDIATELY! Just watch friend. Here he comes, runnin' as fast as he can. Bless his heart. Look at him holding his mouth under the spicket at the sink. Look at him put that water away! Uh-ohhh, here comes his Mother! Good, she's not angry. In fact, she looks amused. What did she just say to him friend? Really? She actually told him to listen next time she said stay out of the food till meal time? NO WAY! I bet he does too, right? Whats that? I already know the answer to that one? Well.....heh-heh...lets just say that I was all boy and let it go at that.

You're asking about the door to the left off the kitchen. Well, lets go in and see. Yes, there are two beds here, and a couple dressers. A door adjoining on the far side enters into Mother and Dads bedroom. Yes, indeed it is cramped. My two sisters sleep on the bed next to the window. My brother and I sleep on the other bed. I once woke in the middle of the night to find my Mother huddled in the room with us. There was a really severe thunderstorm underway. It was severe enough that she wanted all of us to be together. Many years later I would awaken during another thunderstorm to discover my Mother at the foot of my bed as I had never seen her before. We shall visit that night later in this little book of mine. I remember one night us kids looked out of this window in the direction of the lake, just across the road. We saw flashlights over there. They seemed to be comming up the side of the lake towards our house. The imagination of the children we were soon had us in a 'booger bear' frenzy. If that was not enough, about that time my Dad entered the house. That sent us into a screaming fit, which brought our Dad quickly to the room, after which we were relieved and he was a tad upset. Looking out the window he told us the lights we saw was nothing more than some fellas frog gigging. Yes friend, I can look back on that scene now and smile. But on that night, not so much.

Wait, friend, dont go back to the front yet. Believe it or not there is a bit yet to see of this little house. See the tiny hallway there. Lets step over there. On the left is the little bathroom. What? No, no, I dont mind your questions at all. You're right, there is no shower in this bathroom. Just that big ole tub. Kinda looks like the one on Tallassee street, right? In later years my Mother had a standing joke that on Saturday nights all of her kids took a bath in the same bath water, and the last one in could almost walk on the water. You city folk now, y'all just study on that a bit. It will come to ya. Theres a tiny room opposite the bathroom. This, my friend, would be no place for someone who gets the 'trapped in' feeling easily. It was my PaPas bedroom. Bless his heart, he always took the smallest room for himself. See? Theres just barely enough room for his bed and his dresser. By the way, see the back door there? You'll notice it has six little panes of glass starting about half way up. Notice that the bottom right pane is missing. This will cause no small concern for my Mother during an event we shall soon discuss. Lets step out on the back porch friend. You can see that it is screened in too, the door being on the right side. See that fence up in the woods yonder? Someone once raised chickens in that pen. It's a pretty good sized pen too. And straight out into the shallow woods there, we will try our hand at raising hogs.....once.... only once....you'll like that story. But lets walk back up to the front porch. I remember how cool a breeze could be on this porch following a rain in the summer time. We had no air conditioning at all during our stay here. Just open windows, whatever breeze we might be blessed with, and what I call 'automatic fan' power. Explain that one to that city fella standin' next to ya friend, will ya? Thanks

I have a picture in the camcorder of my mind of a scene I took in looking from this porch down towards the curve where my secret fishin' place was. It's a picture of an oncoming storm cloud. The best way to describe it is to call it a light show from God. You see it don't you? Clouds, as though God split open a thunderstorm and let you see the make-up of it. The top layer has off white to deep yellowish color. Then you see how the cloud color changes from that to blue, to deep blue, to almost black the further down the formation you go. Lightning flashes in the midst of the clouds. I know they are moving, but as we watch through the eyes of the boy I was, it seems that God allows them to stand still so that we can see and appreciate His awesome power. I know it had that effect on me friend. How about you? Is it not strange, the things that we retain in our memories, friend? You know, I seldom see the like of the 'electrical storm's' we endured when I was a child. These thing's could blow up, or so it seemed, in a matter of minutes on a hot summer day. They would just pitch a booming light show fit for 15-30 minutes, the the sun would come out again. I could be out in the woods pickin' blackberries friend, and hear just the distant sound of thunder, and it was off to the house for me. I did NOT care to be caught under trees in the woods during one of those storms. Too many lightning rods. You know what I mean, don't you friend?

I forgot to mention the ditch there along the front of the road. My Mother, if there was no thunder or lightning, would allow us to play out in the rain. We tried more than once to dam up that ditch during the rains. I don't think we ever succeeded. And when they finally paved the road, the ditch was covered up anyways. Another way we created our own fun. You know friend, these days we have gotten soft. How many parents do you know who will allow their kids to play in the rain? Or kids who even want to? The boy that I was laughs at them.

REVENGE ON THE BIRDS

I told you earlier about this saying my Mothers Mom had about 'little birds' telling on her and Sister. My own Mother used this same saying on me. It drove me nuts. I decided that this was a problem that had to be addressed. So I discreetly started one year, real early, asking for a B.B. gun for Christmas. Got me one too, a 'Daisy' brand. I immediately declared war on all things winged in the woods around our house. A many a bird paid the ultimate price from that moment friend, without ever knowin' why. But they just didnt get the message. They just kept right on tellin' stuff that was none of their cotton pickin' business! The most stubborn animals on earth, those birds. ALL of'em. Only after I had kids of my own did I find out all of the truth about the 'birds' of life.

GO PLAY, BUT STAY NEAR

On Saturdays, and most any day during the summer, Mother would shoo us young'uns out to play, with but one admonishment. "Y'all just be sure that when I call you in for lunch, you can here me." That seems reasonable enough does it not friend? We could fish on the lake, or pick berries in the hollow, or go bird huntin' in the woods nearby, and any number of other things and still be close enough by to hear Mothers voice. But you know kids. Every now and again our obedience would get sick, and Dr. Green had to be summoned to supply an 'aspirin' that cured all ills. You know what I mean don't you friend? When Mother called you the first time, she would say "Hugh, time to come to lunch!" Now, if she had to call the second time it sounded something like this; "HUBERT BUING OGLE JUNIORRRRRR!!!" Now friend, if your Momma ever called you in that tone of voice you could turn out the lights, the party was over.

Or does 'bathroom revival' ring a bell? Either way, your fate was sealed. I'll say this. We never had a whole bunch of those episodes. That kind of medicine was rather fast acting. You know what I mean don't you friend?

THE HIGHS AND THE LOWS OF THE OLD DIRT ROAD

I remember as a child Mother and Dad taking us up to Aunt Mildred and Uncle Ramon Thrifts home in Clay County. They lived on a dirt road that we had to go about a mile on to get to their house. At least once I remember us having to turn back because there had been a lot of rain, and the road was just impassable. Other times we kids 'enjoyed' as Mother and Dad 'endured' a joy ride trying to keep from getting stuck on that old road. I came to equate 'goin' to the country' with that dirt road. I was sad when they paved that road. To me it took the 'country' out of the trip.

We went through the same back and forth emotions wen we moved onto this dirt road where this precious little green house is. In the summer time we didn't care whether the road was quagmired or not. Either way we were gonna have fun. Our parent's now, not so much. My Dad burned up the motor on an old Packard car tryin' to get it up the road to our house. It was only... what, a hundred yards or a little better as the crow flies from our house to the end of the road. But it could be a pretty steep challenge for any vehicle that tried it's luck after a rain.

During the school year is when we kids had our turn at the frustration trough. You see friend, the school bus would NOT come up this ole dirt road if the rains had been really soaking. This meant that we would have to walk around the curve down yonder and on to the end of the road to catch the bus in the mornin'. And in the afternoon, if the road was not passable for the bus still, we had to walk right back. And if it was still raining, an umbrella was mandatory. I remember walking slap out of my shoes in the mud one day, just as we rounded the curve. Walked all the way home. And walked all the way back down there to retrieve those shoes too when my Dad found it out. And him right in behind me with an occaisional swat to the south end, just for emphasis. Ask me friend. Ask me how many times this happened to me? Thats exactly right. Once. Any questions?

CAN THERE BE FUN ON A PAVED ROAD?

We had our special brand of 'chicken' we played on the old dirt road. Just about all of us had bikes. We would line up at our drive way. The idea was to go down the road as fast as we dared, and turn hard left onto the dirt road that ran the length of the lake without wiping out. The one judged to do it fastest was the winner. The one who backed out, especially if he backed out 'in the process' was declared chicken. Friend, I've seen my share of wipeouts take place at that turn. Wiped out myself a time or two. Once I wiped out trying to make that turn. I spilled over the pasture fence at the foot of a little hill. When I looked up, there stood that onery old bull about fifty or so feet away. Friend, I waited till the next day to get my bike. We had another game we called 'hot foot'. When they paved the dirt road, it was basically with tar and gravel in that day. Cars goin' up and down both lanes would eventually leave a 'tar track' on either side of the road about ten inches wide. Soooo...two of us stand next to the tar tracks. On a count of three, we each got on a tar track and walked till our feet forced us off the road. The first one to bail was called 'hot foot'. Neighbor, I honestly think we could have walked on a bed of tacks in those days. Mind now, this game was best played in the heat of summer, in the middle of the day. I'll say it again youn'uns of today. Y'all would stand no chance against us.

B. B. GUNS AND MISCHIEF

My Mother went through a spell when she would say "a little bird told me about that" when she knew about some mischief I had been in, that I was just SURE I had kept from her. As a small child I clung to her every word. So if Mother said "little birds" were tellin' her things, why, I had a problem. I also had a plan. I started later that year asking for a B.B. gun for Christmas. You know friend, discreetly and all. And on Christmas mornin' I was rewarded with a B.B. pistol. You remember friend, the kind that had to have the air cartridges in them. The best part about the B.B. pistol is that it would shoot rapid fire. With a B.B. rifle it was POP! then pump. With a B.B. pistol your shootin' action was more like POP-POP-POP-POP! And NOW then, my new friend, war was declared on all winged creatures in the woods around our house. Friend, a many a bird paid the ultimate sacrifice, and never knew the reason why. Nor did they get the message. No matter how many I eliminated, they kept right on runnin' their cotton pickin mouths off to my Momma! And even to my Daddy too, more than once. In fact, I went on my most torrid wing clipping binges after they talked to HIM. You know what I mean dont you friend?

Me and my buddy Buck use to have B.B. gun battles. Whats that? Noooo, we battled one another. Shot them at one another. It's a thousand wonders we didn't put an eye out here or there. You think that's extreme dont you friend? You just gave me a hard look. I saw that. Let me tell you about extreme. An uncle of mine use to have cherry bomb battles with his brothers. Got a piece of his heel blowed off once. There now. Still think WE were extreme? Anyways, One day me and Buck were havin' a runnin' B.B. gun battle. You know, hide behind this. Ambush the other fella. Shoot on a dead run. All of that. At one point we lost sight of one another. I had Buck figured. He would come around the corner of his house tryin' to sneak up on me. Boy, would I have a surprise waitin' on him! I edged up to the other corner. I peeeeeked around the corner ever so slowly. Nope, he was yet to show. GREAT! I thought, I'll jes' draw ahead on that cornerand wait him out. When he shows, I'll make it warm for him. I drew down on that far corner. I slowly crouched down so as to steady my aim. And friend, just as my britches tightened up on my south end, I felt what seemed like seven or eight hornets stinging me simultaneously on the tip of my tailbone! I dont know if you have ever felt that sensation friend. But if you have, you probably did exactly what I did. I SCREAMED as I flat footed the bush at the corner there that I had used for cover. I don't remember WHERE my B.B. gun went to. I hit the ground rolling and rolling, reaching back behind me to see if I could grab the hornets or whatever had my tailbone sending out air raid warnings. Then I heard a sound I did not like one bit. The sound of LAUGHTER. Can you believe that friend? Somebody thought this was funny! I looked up to see who this obviously rude person was. And there was Buck. He was rolling around on the ground too. I don't think he knows where his gun went either. He was jes squaling almost, he laughed so hard. I done been out hunted! Bushwhacked! And I was NOT laughing friend, I'll promise you that. Well, when something like this happened among friends, you could count on one thing. Recompense was sure. It might take a while, but be sure reckoning day would arrive. So it was in this case. Some time later Buck and me were in the woods across from his home bird huntin'. Now, Aunt Betty, Bucks Mother, had the same rule for him as Mother dd for us. She called by the first name for lunch the first time. She called by the WHOLE name the second time. And then, Dr. Green would already be there when Buck or his sister got into the house. Are ya with me friend?

So there we are, in the woods. Hunting birds. We had this one bird we really wanted to get. We had just gotten into position to send it to it's final rest when Aunt Betty called Buck to lunch. By the first name. Well, he lit out without another thought for the bird. And as he turned his back on the scene, an idea popped into my head. First, I fired a shot off just to make noise. Luckiest shot I ever made. Knocked that bird right out of the tree. That cemented it right there. This was meant to be. Ordained even, by cracky! I hollered to Buck, "HEY! COME BACK QUICK! I HIT'IM! HE'S FLOPPIN' ON THE GROUND!! HURRY!!! In like fashion I kept it up. Looking through the bushes I saw Buck hesitate. He looked to his house, then back down toward me. Then he started to just tear it up gettin' back to me. I quickly stood up and fired, then sat the ground just as he got to me. The poor bird is already grave-yard dead. And I said, "Awww man, Buck, I just finished him off. Sorry 'bout that. "And about that time Buck's Mother called him to lunch the second time. By his FULL name. He cast me a "Whatever it takes I'll get ya" look as he ran madly for the house, no doubt to helplessly....and hopelessly, plead his case... I was quite satisfied with myself that day friend.

There was a neighbor kid in our little community who was prone to acts of extreme mischief. And from time to time it would cause him no small amount of trouble. One day Aunt Bett, as we called her, answered her car port door to find this kids Father standin' there. He was mad as an ole wet hen. "Your daughter shot my son with a B.B. gun! And I think you need to whup her fanny for her!" Aunt Bett said he was quite determined that justice be done. She called her daughter to the door. She asked whether she did what this man said or not. The daughter now, she had heard the ruckus from an adjoining room. She was ready. "Yes Ma'am I sure did shoot him. He was shootin' at some of us, and had already hit one kid. I told him if he shot me I would take his gun from him and shoot him right back. And Momma, he went and shot me anyways! So I did what I said. I took his gun, and I shot him. And if he shoots me with it again, I'll do the same thing!" Aunt Bett had heard enough. She turned to this Dad, and she said, "I 'spect the best thing for you tol do is to get back down the hill before my husband gets home." Good idea too, friend. Uncle Joe was a big man. About six foot one or a tad better, and around 240 pounds. This Dad? Well, lets just say he was not in the same weight class and let it go at that....

BUCK AND ME

As I think back now on those years we spent in the little green house on the dirt road they finally paved, I have a more full appreciation for the kind of friend Buck was to me. I don't think I ever really appreciated him for his steadfast friendship, and quite possibly took advantage of it more than once. He and I spent a lot of good times together. We played softball and basket ball together. Attended the same church and schools. Lived in the same community. I can still get a chuckle out of some of the things we did. Like the day he called me up and wanted to go riding. He had just bought a jeep, and wanted to go riding around for a while. That was A-OK with me. So off we went. We wound up on a dirt road on the Georgia side of the Chattahoochie River. It came out nearby to a place known as the Frazier Hole, below the dam at Langdale Mill. Soon enough we found ourselves at the foot of a hill staring at a stream that ran across the road. It seemd not to be more than a foot and a half deep. Buck stopped the jeep. We both stood up in it and eyed the little stream. Buck asked, "You think we an make it?" I said "It's your jeep, but I don't see why not."

Buck thought it over for a minute. Then he said, "Well, here we go!" He backed his jeep up several feet for a runnin' start. He put the pedal down, and we went into that stream....and the jeep sat down right there in the middle of that stream, almost so that water could come into the jeep. And there we sat. Buck said, "No problem. This jeep has a wench on the front of it. I'll just hook us up to a tree and pull it out." Only the wench broke on us. And with that we were out of options. No way were we gonna be able to push it out. I wandered if we might have to spend the night. In a little while though, a truck came from down towards the river. Two guys got out and walked over to where we were standing. "You fellas look like you could use a little help." I resisted the urge to say, DUHHH! Buck said "I sure would appreciate it." The guy had a WORKING wench on his truck. He hooked us right up and pulled us out of that mudhole desguised as a stream. We thanked the guys for their help. Then I had to open my mouth with a question. "Say, we come riding down this'a way now and again. Tell me, how do you guy's avoid that quick-sand trap? With a sly grin, this fella says to me, he says "Well, I just always go around it on that track over there." He pointed to our left, and I wanted to crawl in a hole. There was a place where that stream ran across rocky type ground. Aand there was a well worn track where everybody ELSE had been driving around the trap for some time. Me and Buck, all we could do was look sheepishly to the ground and thank the men again for their help.

Buck was the kind of friend who lived the scripture that says "A friend loveth at all times, and a brother is born for adversity." I remember a time when I was 'living stupid'. I dont think anyone knew until many years later, but in a period of self pity I had begun to take my PaPas pain pills. And his muscle relaxers. And anything else I could find. Two over here, one over there, three over yonder. You see friend, I call it a period of self pity instead of an attempt on my own life because anyone who wants to do that will go ahead and take the whole bottle and be done with it. There I was though, unable to do that, but just miserable enought to take meds that were not meant for me.

Further, let me show you what a scoundrel satan is, to give me opportunity to lose my life by my own hands. One, our family was always in church. Two, I had no history of so much as smoking a cigarrete, much less taking drugs. Three, as goofy as I could act sometimes I was generally seen as an easy goin' fella and the class clown to boot. See the cover I had? So when I began to exhibit some rather strange behaviour, there was concern but no alarm. My friend Buck remembers taking me to the Kroger store in Lanett to get something or another, only to watch silently as I got something entirely different. And heres the real coup satan just KNEW would finnish me. My sister took me to a doctor who diagnosed inner ear trouble and prescribed me meds he said "might make you a little sleepy." Yessir neighbor, in cold blood satan wanted to kill me. But God gave me a guardian angel who found those meds stashed in my room, and ditched them. I may never know who it was, but it may have saved my life.

Friends like Buck saw me through that sad time without knowin' what they were seein' me through. Bucks interest in me went further than friendship. We were riding around one day,and he was doing his best to witness to me. I remember sayin' to him, "Buck, I did not get the way I am overnight, and I won't change overnight either!" He thought on that for a moment. Then he said, "I'll give you that. But don't you think it's time to start thinkin' about it?" Years later he would not remember that conversation when I asked him about it. But my friend, Buck, and Mr. Carl, make no mistake, are the kind of friends who planted seeds in my life that grew into salvation for me on March 16, 1980 on a Sunday night at Midway.

I haven't seen Buck for a long spell now. But he was a good enough friend to me, and I am so indebted to him for standing behind me when others turned their backs and walked away, till I wanted to have him enshrined in this little book of mine through the stories I have shared with you. Buck, you are the man! God bless your heart. My love to you and your precious family.

MY LAST BIRD HUNT

Let me take my leave of all things bird huntin' and let Buck help me with it. We went out the car port door one fine day to do a little bird huntin'. There was a fence at the back of their property. We argued over who got to make the first shot. But I was in the lead, and we no sooner got into the yard till I saw a cardinal perched on the top strand of the barbed wire fence. Before Buck could protest anymore, I fired off the luckiest shot of my B.B. gun shootin' career. Dropped it right there. I was beside myself with excitement. I did NOT want to hear anything about a 'lucky shot' either. I wanted to go next door to PaPa Deloaches house and show him what I had done. This was Buck's PaPa.

PaPa Deloach was one of the wisest men I knew. He was a WW2 veteran, having served our nation in the United States Navy. He worked for years at the River View Mill. He was a deacon in our church. As a child, and on through my young adult years till he went Home, I admired and respected him. He was a little over six foot tall. He was a wiry, but by no means skinny man. He had silver / grey hair on both sides of and in the back of his head, cut short, bald on the top. He wore blue jean type britches at home most of the time, and short sleeve denim type shirts. He wore glasses too. I can see him now, plain as day, sitting in his living room in an old ladder back chair. His right leg is crossed over his left. In his right hand is his pipe. His right elbow is on his knee. As I see that now through the eyes of the boy that I was, he was the very picture of a man waiting to dispense some knowlege to a willin' ear. I was about to become that ear.

We went runnin' into his house, Buck and me. I was half out of breath as I exclaimed, "Papa, PaPa, look wht I got!" I let him look into the sack I had put the little cardinal in. To my surprise he did not share my joy. He showed no emotion at all in fact. He said, "That's a pretty one, sho' nuff." Then he looked at me and and said "Hugh, can I ask a question?" I said sure. And he asked me, "Did you find the nest of this bird yet?" I said well of course not. He said, "Well, now that is sad to me. This bird prob'ly left eggs or little ones in that nest not very long ago. It was out mindin' it's own business, probaly looking for food for the babies. They may well be callin' for Momma right now. But Momma ain't never commin' home again. So, them babies will starve to death. If they're lucky. Or another bird will kill them and take over the nest. Or a snake will use them for lunch later today. All because this Momma bird can't help her children."

WELL!

Friend, he almost had me in tears. To be honest, I don't know what I did with that little cardinal. The boy that I was won't even speak to me about it. I hope I buried it proper. But I have consulted with the boy that I was on another question, and on this point we agree. That was the last time I ever raised a B.B. gun to take a winged life. Decades later, when PaPa went Home, I remembered that last bird hunt all those years ago. I remembered his words which, with the added benefit of years of hindsight, now seemed even more sage than then. That kind of wisdom is hard to come by in this day and time friend. I am a better man today because I had that kind of wisdom expounded to me by people like Olin DeLoach. Gosh friend, I'm almost ready to cry right now....

TO CHANGE MY NAME.... OR NOT?

Friend, maybe you don't think PaPa DeLoach was as sage as I do in the story I just told you. So allow me to share with you a story that will put his 'sage-ness' beyond doubt or reproach. To do this though, I must let you have a glimpse into a family dynamic I'm not too proud of. I say that as the man I am now, a bit wiser myself than I was in my young adult years. My Dad and I, as I told you whern we began this little journey of ours, had our moments. Dad was a strict disciplinarian. I have told you he used his belt liberally. But in the eyes of the boy I was he could be just as forceful in his words and his general actions. Over time, as I grew older, I began to scheme friend. I searched diligently for a way to get back at him in a way that he couldn't do a John Brown thing about it. One day I hit on an idea that really got me to reving my vengeance motor up. I was a legal adult now. Able to make my own choices. I was named for my Father. I am a 'Junior.' And I decided one day, "Well maybe I didn't wanna BE a junior no more!"

I began to do some research. I found out that I could indeed legally change my name if I so chose to do that. It would cost money. But I was willing to spend it. I was gonna 'break my dad from suckin' eggs' once and for all. Friend, the angry young man that I was can't even remember what he was gonna change his name to. But we agree that all I had to do was go to the court house at an appointed time and do the deed. The only person I took into my confidence was my Mother. She didn't like the idea. But she said I was an adult now, and the decision was mine. But she was sad about the prospect. I understood that. But my mind was made up. Sometime in the next few days Mother came in from work and said, "PaPa DeLoachsaid he want's to talk to you when you have the time." I asked her what in the world would he want to talk to me about. She said, "Go on over there and find out." It never occured to me that she had shared a troubled heart with MaMa and PaPa. Looking back now, I really have no reason to be surprised. She went to them with many things over the years. So I promised to go over there tne next day. I'll never forget that day. I went to PaPa's house after work, just as care free as ever. I said, "PaPa, Mother said you wanted to talk to me. "Pa Pa was sitting in his regular place by the small gass heater in his living room. He said, "Yeah, Hugh, come on in and sit a while." As I sat down PaPa said, "Your Momma tell's me that you're thinkin' about changin' your name."

AWWW MAAAN, IT'S A SET-UP!! That was my first thought. I said, "I sure am, and the sooner I can do it the better!" I began to list every 'sin' my Dad had committed in my life. This wasn't fair, that should never have happened, he had no right to say those things to me in front of my friends, on and on I vented. PaPa, for his part, sat taking an occaisional puff on his pipe, and humoring me with a nod or two. When I was finnished with my rant, PaPa spoke. "Hugh, I hear what you're sayin.' I even agree with some of your complaint. But I just think you're lookin' for a permanent solution to what might be a temporary problem." I asked him how in the world could he say that? PaPa said, "Well, you are going to get older. So is your Daddy. As mad at him as you are now, you may not feel that way in 25 years. But then, you'll have two problems. One, you're pride won't let you change your name back. Besides all the damage is done. Also, you'll prob'ly be married by then, have a kid or two. You'll be too caught up in raisin' a family to go back and change your name again. And I just think you ought to pray about something like this before you do something you can't take back."

PRAY?? PRAY??? He wanted me to PRAY? Friend, I wasn't saved at this point in my life. The very LAST thing I wanted to do was PRAY about anything! And yet here was PaPa DeLoach, a man I otherwise loved, admired and respected, a man who KNEW I was at least partially right in my complaints, and he wants me to PRAY! Geeez..... when I left his house that day, I was so mad I could have bit a nail in two. Or knawed on it anyways. But as it is when you get Godly advice from a Godly man, friend, I could not ignore what he said. I ended up not changin' my name. And you know what? PaPa was right. When my Dad yook his Place of rest in 2008 he was one of the very best friends I had. He was a mentor and a confidante. I hung on every word he said. It broke my heart when he went Home ten minutes before I got to his hospital room. And in those moments, I thought of the advice that Olin DeLoach gave me that day, all those years ago. And I was thankful. And I emptied my tear ducts one more again, friend. As I said before in this little book of mine, Dad and I forgave one another as an act of faith, and allowed God, and Him alone, to do the healing.

WHAT WE DO FOR A BROTHER

My brother was still very small when we moved to the little green house. Some folk had built a home out away from the road. They had a sort of a hill that their dirt driveway went down to get to their house. One day my brother got into a tri-cycle race with another kid. He was beatinge him pretty good too. This kids sibling came up and started pushing from the back to increase speed. My brother promptly came into the house to get me. Friend, I had NO desire to push a tri-cycle, with or without him on it. But my Mother prevailed on me to do it just once. Grudgingly I went out to have a look. As we watched them from the screened porch, I knew we could take'em. I said to my brother, "This will be easy. The strategy is simple. Hold your feet up off the pedals. Let me do ALL the pushin', and you just steer it. We'll beat'em proper. Got that? Picture us friend, with our bony, bald headed, knobby kneed selves, both of us with smiles on our faces that say "you two are goin' DOWN!" Are you with me friend?

My brother and I walked over to the driveway. He said "NOW, we'll see!" Picture this now friend. I whisper to my brother once more to keep his feet OFF the pedals. He nod's. On the count of three it's 'OFF THEY GO!!' time. And we were almost instantly winning, friend. Can you see it? We were flat out flyin'! Too fast for my brother I guess. He panicked. He tried to put on the brakes as it were. Which required what? Say it with me class. THE PEDALS! When he did that, the tryke jack-knifed. I went flyin' over the handlebars. And landed on the left side of my face. Which then looked like a road map of Georgia basically. Only red. And swollen. I looked like I had the mumps friend. And I had to get on the school bus on Monday mornin'. I spent the rest of the weekend thinkin' up a story to tell about what happened. I knew there would be questions. And there were. But before I could plant a story on them my brother proudly informed everyone that I was helpin' him win a try-cycle race! Friend, I would take you back to the playground and let you see the ribbing I took that morning. But honestly friend, I really don't wanna relive that particular morning again. Trust me, once was enough. And that's all I got to say about that. But I'm smiling right now. Why, look at you friend. You're smiling too!

"ERMA"

We knew and loved good friends whule we lived here friend. Some we claim as family to this day. But I want you to meet a lady who was very special to our family. I must get away from my theme of telling my stories as they happen on our journey. This one has no ending yet. But I'm getting ahead of myself. You have heard me talk of my parents employing a 'maid' from time to time. The one who dressed up like a monster and chased us kids around the house did not last long. The maid who Dad found occupying the spot in his bed where he thought his wife was got gone pretty quick. But this dear lady you will meet now, she is still a precious soul in my life to this day. Her name is Erma. She told me that she heard my parent's were looking for help from a friend. And she went to see Mother. They hit it off from the beginning. Erma has a big heart, and in our childhood she loved kid's too. That was, of course, very important to my parent's. She did about everything for us while Mother and Dad worked their jobs in the mills. She was quite the cook. And she could get after us when the occaision called for it, and with Mothers blessing at that. Erma even got attached to family pet's. We had this ole mutt of a dog we called 'Buster'. He was white except for a big black spot around his left eye and two or three black spots on his side and his belly. It was almost as if God took a Dalmations skin and put it on a half hound / half beagle :). Buster would follow any of us anywhere we went unless someone held him till we got around the curve. One day Erma decided to walk over to Mr. George Will Monk's store. Ole Buster was just not goin' to be left behind. When Erma got over to the main road, she picked Buster up and carried him to the store and back to this little dirt road. She was concerned he would run out in front of a car. Friend, she did not have to do that. But that was Erma.

I have to tell you a story about something stupid I did friend. But ONLY ONCE did I make this ignorant mistake. One day I was being admonished by Erma about something. I don't even remember what it was now. But I was indignant towards whatever she was saying to me to the point that I shouted the "N" word at her. Dont pretend you don't know what I mean, friend. What's that? No, I CAN'T tell you why I did that. Remember though, we lived during a time when our communities, indeed our nation, were going through a very painful transition from a segregated society to an integrated society. I no doubt had heard this hateful word tossed around in the community. I normally would not have dreamed of saying that word. But Erma was on the last nerve of the boy that I was. And...it happened.

Erma could have reacted in a number of ways. But on hearing this word, she immediately stopped talking to me and went on aboout her business. But when my Dad got home that day, she told him what had happened. My Dad did not even wait till after supper. He called me, and in a voice I had not heard in a while. When I got in the house, he didn't say "Hugh, I want to see you in the bathroom, son." He said, "GET IN THE BATHROOM! NOW!" Ohhh, dear friend, the revival started before I even got all the way into the bathroom. The whuppin' I got that day was one of the two or three worst I ever got. Dad whipped me for a while. Then he gave me a severe verbal whuppin'. Then he took me out to where Erma was. He said, "YOU WILL APOLOGIZE!" And apologize I did, and in ernest, friend. Dad said, "FOR WHAT?!" I stammered out, "f-f-f-or c-call---i--n-g y-y-y-ou -that n-n-name..." Dad demanded, "WHAT NAME?!" And I stammered the "N" word out, I promise you friend, for the last time in my life. I have not spoken it again to this day. For her part, I think she had compassion for my predicament. All she said was "Awww child, go on from here.." I think she felt bad for what I went through. But as I look back on it all now, Dad did exactly what needed to be done. And it had the desired result.

Not long ago friend, my youngest had a black friend over to the house. The "N" word came up on a song he and my son thought was pretty cool. My wife happened to hear that word, and immediately demanded to know what group was singing such garbage. Then she asked whether he was offended by that "N" word. He said that mostly he just blocked it out. That got ME started friend. I told him the story I just told you. Then I said this to him. "You don't remember the days when you could not sit down in a restraunt with my son and eat a meal. But I do. You don't remember when laundromats had separate sides for the races, but I do. I LIVED integration of the schools. I was in the seventh grade when I had my first black teacher. I remember my ninth grade year when the schools at long last integrated. I've seen all of it young man. And I want you to know this. Too much has been paid, too much blood lost, too much sacrifice made for you to relegate this word to a minor offence to be 'blocked out'. You are a young black man, and you ought not EVER hear that word that it does not offend you. Don't let that word become 'just another word'. It's not that. And it never will be either." And I showed him one of my most prized possesions. It's a picture of Erma as she is today. And she wrote under it, "To my son, and his family. I love you. Erma Hutchison." Friend, I think I got my point across, don't you?

Erma had already lost her Mother when she worked for Mother and Dad. Her Dad now was very ill. Erma, as much as she enjoyed working for my parent's, her Dad needed her. So there came a day when we had to say good-bye. Both Erma and my Mother cried when she left for the last time. But Mother, having lost her Mother not that many years ago, completely understood. And thats the end of that......or is it?

Fast forward your time machine about 40 years friend. It became my Mother's duty to help her last surviving aunt on her Mothers side get into a nursing home. Aunt Lorene was a dear soul who we all loved and respected. She COULD, however, be a bit testy from time to time. So one day Mother was visiting her at the nursing home. Aunt Lorene said, "Hazel, I want you to meet my new friend." Well, if she had a new friend, Mother indeed wanted to meet them. So Mother pushed Aunt Lorene up to the day-room in her wheel chair. An older black woman sat there in a chair. She had salt and pepper hair, wore glasses, and had a casual pant suit on. Aunt Lorene said to her, "I want you to meet my niece." The black lady said "Oh, I know her already." My Mother said "Oh, really? How is that?" The answer came, "I use to work for you". Mother stood back and looked her over. "Erma?....ERMA!!!" My,my, friend, what a reunion took place that day!

Mother called me at home soon after. She said, "You're not going to believe who I found today?" When she told me who it was, I was almost as excited as Mother was. I couldn't wait to go and see her. And see her I did, the next weekend. Friend, that year we went and got Erma and took her to Mother's house for Christmas Eve dinner. We sat her at the head of the table. We fed her all she could eat. When we opened gifts, Erma had two or three to open too. Mother asked her at one point if she was glad to be with us. Erma said, "Miss Hazel, let me show you how glad I am." She proceeded to stand and do a little 'shuffle step' of a dance that had us all laughing. To top her evening off, we took her sight seeing through our Valley. We took her by the 'Madonna and Child', the Manger scene, we drove her down the boulevard in Shawmut where most of the homes are decorated to the nines every Christmas. All in all it was a grand night indeed. We had no idea at the time that Mother would not be with us by the time next Christmas came around. When Mother went Home, it fell my lot to go and tell Erma. I dreaded it. My family and I made sure she got to go to the visitation at the funeral home. It was a sad time friend.

Erma is still at that nursing home today. When I get to go home from time to time she is a priority visit for me. One day we were talking. Erma had never had children. The only family she had left was a brother who was in failing health. I said to her that day, "Erma, I tell ya what. I'm gonna vollunteer to be your son. Mother and Dad are in Heaven now. I don't think they would mind. So if you'll have me, I am adoptable in the temporary sense." She laughed and said that would be fine. I had no idea just how much she meant that till I was there to see her recently. She wanted me to have a picture of her, as well as an art project she had colored. I said that would be nice on one condition. She asked what that would be. I said, "You're gonna have to autograph it for me." She laughed, then took a pen and wrote on the colored picture, "To my son and his family. I love you. Erma Hutchison" Her picture hangs in a place of honor on my wall these days...right next to my Mother. And friend, that is good enough for me. You know what I mean don't you?

BAD APPLES

You know, friend, it just occured to me that I might be leading you to believe that we lived in a eutopian community that was devoid of any bad behaviour. But we did have a bad apple or two. I shall tell you about one of the two I would put in that category now. This fella lived off the road a piece, in the woods just up from where we lived. He walked almost everywhere he went. He had a big German Sheppard dog that walked with him. He was known to 'sample the suds' to excess, and as we have already seen in this little book of mine 'excess suds' can cause amjor difficulties. And so it was to be on the day I shall tell you about. The first difficulty belonged to my Mother and my two older sisters. The second, and biggest, difficulty belonged to this fella. And looking back on it now, he got off lightly in my opinion.

My Dad had taken my brother and I for one of those G.I. Joe haircuts I had to wear until my ninth grade year. Mother and the girls were at home. This fella came walking up the dirt road there, and stopped at our house. He first asked for my Dad. Mother, who had the front porch door latched, said to him through the screen that he was not home right then. This fella asked then for a glass of water. Mother said she did not think that would be appropriate with my Dad not home. This fella,who Mother would relate was obviously 'three sheet's to the wind', made like he would try to come in anyways. Mother quickly went in the house and locked the door. My Mother watched this fella by peeping through various window curtains. Good thing too. He hid behind a tree for a while, hoping Mother would come out to go somewhere. Then he went around to the back and finding the screen door opened, tried his best to get in the back door. Mother locked the girls in the bathroom and told them not to open it for anyone but her. Meanwhile this stupidly drunk fool was fumbling all over himself trying to find a way into the house. Thankfully he eventually gave up and stumbled on off, I suppose to his house. When my Dad brought us boy's back home Mother was still shaken. She told Dad what had happened. My Dad said "He'll be back. I'll see to him."

Sure enough, one day the next week, Mother was on the porch watching us kids play. Looking down towards the curve, she saw this fella coming up the road. My Dad, a third shift worker just outside of starting his job at the recreation department,was asleep. Mother woke him in plenty of time to get dressed. This sod was about to get the surprise of his life. Friend, do you believe this nut came just as straight up to our porch and knocked on the door?! Mother had shooed us kids into the house. Imagine this fellas shock when he found himself confronted not by a scared Mother, but a highly upset DAD! I had slipped around Dad and was standing over by the swing. And as best I can get it from the boy that I was, this is how the next two or three minutes went.

My Dad burst onto the front porch. He put his face right up against the screen. And he began to speak to this spectacle of inebriation ; "You listen to me, and you listen GOOD! This the second time, and it better, for YOUR sake,be the LAST time, that you come into my yard, much less to my DOOR! I know about your last visit here, and if you had done what you came to do I would have killed you long since. And if you EVER come near my wife or any of my kid's again, at a MINIMUM I will beat you down so fast I can stand back and watch it happen! You see that road right there? Best thing for you to do is to get on it and start walking. You walk till you get to the end of it, then you get into the woods and walk some more. If you come to a creek, get across itany way you can and you KEEP ON walking. But don't you EVER come near my place OR my family again! DO YOU UNDERSTAND THAT?!?

Ohhh, my dear friend, this fella was both too drunk and too horrified to say anything without stuttering. He didnt say a word that he did not have to start over a couple times. Except for once when his dog started growling at Dad, who told this fella if he wanted that dog to live to walk up the hill with him he had better shut it up. He stomped his foot and said, "HESH BOY!" And suddenly Dad was through. He said "Now GIT from here and do NOT come back!!" By now the boy that I was thinks Dad had become like a few cups of coffee to this fella, coz he does not remember him zig zaggin' too much as he left. Looked like a pretty straight line to the boy that I was. He still laughs when we discuss the incident. And so does the man I have become.

Friend, let's walk back into the house for just a sec. Let me show you just how thankfully stupid and discombobulated a drunk fool can be. Let's go back here to the back of the house. See the back door? You will notice that there are eight small panes of glass in that door. You will notice that the bottom right hand pane, JUST ABOVE THE HANDLE, is gone. This is the one time I can be thankful for alchohol friend. The fool, for all his fumbling, never saw the missing pane. That's just scary, is it not? At any rate, I have asked this of the boy that I was many times over the years, but he can not remember seeing that fella again. He does remember they found him one day in his house, dead. And that's all I got to say about that.

MR. BILL SAVES CHRISTMAS

Friend, I'm a firm believer that we ought to allow folk to 'smell the roses' while they are still here to enjoy the aroma. The story I will tell you now involves a man who made a regular habit in his career of 'standin' in the gap' for the less fortunate, and doing it multiple times over the years. I know for a fact that he stood in the gap for my family once during our stay on the Fairfax short-cut road in this precious little green house. The funny thing is, I didnt find out about it until years later after I was grown. Let me tell you about it. The year was 1980. That was an exciting year in our Valley, and a decisive one as well in my opinion. Four mill villages brought one another to an election that year to determine whether or not they should create from themselves one city. It was decidedly not a common thing that you see done, then or now. It was a daunting task that took years of preparation. Long hours were spen gathering information, learning about the nuances of this thing called 'incorporation'. More sacrifice than we will ever know was put into the effort in terms of hours spent going door to door, of creating a working committee to oversee the effort, things like that.

Nor was this a universally embraced idea. More than a gew loud voices were raised saying this was an impossible dream, or that we should not abuse the status quo. Then there were some who were like I had always been to that point, traditionalists who were afraid that the villages would lose their identity in a successful effort like this. I remember some lively debates in Mr. Ralph Siggers barber shop in Fairfax, in those days. But unlike the world we live in now, we debated passionately without making it a contest of personal attacks and character assasinations. I lost not one friend, and neither did the folk I debated with. At the end of the day, the idea of incorporating the four villages was adopted in an election where 79.9% of the voters agreed. I got to work up close with great men like Doss Leak and Bruce Gray, both with the Lord these days. And among many others, there was a man by the name of Bill Hayes. Mr. Bill owned Hayes Hardware in north Langdale.

After the question of incorporation was decided, it was necessary to call an election to seay our first Mayor and council. The council election now, would be an 'at large' election. That council would then be charged with creating voting districts for future elections. So the top vote getters would become the entire council. I was very excited to take part in this election. I do not remember a bad candidate being on the slate. Never-the-less, I wanted to be responsible with every vote I cast. And I was struggling a bit with a couple of my choices. I was living at home still at that time. One day my Dad and I were watching t.v. and I thought to 'pick his brain' about his choices for council. I asked him, "Dad, I was wandering if I could get you to tell me about the thinking that goes into your council votes. Not WHO you're voting for now, but just what kind of thinking goes into your picks in terms of their ability or qualifications. I'm arguing with myself over a couple of mine, so I just thought I would ask you".

My Dad did not hesitate to answer. He needed no thought at all. He said to me, "Son, the first person I'm going to be voting for, is going to be Bill Hayes." I said "Bill Hayes, he runs the hardware store in Langdale, right?" Dad said "Yes, you know Mr. Bill well. You went to school with his boy Johnny." I said "I think you're right. But let me ask this question. Mr. Bill is a good man. Good businesman too. I promise I won't be disappointed if he get's elacted, I really won't.

But there are some folk on this slate of candidates who already have some public service under their belts. And I'm just wandering how Mr. Bill jumped over them to get at the top of your list." Dad looked at me for a moment as though deciding what to say next. Then he said "Son, turn the t.v. off for a bit and I'll tell you a story. I've never told you this before. But now is as good a time as any for you to hear it." Friend, I turned that t.v. off pretty quick. I had a feeling the story I was about to hear would be on the unforgettable list. And it was, friend. It was. As near as I can remember his words, this the story of how Mr. Bill saved Christmas.

Dad began; "There was a time, many years ago, when you were very small, when your Momma and me had a tough year. Your Momma was in the hospital for a time. In fact, we nearly lost her. Her recovery was in months, not days. Then just when she got able to get into a normal routine again, I got down. Oh, I didn't have to go to the hospital or nothing like that. But all of a sudden I wasn't able to work the double shifts in the mill that was use to working when times got hard,and I sure wasn'table to work a part time job on the side like I did from time to time when our circumstances required it. We were behind on everything from our tithe to our rent. And one day we looked up and there came Christmas like a run-away train. It had done sneaked up on us. Your Momma and me decided we needed to get it in gear pretty quick. Son, it never occured to us to do anything other than start shoppin'. We went to West Point Georgia where everybody did their shoppin' in that day. All over town we went. We discovered a problem. The more we compared what the stores wanted us to pay for the stuff you kids were askin' for, with the money we had to spend on that stuff, the more out of balance it got. We made more than one trip up town too. Waited for the Christmas sales to kick in. And son, it just wasn't happening. I even waited for the last second sales to come around. Even then we were just not going to have the kind of Christmas we wanted for you kids.

Son, you have heard me talk of Christmas in my home at Christmas when I was a boy. My Daddy was a share-cropper, and a share-cropper was not a well to do fella. A good Christmas for us, we would get a sack full of fruit, and maybe some nuts, and a little candy. I'm not ashamed of the Christmas times we had son. But like any parent, I always said I wanted to give my kid's more than we got. But this year, for the first time, it looked as though we might be near to having to do for you guys what my Dady did for us. Call me vain, but that is not what I wanted.There came a Saturday, son, when I left West Point Georgia for what I told myself would be the last time. The Top Dollar Store could not help me. Kesslers could not help me. The prices were as low as they were gonna be, and my money was as high as it was gonna be. I would just have to go home and talk to your Momma. And I would almost prefer one of my Daddys thrashings with that horse-strap of his. I drove back down high-way 29 towards home. I was feeling pretty defeated, like I was lettinr you kids down. As I got into Langdale, I saw a sign that said Youngs Sno-Cap."

Dad paused right here, and for a few moments the smile came back to his eyes. He asked, "You remember Youngs Sno-Cap, don't ya son?" I said, "Ahh yes, how could anybody forget Youngs? They had the Indian themed burgers, right? Let's see, there was the biggest burger they had, a 'Chief Burger'. Then a brave burger, a squaw burger, and finally a papoose burger. Good burgers too. And don't forget about the banana split's Dad. Awesome diet bustin' food indeed!"

My Dad said, "Thats right son. But I bet you dont remember how you use to stay on me about lettin' you have a Chief burger, do ya? You almost begged at times, but I said they were too much burger for you." I told Dad with a touch of embarasment that I did seem to remember something like that. Dad wasn't through with me just yet. He said "There was a Sunday night after church when we went to the Sno-Cap for supper. You were after me about that Chief burger again. And I made a deal with ya. I said I would buy you a brave burger on this night. If you got it all down, I would buy you a Chief burger the next time out. If you did NOT get it all down, you had to wait till after your next birthday to ask again. You might just remember being game for the challenge. But I measure you don't remember that I had to help you finnish that brave burger, do ya? I said, "Now dad, you did NOT have to bring all that up, now." With a smile and a twinkle in his eye Dad said he just wanted to make sure we were 'on the same page.' Then, his eyes told me he was back to his story. It was almost as if he was reliving it right in front of me.

He said, "The next sign I saw was 'Hayes Hardware'. Son, you remember how Mr. Bills store looked like a Santas workshop at Christmas don't you? Seemed like anything a kid could want could be found there." I said "Oh, yeah Dad, who could forget that? I've had a few cases of the 'goo-goo eyes' walking up and down those aisles." Dad said, "That's exactly what I thought of when I saw that sign. It's not like I had a whole lot to lose. I was on the way home to have a sad talk with your Momma. And I wanted to know that I had done everything I could before I had that talk. So, I pulled into the parking lot and went in. And you know, I liked what I saw as I walked around in there. Only thing was, I had no more money then than I did when I left West Point not twenty minutes ago. I decided to go and talk to Mr. Bill. He wasn't too hard to find. When I found him I asked if I could talk to him for a few minutes. He said "sure Hubert, come on back to my office and we'll talk'." So we went back to the little office he had. He sat down at his desk, and I took a chair on the other side. He asked, "Now then Hubert, what can I do for you?"

My dear friend, can you even imagine how hard it must have been for my Dad to come to a place of asking for help? I've told you in this little book of mine about how fiercely independent share-cropper families were. Dad was an apple that didn't fall far from the tree. He and Mother liked to take care of their own business. Over the years I have known my Dad to work double shifts or even two jobs at a time so that he could take care of his own. Yet here he sat, in the office of a local business man, about to bare his troubles to him hoping for help he could not have known whether he would get. Dad just blurted out to Mr. Bill all he and Mother had faced in this year. He told him about what he had left to spend, and how short that was from being able to have Christmas for his kid's. Then, at some point, he had nothing to do but sit back and wait to see what Mr. Bill would say. I imagine there may well have been a 'pregnant pause' there, though Dad didn't say so. I do know that when Mr. Bill spoke, a thousand pounds of emotional weight began to lift from dad's shoulders.

Mr. Bill said, "Hubert, heres what I want you to do. I want you to go out into my store and get yourself a buggy. Get two if you need to. I want you to go all over the store and get everything you need to give you kids a good Christmas. Now hubert", he said with a smile, "you got a wife too. I 'spect you better get her a little something. And by the way Hubert, get yourself something too. It's Christmas for everybody you know." Friend, my Dad would have been ecstatic with that much. But Mr. Bill wasn't through yet. He said, "Now, when you get everything you need, I don't want you to go through the check-out line. You bring everything back here to my office. I'll write the bill up right here, and stick it in my desk. After Christmas, why, you and Hazel will get back on your feet. You just come by every week along and pay a little on your bill, and you'll have it paid off in no time."

Friend, as we sat there in our living room that day, I saw my Dad about as humble as I've ever seen him as he relived that day. He was not an emotional man most of the time. I only remember seeing him cry two or three times my entire life. He looked away for a moment, then he turned back to me again. "Son, Mr. Bill said something to me before I left that day that has stayed with me all these years. I've never forgotten it. He said, "Hubert, you are a hard worker. Everybody knows that. And you're as honest as the day is long. I'm not going to worry about one dime of my money coming back to me, as long as it's a fella like you payin' it back." My Dad looked down again, and I swear I thought I saw his bottom lip tremble just a bit. Then he caught himself. He looked at me, and I'll never forget these word's. "Son, I told you when you asked me, and I'll tell you now again. The FIRST person I'll be voting for in this election, is going to be Bill Hayes"

Well.

Friend, do I really have to tell you who got the first vote I cast in that election? Didn't think so. Oh, I know we'll have some readers friend, who will take me to task for telling this little story form that Christmas long ago. They'll say that Mr. Bill and others like him in our community did not do their good deeds to be seen of men. And I understand that, I really do. Why do you think I sat on this story more than 30 years after Dad told it to me? Listen friend, Mr. Bill Hayes and his dear wife Virginia are a part of what Tom Brokaw called 'Americas Greatest Generation.' That generation is getting away from us way too fast. Many of them did this kind of unseen kindness behind the scenes, never wanting or needing any attention at all. Truth be known they are the strongest part of the fabric of the mill villages I was raised in. And I just think it to be time, high time, and PAST time that we take the time and give THEM some time where we say that somebody noticed. Somebody remembers. Somebody appreciates what you did. And if any reader can't wrap their mind around that, well, the only thing left for them is a hearty suck of the ole thumb, friend. Too many people have gone into eternity without ever hearing words like those I speak now about Bill and Virginia Hayes. Dear God, what I would give to know that somebody, ANYBODY, would speak thus of me when I am in the winter of my life.

I know that Mr. Bill and Virginia are still with us as I type these words. I told this little story on a face-book page last year. They have seen it. And they loved it. Mrs. Virginia said so to me via a face-book message. Perhaps by the time our readers have read this little book of mine friend, I will have had the honor of meeting them and giving them both a big hug. And I would hope to say to Mr. Bill that he started something that Christmas, though I didn't know it till years later. As I think back across the years, I remember very few Christmas seasons wher our family did not help at least one family have a good Christmas. My parents raised five children, the youngest possibly not having heard this story till she reads it in this little book of mine. All of us have tried to be a blessing to others at Christmas and other times as well. My bride and I have almost without exception helped someone at Christmas during our 25 + years of marriage. My two boys have heard this story more than once during their raising. I have no doubt that they will continue the tradition of always remembering those less fortunate at Christmas. So Mr. Bill, you might say that your kindness to our family that Christmas is a gift that just keeps on giving. My boys will be the third generation of our family to do the kind of giving you did for us.

Mr. Bill Hayes lived out, many times, that old addage we have all heard in one form or another; No man ever stands higher than when he stoops down to help another man out of the ditch of despair, and helps put him on a solid ground called hope. You can believe me friend, as I listened and watched as Dad told his story that day, I saw him go through all the emotions all over again. In his selfless act of service, Mr. Bill restored hope to my Dad. Thank you, Bill and Virginia Hayes, for what you did for our family that Christmas long decades ago. Hubert B. Ogle Sr. never forgot your kindness. And by the way, Hubert B. Ogle JUNIOR will never forget it either. Nor will your service be forgotten, God willing, in the years to come. May it be reborn in some heart afresh, every time someone reads this little book of mine.

WHY DO WE GIVE?

That story had not one thing to do with our little green house or River View, other that I have ciphered out as best I can a timeline that says that the Christmas in question probably happened during our early years there. But allow me to chase another of my rabbits here, just for a moment or two. A question for you friend. And for our readers too. Why do we give? For those of us who follow Christ, we give because we are commanded to. God asks one dime out of each dollar we make. Just a dime. I mean, He gave us the whole dollar. He could take it all if He wanted. But He only asks for a dime. Secondly, we give our small tithe because of the giant gift Jesus gave us by vollunteering to go to the Cross for us. And it was Jesus Who taught, "Inasmuch as ye have done it unto the least of these my brethren, ye have done it also unto Me. Why do we give? Why did the early Midway Baptist Church family continuously reach out to families in need the way Clifford Hamers family reached out to us when Mother was in the hospital? Why did they once stop a Sunday night service so the men could go help fight a fire at George Will Monks store? Why did Brother Charlie Bohannon, on NUMEROUS occaisions, say to my parents or some other struggling person "God will see you through this" and slip them a twenty dollar bill as he shook their hand?

Friend, over the years I have watched about every t.v. telethon you can think of. I've watched CEO's look into a camera and proudly tell the world how many hundreds, or even millions of dollars they had given to some effort. God bless'em. Good! But I make no apologies for saying that my heart will always be first towards the faceless, nameless people who do true sacrificial giving all the time and not just during a special fund raiser. You don't see them on t.v. You dont see them on the front page of your local paper. But no community, I measure, could survive without them. Every second of every day one of them is performing small and large acts of kindness. Without them, state and local agencies would be even more overloaded than they are. But why? Why do they bother?

One, most folk who give of themselves know what it's like to need the giving of others to help them get back on their feet. Others realize that "except for the grace of God there go I". They live the principle of not letting their left hand know what their right hand is doing. They don't NEED any credit. They don't NEED a t.v. camera. They don't NEED to have their smiling faces splashed across the front page of their local paper. At the end of the day all we NEED is to know that we made a difference in at least ONE life. A mouth fed, a wish granted, a need met. Then we just slip on out and go on with our lives. It is, after all, an affair of the heart, this thing about giving. The 'bah humbugs' of this world miss out on so much. The 'look at me' types don't have a clue once the spotlight is gone. To get the real effect of this thing called giving you must have a heart for it. And you must be happy 'giving' outside the spotlight, where the real needs often are anyway. So for me, the retired lady who gives ten of the last twenty dollars she has till till the next two weeks when she gets her next retirement check carries much more weight with me than the CEO or the celebrity who writes the big checks. The retired lady gave sacrificially. The CEO or the celebrity gave of their plenty. Which isn't a bad thing, friend. But the sacrificial giver is going to be there no matter what. The rich guys have to have a 'cause'. At any rate, as I said, the gift of giving is an affair of the heart. Those who give sacrificially by grace, silently, not seeking attention, have the greatest reward. And thats all I have to say about that.

CHRISTMAS IN OUR VALLEY

Friend, our Valley is a unique place in many ways. Unfortunately we live in a day where it is fashionable, even preferable to some misguided types, to spend one stime in the politics of personal destruction. They cant find even one positive thing to talk about in their community. I have made a concious choice to prompt my readers who may never have been to our Valley to try us out sometime. And Christmas, to me, is the perfect time.

We have a few decades long attractions that you don't get to see anymore in way too many communities. Two are in the Langdale area of Valley Alabama. If you are comming north on highway 29 from the Auburn-Opelika area, about a half mile past Valley High School you will see a huge picture of Mary and Jesus, created by Christmas lights. We call it "Madonna and Child". This has been a regular attraction in our Valley since the 1960's to the best of my knowlege. There was one time when Mary and Jesus were moved to I-85 in front of Lanier-Carter Mills, and was replaced with a giant candle. The people of our Valley, I'm told, were not too keen on that idea, to the extent that Mary and Jesus were back in their place the next year. What happened to the candle I can't say. And I have to say, from the heart of a traditionalist, I dont give a fast swim through a slow moving group of pirrhana fish either :). I'm jes sayin'....

Another and arguably even more revered ytradition in our Valley is the life sized Manger scene you can see each year in what little is left of the meadow. This has been an annual thing since my Mothers childhood. Just this past Christmas (2012) the figurines in this display appeared with a fresh touching up in both paint and costumes. It is wasily seen from Highway 29 any hight you want to go by there friend. I think that's good. A constant reminder, in the middle of all the commercialism of theseason, of THE reason for this season. May it ever be so.

By far the most attended tradition in our Valley each year is the Merry Go Round. This has also been around since just before I was born In my childhood this event was held at a small ballfield in Fairfax across from the mill. Christmas trees adorned the ball field. We got our free tickets to ride at a huge candle on one side. You caould, and still can, ride the Merry Go Round as many times as you can stand to wait in line. It's current home each year is in front of Langdale Mill where the tennis courts use to be, Last year over 10,000 people rode it. Folk from as far away as Alaska have ridden this ride friend. Three generations of our family have taken rides on the Merry Go Round. Friend, that almost makes me feel old. ALMOST, I said.There is a street in our Valley that is a must drive through at Christmas in our Valley. It's called 'the boulevard' in the Shawmut area of Valley. You will come to a Burger King on the right side of highway 29. Directly across from there you will see three roads. The road furthest right is the one you want. Almost every house on this street is decorated to the nines for the season. All the way to the Nazarene church you can admire the yards and the enthusiasm of these citizens for Christmas. Those, my faithful traveling partner, are just the highlights. Our Valley is full of celebrations of Christmas if you know where to look. But I think Madonna and Child and the Manger Scene are powerful examples of how our people still remember that the real Reason for the season still revolves around a manger in a barn that served as a room because the inn was out of rooms. Out of that first Christmas was born Hope for every single one of us. A Hope that endures to this day. It is a free Hope to anyone who will accept it. It is a real Hope to anyone who embraces it. And it is an eternal Hope for anyone who has asked for it. And still there are many who refuse it, who mock it, who laugh at it. But some day my dear friend, the laughing will be over for them. The pleading will begin. And eternal rejection will be their only answer. Friend, I am so glad you and I will not be among them. Aren't you?

THE SANDS OF TIME MOVE ON....

Those are the things I enjoyed, especially in my childhood friend. I enjoyed living on this little road too. I enjoyed it when it was dirt. I enjoyed it when they paved it. Now the time is near when we must take our leave of it and move on down to River View, the recreation department and the school. As we stand beside the road next to the driveway where I was coerced by a fair minded Mother into a tri-cycle race thet caused my face to look like a roadmap of Georgia, my heart is heavy. This place, in it's own way, is just a hard to leave as Tallassee Street was. Looky there, it's ole Buster runnin' at us! Hey there boy! Buster...BUSTER!! Can you believe that friend? He just ran by me like he never saw me before. Right down towards the far end of the lake......hey, friend, get a load of that! Look at that bony,buck toothed, bald headed boy that I was. He's done hung him a big fish on that cane pole of his. Get'im out'a there! OOPS, dont let him get away! See there friend? See how big that bream is? Looky there at it's yella belly. Some folk told that boy it was a sunfish. He don't care what they call it, as long as it's on his plate at suppertime! Good thing we walked down towards where he is. I want you to get a good look at this fish. That boy has had it on the hook a number of times, only to see it flop off at the last possible moment. It's the biggest bream in the lake. That boy will tell you that catching the biggest of ANY fish in the lake seems to take something out of the fishin' trip, ya know? It's like, what will be the challenge now? Lets get a little closer friend. But let me tie this infernal shoestring that keeps coming untied. I'll be just a sec......

HEY! WHATS THE BIG DEAL? What happened to my lake? We ARE standing on the road that goes across the dam of this lake, right? But it CAN'T be the same place! Theres no water in the lake at all! GEEEZ, theres weeds growin' in the lake bottom for Petes sake! And look, trees and brush all over the red dirt ground that we played on so freely. This aint right friend. Wait, I bet if I turn around....OH,NOOOO!! The pasture is gone too! Why, it's nothing but a marshy lookin' place with huge brush growth. Not a cow in sight, much less that onery old bull. Can you believe it friend?! Mr. John McCulloughs barn and pig pen are absolutely GONE TOO! C'mon, friend, what happened here? Looky yonder, even the 'secret' fishin' hole looks like nothin' more than a glorified mudhole now. This aint right friend! It just ain't right! Well at least I can walk back to the road and look at that precious little green.......NO! NO! NO! NO! The little green house is gone too. It looks as if a house never DID sit there. But we went inside friend, right? I gave you a tour, right? Well what in the name of banana puddin' at church home-comin' HAPPENED here?!? Whats that friend? Lord help me, you're right of course. TIME happened. But I don't like it friend. I don't like it one bit. The sand's of time....they wait for no man. And sadly, we must be going now. Maybe we will yet get another glimpse of this place, and the little green house. But for now, let us be on our way...

CHANGING SCHOOLS

ONE HUNDRED YEARS, AND THE GREAT RACE

I wanted to take a break right here friend, and tell you a couple stories that took place during my time at River View School. The first concerns a celebration they called 100 years of good living. There were all sorts of events at the school, including a gospel singing and a lot of fun for students. There is one thing that stands out in my mind about that day. It was the hundred yard dash contest. Specifically, the girls division is where the 'Great Race' came from. It got down to two girls. I hesitate to use their names here. One is in Heaven now. The other I haven't seen in many years, so I could not ask permission. One was a regular tom-boy, as we say it here in the south. She could run like the wind. The other was as pretty as a picture, the very image of a young lady. But ohhh, my dear friend, you didn't need to let her fool you. She could flat out run. Girl #1 was a mite brash, enjoyed talkin' her race up with her opponent as they walked to the starting line. Girl #2 was more quiet, preferring to let her racing do her talking for her.

When it came down to the two of them to see who was the fastest girl in the school then, you can see them, can't you friend, as they got ready to race. And goodness gracious, gret goo-ga-moogies what a race it was. It was so close that a winner could not be determined. Neither girl wanted anything to do with that. So they took a break, then raced again. And again, the race was too close to call. There was a third race, this time more encouraged by the 'fans', not the girls. So off they went again. With the same result. Friend, I've watched a lot of racing in my day. I've seen the greatest in the world at the amateur and professional level. But to this day, I have to say that I have never, EVER seen a spectacle like that again. In the m,emory of the boy that I was I can still see them, flying across the outfield of that playground, each determined to win or bust. Friend, the both of them almost 'busted' before they decided to let it be for the day.

The funniest race of the day, however, was a 'walking race'. It involved three teachers. Mr. Crook, Coach McCarley, and a lady teacher. I have strongly encouraged the boy that I was every way I can, but he can NOT remember her name. Thats sad too, because as the race unfolded the two men were so concerned with one another till they completely forgot about the lady. And she nipped the both of them at the end of the race! She won, friend! The boy I use to be near about died laughing. All in all it was a fun day thet he still reminds me of from time to time.

CHOICES ARE FOREVER

Friend, I know I'm chasin' a rabbit here. But just bear with my ADHD once more, would ya? Thanks. One of these girls was a friend of mine. We grew up in the same church. Went to the same schools. She possesed stunning good looks. She had a winning, outgoing personality. She went on to win her share of beauty contests, got to be a cheerleader in high school, and was extremely popular. Yet she never forgot where she came from. And she never, ever forgot a friend, even if that friend didn't grow up to be like her. For example, one day she was standing in the parking lot at the high school gym talking with my oldest sister and some others. Another cheer-leader watched from a distance. When my friends conversation with my sister and others was done, she walked off, I suppose to go to cheer-leader practice. The cheer-leader who had watched her from a distance took her to task; "Why do you spend time with people like them? They're not in your class at all." My friend had a short, blunt answer. "Dad-burn it, because they're my friends!!!" Any questions?Friend, that event happened over 40 years ago, and I assure you my sister still remembered it right on up to the day she went to Heaven. I remember that 'better than you' cheer-leader too. You have no idea how much I would love to put her name out there for all to know. But over the years I became a Christian. I know well the do's and dont's of my faith. Better to let this person, if she hasn't changed in all these years be judged by One whose judgement leaves no room for appeal. And per chance she HAS changed, it would give me no joy to discover that I unnecessarily drug her through her past conduct again.

It was a Saturday morning, several years later, when my friend ran into my sister somewhere in town. You know how it is when you see a friend you've lost touch with for a while don't you friend? There is much to 'catch up on'. Too much, in fact, for a brief encounter out in public. My friend said to my sister, "If y'all want to, we'll get together next weekend and do something together. I can't tonight. I have a date." They made plans for the next weekend, and my friend and my sister went their ways. It was the last time they would see one another. My friend was killed in an automobile accident that night. The young man she was with ran a stop sign and hit an embankment at a high rate of speed. My friend died at the scene. He died on the operating table. The tragic thing is that alchohol was involved. This is a poster story for abstaining from alchohol. That young mans faculties were impaired enough that he either missed or mis-read the stop sign. The results tore apart two families.Young folk, I know that in todays world I'm not much more than a voice crying out in the wilderness, but this kind of tragedy will not involve you if you just never take that first drink of alchohol. "Responsible drinking" is the phrase of the day. But the only true way to stay out of this kind of tragedy is to invest your money in a more constructive way. I know more than a few families that will agree with me on that. And yes, friend, I know, I know about those who are going to crucify me for what I've said here. You know what they can do for me, don't you friend? Let's say it together..."GO SUCK YO THUMB!!!" There, I feel much better now.

One final thing here and we'll move on. I fully believe, with every fiber of my mind, soul, body, and spirit that my friend is in Heaven today. Does that surprise you, friend? Get out your Bible. Find the story of Samson. Strongest man who ever lived. He defied his God, disobeyed his parents, married outside his faith, gave away the secret to his strength. It cost him his freedom. it cost him his eyesight. It cost him his life eventually. He died correcting his wrongs. Do I even have to remind you of the wrong committed by King David, and the consequences of that wrong? Yet I will be seeing both of them in Heaven. They both did much, but both could have done much more. So it is with Christians today. Choices, my dear friend, are forever. Once you make'em, there they are. You can apologize for some. You can fix some. But once the choice is made, it's part of your life record forever. But thank's be to a merciful God, who can blot out that choice when you come to Him, and put your feet back on solid ground! Chose your friends carefully. You will become, at least in part, what they are. Remember, my Grand-father said "If you hang 'round it long enough, you'll go to smellin' like it." ' 'Nuff said.

MR. FRAZIER

Mr. Frazier was a tough but fair 'old school' administrator. He was as 'black and white' as they come. Right is right, wrong is wrong. Very little 'gray area', if any at all. But he was not without compassion. For example, one afternoon, while we were waiting for our bus to come, we were on the ball field playing. The boy I use to be can't remember now how it happened, but he hurt his leg, probably in a fall. It wasn't as bad as all that friend, but he was 'puttin' on' like he was hurt much worse than he was. Pretty good job he was doin' too, coz he got help gettin' on the bus, and even his dear Mother made him lie down on the couch when he got home. In just a little while there was a knock on the front door. Who do you reckon was standin' there? It was Mr. Frazier, who was concerned enough to come by and check on him. Mr. Fraziers daughter Amelia, several yeras the senior of the boy I use to be, defended him on the school bus more than once. She was pretty as a picture, a majorette in the high school band. What about that friend, to have a defender like that? The boy I use to be never forgot that. Neither has the man writin' this little book right now.

Mr. Fraziers last year at River View was my seventh grade year. Looking back, thats a shame, because he had been there a really long time. He didn't move far though, going to Langdale School where he was when he retired. I saw him a good bit though, after retirement. My Dad started a domino club at the gym in River View. Mr. Frazier was a member of that group. He was a pretty darn good domino player too as I recall. When he went to be with the Lord, River View was diminished just a bit in my opinion. He was an integral part of the community in my childhood, and affected the lives of many, many students. Mrs. Frazier lived several years after Mr. Frazier went Home. She enjoyed going for walks at a little park near Fob James Drive, not far from city hall. Thats where she was found one day, having collapsed during one of those walks. By the time someone found her, she was already hugging Jesus, friend.

Replacing people of the integrity and character of Mr. and Mrs. Frazier is nigh on to impossible. The boy I use to be and the man I am today agree on that point. They were vital and active members of our community, never 'above' their neighbors but considering themselves to be just another part of the community. When people like them move on from this life to Home, you find yourself in shock, actually, that they would dare to leave before you, even if you have been moved away for some years. I think of them often, even now. Do I miss them? You bet I do....

YOU CAN'T DO THAT NO MORE

I was destined to be a part of the last eigth grade class at River View School, ever. Integrating our schools meant that the school that had been Rehobeth High, where the African American students had attended, would now be Valley Junior High School, hosting all students from grades seven through nine. River View would now host grades one through six. Mr. Frazier was at Langdale School now. He was replaced by Mr. Carey Philpott. The boy I use to be remembers Mr. Philpott as a man who could be just as 'old school' as Mr. Frazier. But he could also be very personable with his students from time to time. And the boys in particular got a bonus or two that year that would get an education professional fired in short order today.

For example, one day Mr. Philpott gathered us boys into his truck and off we went to a place where he had some hogs, a horse or two, things like that. They had managed to get out of the fence somewhere on the property. We were to help get them all back in. The boy I use to be can't for the life of him remember who it was, but at some point a fella could be heard yellin' at the top of his voice for help. There was a crashing sound that came through the brush. Then there they were. The boy, hangin' on to one of them hogs for dear life, and that hog pullin' him along like a rag doll. But give the kid credit. He 'twernt about to let go. There was both laughter and work that day.

Another time Mr. Philpott got word that he had himself a fire burnin' on his place somewhere. So the boys got to be a 'vollunteer drafted fire department' as it were. If that boy I was is rememberin' right (and I'm not real sure of this), they went at that fire with shovels and rakes, and youthful exuberance, and not much else. As it turned out some more official fire fighters came on the scene and shortly had the fire contained.

Another bonus we got was that any time we went on one of these adventures, our lunch was waiting for us when we got back. So we got to eat before we went back to class. Friend, I can see the new age academic intelligentia now. They're foamin' at the mouth, so enraged they are that boys like those would be 'abused' in that way. To them, the boy that I was would stick his tongue out and say "Awwww, go suck yo thumbs, the lot'a ya!" We still got our class-work in. And every one of us passed. And don't even go there neighbor insinuating or stating outright that we got 'special treatment' on grades. We worked hard at school. We were required to work hard at our homework, at home. We were held to accountability standards in every area of our lives that would be considered abuse by todays wuss raising generation. So stop choking on your 'enlightened' rules and regulations modernists! We did o.k., us boys. So get over yourself.

Listen, there was no such thing as a 'social promotion' when the boy I use to be was in grade school. Either you passed, or you repeated. We had home-work, HOME-WORK, students, EVERY single day. Our parents stayed on one side of our rear ends, and the school stayed on the other. Failure to turn in home-work could cause some genuine trouble at school. It caused that boy I use to be even more when he got home too, let me tell you. All that had to happen was for the school to call and make such a report to his parents, and believe me a bath-room revival was soon convened. No, my two boys have never been asked or able to do the kinds of things we did all those years ago. Nor would I venture that in todays world a student should. But I speak of those days now wistfully. I have nothing but respect for Mr. Philpott. As I said, the words 'tough' and 'fair' could be equally used to describe his style of administration. The boy I was counted it a privelege to have him as a principal and instructor. And if you want to make a very unhappy camper out of your author, just say a bad word about him in my presence. You decidedly will NOT like my reply. All that said, I do have one item of good natured unfinnished business with Mr. Philpott, as well as a bunch'a folk I went to River View School with. This needs to be a story all unto itself, and that's the way I'll tell it. I call this little story....

THE END OF THE CAT STORY - ENOUGH ALREADY!!

A story got out into the school about me and a cat. It seems that I threw this cat into Mr. John McCulloughs lake, across the road from our little green house. The story goes that the cat swam back. And I threw it back into the lake. The story goes that this process continued until the poor cat drowned. Now friend, that's nasty. Mr. Philpott, along with more than a few others, got hold of this story. I havent seen Mr. Philpott in many years. But long after I left River View School, he would give me the business about that confounded cat! Friend, as a boy of that time I have had to stay real close to my Dad at more than one softball game to keep from bein' beat up over that infernal cat! The boy I was still thinks the cat story was more a convenience for his tormentors than any belief in the story itself. At any rate, for a time I was a target for an act that did not come close to happening like it was told.

Well friend, I have lived over half my life at this point. Regretably I don't live in River View or the Valley area for that matter, anymore. But I have decided to put this story, which caused me more than a little grief, to bed permanently. Lets do it in detail, shall we? We'll handle it one question at a time if that's o.k. with you all. Or even if it ain't alright. Did I toss a cat into Mr. Johns lake? The answer is yes. Did I toss it in the lake more than once? The answer is NO! Did I drown the pore thang? The answer is an emphatic NO!! And now, for the first time, I will tell you why the cat lived to swim another day. The cat had no sooner left my hands than I heard these words; "HUBERT BUING OGLE JUNIOR!!!" It was my Mother. She saw the deed, and my toast right then was more than done. It was BURNT! And that ain't all that was burnt before my Mother was done. I was required to fetch the cat. I was to completely dry the cat with a towel. I was required then to set it free, at which point it departed so fast till I was almost left to wander why I was holding a damp towel in my hand's. And then I was required to attend a soul stirring bathroom revival I have never forgotten.

Friend, you're frownin' at me right now. I don't blame you really. I've heard all the 'how could you' questions, in all their forms, over the years. And I say to you what I have said often to others. Heck, I don't know! Why is it that all the trash cans around River View School got scattered all around, especially at Halloween? Why did a person who I really ought to name here but won't, once take an apple, rub it in doggie dooo, clean it up, give it to me, then laugh with his co-horts when I ate it? Why did some idiots vandalize most of the windows on the back side of River View School, and spray paint a couple of the rooms, when good people like Ray Anthony and many others were trying to restore it for historic purposes? Listen, all boys are born, I believe, with what I will call a 'stupid thermometer'. On the day of this cat incident, my 'stupid thermometer' burst at the top. And I'll tell you something else too. You could have burst any thermometer you wanted, using me to do it, when my Mother got through with me that day. All you would have to do is stick it....well, you get the idea, don't you friend?

At any rate, I can report to Mr. Philpott and my tormentors all those years ago that this cat lived to a ripe old age as a cat's life goes. And trust me, it was a long, loooong time before I handled another cat at all without someone bein' in the room to verify my actions. Now then, the truth has finally been told. The cat is truly 'out of the bag'. That is the truth, the whole truth, and nuttin' but the truth, so help me God! It's my (true) story, and I'm stickin' to it. And that's all I've got to say about that.... :)

REFLECTIONS ON THE SCHOOL...

Ohhh friend, there is so much to tell that I could stay here at this precious little school building for a very long time. I still think about folk like Miss Christine, who worked in the office, or Miss Kate, who was over the lunch room. There are so many stories about friends from this school that it would take another book to tell them all. River View School is not a school anymore. It now belongs to the City of Valley. It was sold to them on the condition that it would never again be a school. So a group called the River View School Restoration Committee has for some years now done yeomans work with little resources in trying to restore the school to how it looked when folk like me went there.

I was back there a few years ago for a reunion of Dads womens softball team. Last year I went back for the annual River View Reunion. By then my Dad was three years in Heaven enjoying a greatly deserved rest. It's sad to me when I walk down the halls of the old school now. No students. No teachers. The silence is deafening. Mrs. Spears third grade class-room is one of those that got vandalized a few years ago. A pox on the low lifes who did that. Chicken pox would do the trick. With a full recovery of course. But only after seeeing the ugly face of death up close.

Ray and the Committee are doing a really marvelous job of restoring the school, if vandals will only leave them be. As I walked through the school on one of my occaisions to be back, I noticed that the fifth grade class-room which had been such a torture chamber for me was one of the first to be restored. The flooring has been varnished, and the desk's give the look of a class-room that could open just any day. I walked over to the cloak room where I was humiliated over a spelling test. I remembered the feeling I had when I got to my desk the next day and found that big fat zero marked through and replaced with the 85 I deserved. And I smiled. Again. No reason. No apology ever made. None needed. The corrected test paper spoke for itself. The absence of the teacher the next year confirmed it all. 'Nuff said.

The old cafeteria inside the school had been refinnished the last time I was there too. I was at River View School when the new cafeteria was built. We thought we had done got up town then, friend! I walked into that 'new' lunchroom at the door opposite a door at the school. And I had a memory come back from the boy I was, and we both smiled. Well, the boy now, he laughed out loud. You see, us boys would be allowed to clean the lunch room from time to time. We were expected to sweep the floors, then mop them. I have to say though that boys were boys then just as they are now, and mischief did it's impish work more than once. One day one of the guys had got a hold of the curtain up on the stage (the lunch room doubled as an auditorium), and swung way out over the floor, soundin' out his very best Tarzan yell. Then he looked towards the door. And who should be standin' there but Coach Calvin McCarley. With his arms folded. And that stilleto steel gaze in his eyes. Nowhere for the pore fella to run. No way to blame his folly on someone else. BUSTED! Actually, he was 'caught'. He got 'busted' shortly thereafter.

I made arrangements to meet Ray at the school when we were planning Dads softball reunion. He and I were standing in front of the school at the top of the steps that led down to the softball field. Today it's just a field of grass. A bar-b-que pit sits where home plate use to be.The tall fence that stood in right field is gone.So is the basketball goal that stood in deep left field. The schools closing was the product of downsizing to cut costs. Our little village has paid a severe price due to that kind of thing. The theater? Gone. The general store? Gone. The barber shop? Gone. The gym? deteriorating, and without a miracle, destruction will find it's way to that grand ole building. The mill is slated for destruction. Then, there will be only the school. God forbid it suffer the same fate.

At any rate, as Ray and I stood there that day, I remember him asking, "It looks different now,dosen't it? "That day, I agreed with him. But I have since changed my mind about that. Since that day I have learned that sometimes it is better to see things with the heart rather than with the eyes. And in my heart there will always, always be a softball field with kids runnin' about, playin' the games that kids play. I can still see Mrs. Spears tryin to do the twist 'tween two desks. The faces of Mr Crook, Coach McCarley, and Mr. Frazier are as fresh to me as though they were still tryin' to teach me. I can still watch students receiving their yearly free pencils and tablets from the Coca Cola company. Two girls still race the closest 100 yard dash in the history of River View School. As long as the boy I use to be will stay with me, these scenes will always be indellible in my heart. And if he should one day go away...well then friend, it's time for God to take me Home, where I'll have no need of any earthly memory.

God bless you River View School. And God grant you the privelege of enjoying the completion of the restoration now underway. God grant you the people who will give of their time, their money, and their talent in making that happen. I will never forget you. I love you now. I loved you then. We all did. We never thought the day would come when you would be unwanted by education professionals. But that day did come. And it is left to us now to see to it that you can at least be a museum that folk can look into and see the roots of their present opportunities. You will soon be all we have left. I make a solemn promise that if this little book of mine just takes off and does really well, I will some-day do a book signing there, maybe at a reunion of some sort, and make a donation to the school for every book sold. We MUST make sure that you, old friend, can continue to be a window into the history of education in our Valley. God let it be so..... and thats all I got to say about that.....

TIME FOR A REST

Friend, we've covered quite a few miles on our journey through this life I have lived, have we not? I see the weariness in your eyes. You look like I feel. I think we might just need a rest right along in here. There is SO much more to tell in this life I have lived. But I am tired from this journey. And I need to refresh myself. Can we resume this journey together in the not too distant future? You have been a lot of fun to travel with, and patient to a fault with me. But you look ready for a rest too. But what of our readers? Will they forget us, I wander? That would be a shame. The more I look at it, this life I have lived hasnt been the total bore I thought it had been. I measure that they have smiled a few times thus far. And maybe they cried once or twice. There is more of both waiting in the second part of our journey friend. So be sure to bring along your hankies, ya hear?

Friend, can we stand for just a moment and look back on our journey? Can I take one last peek at Tallassee Street, where I got a 'come to Jesus' reminder from my PaPa AND my Dad not to run from an adult, even if you ARE about to be whooped! Can I stand at the top of the playground at the River View School and watch the kids I was raised with playin' before school started, just ONE more again? Lets go to Granny White Springs friend and dip our hands just one more time, into that cool spring water and take a sip. And OHHH, what a joy it would be to my taste buds to have just one drum stick off the table, outdoors, at a Midway Homecoming Day. And wash it down with just one more bowl of home-made from scratch banana puddin'? Made by my dear Mother, of course. Aint it sad friend, that it's only after we CANT go back and visit people and places we loved, that we appreciate them for the blessing they were in our lives? How many of those people got away into Eternity without me saying 'thank you' to them? The very thought breaks my heart. Whats that? Yes, I know....we need to go now.....the sands of time, after all, wait for no man. They just keep right on siftin'.

It's just as well. We're at the place where I drop you off anyway friend. You enjoy your rest. I owe you a huge debt of gratitude for your company. At my age company gets to be more important than it use to be, if you know what I mean. I'll be along not too many days hence and meet you right here. And we shall resume our journey. God bless, my friend, till we meet again....

Hubert B. Ogle Jr.